STREET FIGHTING MAN

STREET FIGHTING MAN

PADDY MONAGHAN
WITH FOREWORD BY
MUHAMMAD ALI

JOHN BLAKE

Published by John Blake Publishing Ltd,
3 Bramber Court, 2 Bramber Road,
London W14 9PB, England

www.johnblakepublishing.co.uk

www.facebook.com/Johnblakepub `facebook`
twitter.com/johnblakepub `twitter`

First published in hardback in 2008
This edition published in 2013

ISBN: 978 1 78219 425 5

British Library Cataloguing-in-Publication Data:

A catalogue record for this book is available from the British Library.

Design by www.envydesign.co.uk

Printed and bound in Great Britain by CPI Group (UK) Ltd

1 3 5 7 9 10 8 6 4 2

Papers used by John Blake Publishing are natural, recyclable products
made from wood grown in sustainable forests. The manufacturing processes
conform to the environmental regulations of the country of origin.

Every attempt has been made to contact the relevant copyright-holders,
but some were unobtainable. We would be grateful if the
appropriate people could contact us.

CONTENTS

ACKNOWLEDGEMENTS

The greatest thanks must go to my wonderful wife Sandra, my dear children and all of my other family. A huge thanks also to all of my friends (you know who you are).

My respect and thanks must also go to the world's foremost ambassador of Wing Chun, Grand Master Samuel Kwok. I am honoured to have known this man and his teachings for a number of years now. We have developed an unbreakable bond over the years, a bond only fighters can share. He is truly a great warrior and my brother in spirit.

Thanks as well to Ian Widley, who was once an opponent, but now is a true friend. And to Naim Munshi, another true friend.

Johnny Najjar and Masisboxingbelts – thank you for all the hard work you put into making the finest world championship belt you have ever made. I must also add sincere gratitude to the syndicate who contributed towards the belt: Tyrone Monaghan; Adrian Frazer, Lakeland Tyres in Lisnaskea; Niall McNulty, UK Direct Cars in Enniskillen; Tom Mollan, Mollan Brothers Furniture in Irvinestown.

Further thanks to Peter Gerrard, the co-writer of my book, for his patience. And to my long time agent Fiona Williams of Berlin Associates.

Special thanks to my son Tyrone, who not only organises all my business, but, of all the scripts I have been offered over the years, has single-handedly written the only worthwhile screenplay I have seen for the proposed film of my story. He has entitled it, 'The Rough Diamond'.

This book is dedicated with loving memory, thanks and appreciation to my manager, trainer, promoter and dear friend, Tommy Heard. And finally to my beloved mamma and dadda – may they rest in peace.

* * *

Peter Gerrard would like to thank Colin and Sandie Johnson for all their help. And to express his gratitude to Vicky McGeown, the editor, for her invaluable comments and suggestions.

FOREWORD

by
Muhammad Ali

Friendship is a word I do not use lightly. Paddy Monaghan and I have been friends since the early 1960s.

Some years ago we were speaking together at my home and he told me that he intended to write his autobiography and it would include the story of our friendship. Although I did not think it necessary, he said he would submit the manuscript to me for my approval before publishing it.

I said to him, 'Paddy, I'll read it, but I don't really need to until it's published. We are friends and I know that anything you say or write will be one hundred per cent the truth.'

A great deal has been written about me over the years. Some of it has been authentic, but just as much has been no more than highly-coloured fiction. Had I been in a position to check each word before it appeared in print, I can assure you that a lot would never have seen the light of day. But these pages are different.

Not only is Paddy my good friend, he is my main man over there in Great Britain. From this man, from that little town in England, came the title, 'The People's Champ'.

Then it was a title that no one had heard of. Now it is known throughout the world.

Paddy, from my heart, I wish you the greatest success with your book.

Muhammad Ali

FOREWORD

by
Sifu Samuel Kwok

It is with great honour that I write this foreword to my friend Paddy Monaghan's book.

I have known Paddy for many years, and in that time we have forged a friendship based on trust and mutual respect.

I have spent most of my life as an ambassador to the world, spreading the Ip Man Wing Chun Kung Fu system. Grandmaster Ip Man was the teacher of the legendary Bruce Lee. I have had the very great fortune of being the foremost authority of this Kung Fu system as it has been passed by both sons of Ip Man: Grandmasters Ip Chun and Ip Ching.

Wing Chun, unlike many other Martial Art systems, is still a combat oriented system, not a sport. Being a combat system, it still adheres to the training methods and ethics of the warrior. It is these ethics and the warrior mind set that forged my great respect for Paddy.

Paddy Monaghan is not your ordinary boxer. He is truly a warrior in every sense of the word. He has demonstrated his courage, dedication, and discipline and shown the respect that is the cornerstone of the warrior life. These are the virtues I have seen in Paddy.

When Paddy's son Tyrone told me that his father's world title belt had been stolen in 1975 in New York, and that he was looking for someone to make a replica, I felt I had to find a way to replace it for him. With this in mind I contacted a friend in the United States and commissioned him to make the replica.

This book on his life is sure to be as instructional in the ways of the warrior as it will be entertaining and educational.

Paddy you are a true gentleman. Thank you for your friendship and for walking the path of the warrior.

Samuel Kwok
2nd Generation Master – Ip Man Wing Chun Kung Fu
www.kwokwingchun.com

INTRODUCTION

For a guy who loves his family more than life itself, paints for a hobby, can't stand cruelty to children or animals and hates bullying of any sort, it's strange how extreme violence became part of my life for almost 40 years.

I came across a couple of lines in a book that went something like, 'Some seek greatness, others have greatness thrust on them.' Okay, I never achieved greatness, and never expected to, but the taking and dishing out of violence was definitely thrust on me.

I can understand that a lot of guys, built like brick shithouses with a chip on their shoulders, are tailor-made for the game I ended up in – but me? Check out my photographs. My fighting weight was never more than 11 stone 5 pounds, yet I put on their backs countless opponents who were getting on for twice that weight. All I can think is that him up there looked down and thought to himself, 'Paddy my son, you've got fuck-all else going for you so what I'll do is give you a bit of a leg up in the fighting business.' Looking back, it's a pity he didn't hand out some less damaging skills, but there you go, you make the best of the hand you're dealt. My bare-knuckle boxing record says you can't argue the fact that I sure as hell made the best of what I was given.

What I've found is that while you're living life, you take what's thrown at you and get on with it when you haven't got the time or inclination to give it much thought. It's only now that I have returned to Ederney, the village of my birth in Ireland, that I've slowed down, chilled out and begun to reflect on my past life.

What strikes me is that my life seems to have been split into three parts. First, there's my family. I got love and support from my ma and da, then later the same from my wife and kids. No question, I've been blessed on that score.

Then there's the fighting that I always kept away from my family. You see, if I'd achieved what I did in the legitimate ring I'd have been a bit of a hero: picture in the papers, credit for being the champion I was and a nice few quid in the bank. Even today, now I've been retired for over 20 years, I might have been a TV fight commentator … But – a very big but – working on the other side of the law meant everything I fought for and won inside the ropes was kept a closely-guarded secret in the underworld it entertained. My ma didn't like it when she found out I was a bare-knuckle fighter and my Sandra was the same. Once I married her she hated every fight I took on. It never changed, no matter how many years passed.

The third part of my life involved my long-term friendship with one of the most famous men on the planet. As you'll see, there isn't anybody more ordinary and down to earth than me and the fact that Muhammad Ali and me became the best of mates is a strange thing in itself. He didn't look down on me because I was an unemployed labourer and no way did I look up to him, but how it all happened will always be a bit of a mystery to me – and one that took me on adventures halfway around the planet. It was all a far cry from my own beginnings.

CHAPTER ONE
Trouble from the Start

On 19 February 1944, I was born in the small farming village of Ederney, Co Fermanagh, in Northern Ireland. One of its claims to fame, if you can call it that, was that a local guy, the Fenian Michael Barrett, was the last man to be publicly hanged. He was strung up for bombing Clerkenwell prison sometime around the middle of the 1800s. Whether you're hung in public or private makes no difference in the end, but three days after he was topped, public hanging was banned. I'm no historian but that little fact has always stuck in my mind.

I was the third son and the youngest of six children, making up the score of three boys and three girls for my parents: Jim and Mary Anne Monaghan. Weighing in at a whopping 11 pounds 3 ounces, Ma and Da still hadn't made their minds up what to name me. I've often heard Mamma tell the tale of how Dadda came up with the idea of calling me by the name of the very first man to pass our house that morning. Mamma agreed and that man turned out to be one whose name was Paddy Gormley.

'That was a terrible odd way to name a child,' Mamma would

say. Then follow up with her punch line. 'Ahhh to be sure, an' he's been nothing but an odd bugger ever since.' It could've been worse. I'm told there was an old fella regularly walked by our house and he was called Diarmuid and if they'd given me that name I wouldn't have been able to spell it for years.

I don't remember ever having lived in Ireland as a child, it was always being talked about in the family that the Monaghans in the past were absolutely minted – my grandfather owned most of the land round Ederney. He owned the local mill as well and almost everybody in the village worked for the 'Monaghans of the Mill'. With his parents both dying when my dadda was about ten, all the money and land was left to him, though everything was put in the hands of executors.

Da was put in the care of his Auntie Rose but she died three years later. He and his mate Manus McGuire ran away from Black Rock College in Dublin and led the life of a young playboy, a life that made a big hole in his inheritance. He was generous and trusting with everybody, but if there had been an Olympic gold medal for drinking and gambling he'd have won it. His executors thought, 'Oh bollocks, if he can waste his money without a second's thought we might as well have some of it.' So they robbed him blind. By the time he met and married my ma he was on his arse and had to work as a farm labourer for someone who'd worked for him and his family in the past.

He suffered that for years until my birth. His pride wouldn't let him take any more and he made up his mind to go to England to find work. To raise the fare and get a bit of money to keep us all going until he found work, Da sold off two acres of the last three that were left from his legacy. I'm talking roughly about 1947 here, so I doubt the land was worth much in Ireland at the time. Still, it must have been enough for what he needed because off he went, leaving Mamma and six kids behind.

The Monaghans were never to be landowners ever again.

Many years later, sometime after Dadda had passed away, I went back to Ederney with Mamma because she had the idea she'd like to look at that one acre that still belonged to the family. I dunno, perhaps she had a dream of putting a little bungalow on it where she could spend her last years.

What did we find? Yeah, her piece of land had been nicked.

The people who had bought the other two acres had stuck a fence around what must have looked like an abandoned plot. The law being as it is, if you have uninterrupted use of a piece of land for 12 years then it legally becomes yours: no argument. Ma was gutted and I was fucking mad to put it mildly.

I kicked up a bit of a fuss with the result I got a few phone calls at the hotel we were staying in telling me to get out of town. Each time it was, 'This is the IRA – if you want to live get out now.'

I said, 'Listen you wanker, like I told the last c**t, I don't care if you're the IRA, UDA or the WRI – I'm going nowhere so fuck off.' IRA my arse. Every weasily little twat with a grievance in Ireland uses those initials to put the frighteners on. As I guessed, the calls were nothing to do with the Republican Army but they didn't half have my ma flustered. Truth is, after that knockback, Ma and me were both ready to go back to England, but to spite whoever was making the threats we stayed another four days and heard nothing more.

Around the time I turned five, Dadda sent for us all to join him in England. He had ended up in Abingdon near Oxford, but I've no idea why. This is where Mamma and six kids arrived to move into one large room. Sounds unbelievable – eight of us managed to eat, sleep and live in such a cramped little space. It didn't bother me at all because at that age I knew no better, but from that first week Ma and Da searched the whole town for somewhere bigger.

Discrimination or racism, whatever you want to call it, might be a dirty word today, but back in the 50s it was as normal as breathing. Young as I was, it made an impact on me that I've never forgotten. I was dragged around by Ma and Da, looking for decent lodgings. I'd hear Ma say, 'Waste of time knocking there Jim, look,' and she'd be pointing at a big handwritten notice in a window.

I couldn't read and wouldn't be able to for another dozen years so I'd say to Da, 'What does it say Dadda?'

Ma said, 'He's too young to know.' But Da told me anyway.

'Son,' he said, 'that sign says that them that own the house don't want no black people, no dogs and no Irish people like us.'

Eventually we got fixed up in a bigger place but even then it was only one bedroom and a kitchenette. It was from this little place that I started school.

St Edmund's School, Abingdon. If I'd known then what my education would turn out to be I would have stayed at home until I was 15. I wasn't stupid and I was ready to start learning like most kids are at that age, but what with being the only Irish kid in the place, and one with a strong Northern Ireland accent at that, I didn't stand a chance.

From day one I had the piss ripped out of me, so I had to fight. It was a primary school for age five to eleven, but when you're five, an eleven-year-old looks like a twenty-year-old. There was nothing of me really, probably three-and-a-half stone soaking wet, but I got stuck into any of them who asked for it. And it was always like that – I never did grow into the sort of guy you'd expect to be a bare-knuckle fighter. At my best I don't think I ever weighed in at really more than 11-and-a-half stone, but when it comes to a tear-up, size doesn't matter: it's what's inside that counts.

Well, I must've had that something inside me because I never bottled a fight, then or in the years to come, but where that something came from I've no idea. Nothing burned inside me like

4

it did in some guys who had a childhood of abuse or neglect. I didn't have a chip on my shoulder or feeling of inferiority, so it's a puzzle. Still, didn't matter where it came from, I had it – as the piss-takers and bullies found out.

One thing led to another and soon other kids were bribing me to take on older boys who'd threatened to get them after school. Sweets and chocolate bars were the currency, and when Mamma questioned how I always seemed to have a pocketful of sweets when I came home from school, I told a white lie and said the other boys liked me. Those times when it didn't go my way until the end and I suffered a black eye or cut lip, I'd have to tell Ma that one or two of the other boys didn't like me quite as much.

This went on until I was 11 and it was time to move onto the bigger school and then guess what? Yeah, the secondary modern school had twice the amount of bullies and I started all over again. Those daily fights got me classed as a stroppy little fucker, a nuisance and a troublemaker. The teachers always singled me out to help the gardener or the caretaker, anything to get me out of the classroom. I had a natural ability to draw and paint, but it was completely ignored. They didn't give a shit back in those days. None of them considered that they were screwing up my future. My education was practically zero.

I'll give you an idea of how I was treated. There was an old science teacher at school who, no doubt, was a clever man. But he was also typical of a lot of teachers back then in that he didn't like children. In fact, he was a heartless old bastard who dug me out whenever he could. One time I was shovelling horse shit on the school rose garden and the sweat was dripping off me. This was in sight of a class who were doing what they called field studies. He walked towards me holding his nose, but I ignored him and carried on shovelling.

Suddenly I heard him say, 'Monaghan, drop that shovel and come over here with me.' I felt quite chuffed, because I thought he was going to let me join the class and have the same tuition as the rest. But instead he said, 'Monaghan, tell me boy, what is a meteorite?' I didn't have a clue, but I knew I'd get a whack round the head if I stood there dumb, so I blurted out the first thing that came into my head

'Er ... I think ... I ... a meteorite is someone who to eats meat.'

The whole class of about 30 boys pissed themselves, which didn't stop him even for a second. 'Monaghan, I never ever have – and I never ever will – encounted anyone quite as stupid as you are.' Then he stuck his face right into mine and shouted 'Am I right?'

Not many years later I would've torn his face off, but then I just mumbled, 'No, sir, you're wrong.'

Bang. He gave me a right-hander across the face, pointed to the dung-heap and screamed at me: 'Get back to the only thing you're fit for.'

The sneering giggles of the rest of the class hurt me more than his clout.

My summers were taken up with mowing the playing field, digging wherever I was told to and weeding the gardener's private vegetable patch. Winter days were taken up with stoking the massive boiler in the basement for the caretaker plus any other shitty jobs he didn't want to do himself. I should've worn a brown coat at school because for the best part of four years I was an unpaid skivvie and school assistant.

You'd think Ma and Da would wonder why their youngest son couldn't read or write, but they never questioned it. I can only think they thought I was a little bit backward when it came to learning and didn't want to embarrass me by bringing it up. I was to blame as well because I never did take home the way I was treated at school. I suppose in a way I thought it was my own fault and didn't want to say how I had been humiliated.

So, at age 15 I was signed off from school and chucked out into the big wide world, proudly carrying the skills that ten years of education had given me: the artistic use of a shovel and a fighting ability that would shape my future life.

Other kids might have dreamed of being train drivers or pilots, but for me there was nothing else I wanted to be other than a boxer. This ambition had nothing to do with my constant scrapping at school; I just did what I had to do. So I knew how to fight but never had the opportunity to pick up the skill of boxing proper, because there wasn't a boxing club in Abingdon when I was a youngster.

While most kids were reading comics like *The Beano* and *The Dandy*, I couldn't get enough of *Boxing News* and *The Ring*. Only difference was, unlike most youngsters, I couldn't nose through them myself and had to rely on the patience of Mamma to read them out loud to me from cover to cover.

When a fight was broadcast from America during my school days, Dadda would let me stay up into the small hours to catch every magic moment. We had a battered, wooden-cased wireless and I sat with my ear pressed to the gauze front and was in the ring with Joe Louis, Rocky Marciano, Sugar Ray Robinson – one of the greatest fighters ever – and Jake La Motta beating Marcel Cerdan.

Ma didn't approve: 'Jim, the lad's got school tomorrow,' but she knew it was the only real interest in my life so always let Dadda overrule her. Oh yeah, fucking school: be a shame if I missed filling the boiler or digging shit into the roses.

There didn't seem to be much change when I left school. My first job was with, you've guessed it, a shovel, digging electric cable trenches alongside my father and brothers, Seamus and Brendan. Dadda wanted me to be an electrician, so I put in for an apprenticeship but I was turned down because I couldn't read or write. This bothered Dadda, but honestly and, I can see now, stupidly, I didn't give a fuck. I had a lot to learn about life at age 15.

Within a year I was in trouble with the law after flattening a bouncer called 'Jumbo' Denton at a Saturday night dance. This guy wasn't called Jumbo for nothing. He was built like a brick shithouse and was known as a bit of a handful and a right bully.

I'd gone to a local dance with a few of the boys, even though dancing wasn't my thing at all. So that meant standing against the wall, looking mean and moody like James Dean in his films; seemed to work all right with the birds. I knew this Denton fella, we all did, 'cos he'd been the bouncer in the place for a couple of years: cocky sod, all brawn and his brain up his arse.

I'd never come up against him in any way because honestly I was completely indifferent to the prick. At the same time his reputation meant almost all the kids and older fellas was shit scared of him. I reckon it was just rumour and gossip, but it was all believed – the word was he was a bare-knuckle fighter who took on all comers from around the country. Apparently he was ex-SAS and had done time for killing somebody in a fight – you get the picture. It gave him free reign to take any liberty he fancied and nobody had the balls to tackle him.

Funny thing reputation. If word goes out that some weedy fella is a bit of a nut-case and goes from Clarke Kent to Superman in the blink of an eye – what are people gonna do? They ain't gonna risk checking it out just in case it's true, so they steer well clear of some nine-stone streak of piss. So, in the same way, big as he was, Jumbo's rep might have been fuck all but most people thought it was wise to believe it.

Anyway, I'm minding my own business and having a crack with the lads, when through the crowd I saw Jumbo, the fat twat, walking over to a young fella who happened to be sitting with a very attractive girl. I was too far away to hear what was said but had a good idea that, typical Denton, he was showing off and trying his luck with this young girl. Give him his due, the boyfriend, if that's what he was, stood up and appeared to be having a few words. Next thing Denton gave him a shove that nearly had the fella over. Just as I noticed the lad had one arm in a plaster, big man Jumbo slapped him full in the face.

I hate bullies, as my school record showed, so without even thinking I ran through the dancers and got myself between the two of them, saying, 'C'mon, you fat c**t, try it on with somebody your own size.' I was so wound up I obviously didn't choose my words too well. Somebody his own size would've been a foot taller than me and around five stone heavier. He looked at me as though I was gone out, grinned all over his fat mug and swung a punch at my head. Talk about telegraphing a message ahead, he was so slow I saw his fist coming long before it got anywhere near me.

I ducked and threw a hard right into his bread sack – he whoofed like a dog and his eyes crossed. There was no doubt that if his meaty fist had connected with my head I'd have been spark out, but I never gave him the chance. He came lumbering towards me, spitting, swearing, his arms going like windmills. I swerved to one side and hit him just below the ear with a powerful left and as the power of the punch turned him sideways I curled a vicious right into his kidney. I knew that if I didn't finish him I was in trouble, so I pistoned punch after punch into him until he went down on his knees – finished – but I wasn't.

What with the height difference I'd been punching upwards, now he was on the perfect level for a two-handed haymaker – and boy, did I make it count? His eyes rolled up into his head and he fell sideways in slow motion.

The music still blared out, but the dancing had stopped and the crowd surrounded us all whistling and shouting. Two of my mates pulled me away in case I had ideas of kicking the shit out of the unconscious bouncer and perhaps accidentally killing him. But that was the last thing on my mind. I fight hard – fucking hard – but I fight fair.

Apart from skinned knuckles I was unmarked, so I had no problem saying goodnight to Ma and Da, keeping both hands in my pockets, before I sloped off to bed.

In the early hours of the morning, we were woken by loud knocking on the front door and I could hear shouts of, 'Police – open up.' It wasn't difficult to work out why the law was banging on our door, but before I could get out of bed I could hear my Da opening the front door and loudly telling the coppers to fuck off. Then I heard Mamma's voice joining in, so I pulled on my trousers and ran down the stairs. There was some scuffling going on as Dadda blocked the door to keep them out.

As I got to the bottom of the stairs Ma was crying and shouting to the three cops, 'You're not taking my boy, he's a good lad.' I put my arm around her shoulder and told her not to worry. It was some sort of misunderstanding and the sooner I went with them the quicker it would be sorted out. Da was kicking off, demanding an explanation but they just ignored him and that made him even angrier. I grabbed my jacket off the coat rail by the door, stepped outside and told the coppers I was coming quietly. I wasn't in a great rush to get nicked but at the same time I wanted to get away before Dadda was himself in trouble with the law.

I was handcuffed, stuck in the police van and whipped off to the local nick. If I hadn't already guessed, once I'd gone through the business of being photographed and printed, I was told that Denton, spineless bastard, had grassed me up. Him, a guy who'd created aggravation and committed GBH on a regular basis, had gone crying to the law.

Cut a long story short, a month later I was up in court listening to a load of bollocks about my unprovoked and vicious assault on an innocent man who was quietly doing his job in the dance hall. My mates searched every corner of Abingdon in an effort to find the young guy with his arm in plaster for him to speak in my defence, but he'd disappeared. Paid off or frightened off? You tell me.

Big Jumbo Denton was given a police escort out of town and has never been back since.

The judge, a miserable looking old git, didn't even look at me let alone wanna hear what I had to say for myself. His mission in life was to rid the streets of gangsters and violent criminals and standing in front of him, he believed, was one of the worst. So to be honest, I only opened my mouth to give my name and address and a very firm 'Not guilty'. I'll swear he smirked when I said that.

So I didn't say much, but no way was my Dadda gonna be gagged. He gave it plenty. Chipping in every few minutes with shouted questions and advice for the judge. I could see the judge was getting the right arsehole and it was the last straw when Da shouted, 'What was the point of people putting their lives on the line in the War for a country that had turned into a police state?'

I just groaned inside thinking, 'Da, I love you for defending me, but for fuck's sake give it a rest before you're up here in the dock with me.' The threat of being held in contempt of court and a good dig in the ribs from Mamma shut him up in the end.

It was a foregone conclusion. The judge casually announced I was guilty of assault and sentenced me to three months in a detention centre. It was a bastard, I thought, but with a detention centre based just out of town, at Kiddlington near Oxford, at least I'd get plenty of visitors. But unfortunately this was not to be.

How green was I to how the system worked. What they do is get a compass and set the radius at roughly a hundred miles. Then they put one point on a map of the nearest borstal or prison to your home. Then striking a radius, choose the nearest place to the other point that, like I said, is about a hundred miles away.

I never got a chance to say goodbye to Ma or Da as I was escorted straight out of the court and stuck in a holding cell with about half-a-dozen other young guys. A notice on the wall said, 'No talking and no singing'. I wondered if somebody was having a fucking laugh with us. No fucking *singing*? We've all just been ripped away from our families and haven't got a clue what lay ahead and some bright spark thinks we might fancy breaking into song?

Three tea-less hours later I was squeezed into a car with four copper escorts heading for Goudhurst, in Kent and my new home – HMP (Her Majesty's Prison) Blantyre House.

The place we ended up at some four hours later was built just before the First World War as a training centre for deprived boys to learn about coal mining. Then, around 1954, it was taken over as a prison. Did I give a fuck about its history – no, but that was part of the induction speech given by the assistant governor. The rest, that I barely listened to, was how we would look back on our forthcoming experience as a breath of fresh air in our horrible criminal lives.

Nobody questioned why me, aged 16, should be banged up in a place for age groups 18 to 21. Turned out I was the youngest ever prisoner in the place.

Well, if any of those older guys thought that because of my age I was some sort of prick and a pushover for piss-taking, bullying or robbing, I opened their eyes at the very first dinner I sat down to.

I managed to be late into the canteen hall and the only seat left was right opposite some shaven-headed fat bastard. His forehead was about an inch wide and if his eyes had been any closer together he'd have looked like he only had one. But, I thought to myself, don't jump to conclusions based on appearance, 'cos he might be the nicest guy in the world. So, benefit of the doubt and all that, I gave him a nod.

Fucking hell, it was like poking a bear with a stick. He gave a sort of growl and, food spilling out of his mouth, shouted, 'Custard!' He was gulping down a pudding and I hadn't even started my dinner yet.

'Do what?'

And like some animal he shouted again, 'More custard!'

I looked behind me in case he was talking to somebody else, but then he leaned across the table, jabbed his finger in my chest and said, 'You fuckin' deaf? Get me more custard.'

Before I could open my mouth or react, some soft-looking fella beside him jumped in: 'I'll get it. I'll get it for you.' He got a backhander in the mouth and that was enough to wind me up, but when the fat fella said, 'I want this new young prick to get it.' I saw red and at the same time thought … here I go again.

I said to him, 'Tell you what, mush, why don't you have my custard?' and slung my plate right into his face; nice and hot.

He screamed at the top of his voice and tried scrambling across the table to get at me, but slipping and sliding in the custard he ended up laying across it with his face at fist height. Yeah, no messing, I hit him as hard as I could. When necessary I can deliver a proper knockout punch. He just put his head down and closed his eyes. Game over. Straight off, I felt myself gripped in a headlock from behind by one of the screws and 'No fucking dinner for you'. Later I was down the block – the punishment wing – thinking, Good start, Paddy, my old son.

That bout set the pattern for the rest of my time in Blantyre House. I never got another squeak out of custard bollocks but many others wanted to prove they were top dog or the daddy. I had them queuing up to take me on and not one of them managed to beat me.

I'm not saying every battle was easy, because there was some very tasty fellas in there. I often took some heavy beatings and ended up looking like I'd been run over, but, at the finish, I always managed to dig deep and find that bit extra to finish off my opponent. Like I said before, it's what's inside that makes a fighter. It didn't take too long for me to lose every day of my remission. I spent so much time down the block it was like having my own private cell.

I could've done without being banged up, but I can't say the experience was too bad. Apart from the loss of freedom and being away from family and friends, I think the worst fear for most serving at Her Majesty's Pleasure is the threat of violence from other prisoners. But what with me being a bit handy when it came to a scrap and not having the sense to fear anybody, I sailed through the whole thing, no problem.

I got the usual sarcastic 'See you soon' when I was finally let out of the gate, gave the screw a quick 'Fuck off' and at the same time told myself that was the last time – and it was.

A few weeks after I was released, I happened to bump into some traveller friends I hadn't seen for quite a while. These fellas knew what I could do with my fists and when it came out that I didn't have a pot to piss in these travelling boys talked me into showing up in a couple of weeks time for a bare knuckle fight about a hundred miles away at a horse fair near Cambridge; cash-in-hand. Only thing was, I had to say I was 19 otherwise none of the fellas would even consider taking me on.

In my favour, during my spell behind the door, where every move you made was on the hurry up, plus my time in solitary down the block, I'd nothing else to do but shape myself up by doing endless press-ups and any exercise that I could do in the confined space. Result was I toned up and was as fit as I'd ever be.

Taking on grown men, and rough, tough bastards at that, didn't make me lose any sleep at all. I was very confident in my own ability to do the business when it came to it. Not young, cocky confident that would all fall apart when I was put to the test, but a feeling inside that being sure footed, fast and with the trump card of a deadly knockout punch I could take on and beat anybody: game on!

I spent the next couple of weeks running for miles to strengthen my legs up and improve my wind. Not that I needed to, but, without work to go to, I couldn't sit around with my thumb in my arse. I never told Ma and Da what I was up to – well, you wouldn't would you? So they both thought I was out looking for work.

Come the day, I was picked up early by two of the travelling fellas in a battered old tarmac lorry. That put Mamma in a panic 'cos she thought I was off to work and spent five minutes running around shoving cakes and biscuits into a bag for my lunch. I felt bad that I wasn't telling the complete truth but at the end of the day I *was* going to work, just not the sort she would've approved of. A couple of hours later we pulled into a secluded area that I think was an airfield at some time. It was rammed with people, lorries, trailers and horses. I'd never heard it said that there was any gypsy or tinker blood in our family, but I had a sort of swarthy, traveller look about me, so at least I didn't stick out like a sore dick when we got ourselves mingling with the crowd.

Every which way I turned there was some kind of deal going on, whether it was selling a horse, a dog, gold or something dodgy. Each was completed by spitting in the palm and a quick handshake between the two parties.

There was a fair danger of being either killed or injured, because bareback riders were galloping semi-wild horses through the crowd, yelling and screaming and youngsters as young as seven were hanging onto the reins of massive horses that were pulling flimsy-looking two wheeled carts. I'll swear these kids were doing in the region of 40 miles an hour. The smell of wood smoke, food-cooking, horse shit and people hung over the place in a cloud. There was a carnival atmosphere and though, like I said, I'm no gypsy, I felt I was one of them.

About 11.30am, my two mates interrupted me chatting up some traveller girl to tell me they'd put out a challenge to one of the fighters and it had been accepted. All in, winner takes all, loser dragged out by the heels. We made our way over to where some trailers were parked up in a three-sided box, the open side facing a small group of trees that hid the area nicely. Not that there was any fear of the Old Bill showing their faces, but there was no sense in being too obvious. I've gotta say I was buzzing with adrenaline.

There must've been about 20 guys milling about between the trailers and I guessed my opponent was the one stripped to the waist and hopping from one foot to another. A fight in the ring, whether licensed or unlicensed, usually means you go up against somebody within your own weight range. When the choice is your own to throw out a challenge it's up to you. If you want to take on a guy built like the side of a hill, well, nobody forced you into it. Sizing up the guy over in the corner, I guessed he was about the same as my 11-stone-plus, but he must've been about six-foot-three: a long, rangy character. Not the easiest type to fight because of their reach.

I wasn't too sure how the game worked but my mates left me standing there and walked over to the group surrounding the guy they'd challenged. They didn't speak to him, but, with a lot of head-nodding and arm-waving, they spoke to an older guy for a few minutes. After spitting into palms and shaking hands they came back to me saying, 'Okay, Paddy, son, all up to you now.' By this time, the tall fella had got himself into the centre of the space and was shadow-boxing and giving me the come-on, beckoning me with his fingers. I stripped off the old jumper I was wearing over an equally old t-shirt, took a deep breath and, without any fucking about, I went for him.

We feinted around for a little while as we got the measure of each other; then one of his spidery arms came shooting at me and his fist caught me square on the forehead. He might have been a skinny c**t, but shit, my brains rattled like peas in a bag. Perhaps he didn't have too much experience because he didn't follow through, which was lucky, as he'd have caught me on the hop before my eyes uncrossed.

I went into a crouching position with my guard well up and dodged around waiting for him to leave me an opening. Curled up low as I was, he couldn't resist dropping a couple of hammer blows to the top of my head, but while he wasted his time pounding that block of wood he left his belly and midriff exposed and I took advantage of the opening.

Bang! I gave him a solid belt just below the sternum and having had a few of those in my time, I can tell you it's a paralysing blow. He went rigid and clutched his middle: bad move. I drove a punch upwards, missed the point of his chin and caught him on the temple. That's another one I know from experience it's hard to come back from. His face went a sort of blue colour and, holding one hand to his head and the other to his belly, he just stood there, half doubled over, swaying like a tree ready to fall. Now I wanted to make sure that I earned every penny that was coming my way without any argument. Fair play or not, I delivered two devastating punches to his midriff and he slumped to the ground. The older guy who seemed to be fronting the deal dived forward and stood between me and his boy to signal that it was all over, as if that wasn't obvious to anybody watching.

I thought to myself, Now I'm gonna have to fight my way out of this lot, but it turned out it doesn't work that way, or very rarely. There's an unwritten code that if a fighter gets beaten fair and square that's the end of it. I grabbed my jumper, left my mates to sort out the cash and made my through the crowd to the lorry.

Money wasn't mentioned until we pulled up outside my house in Abingdon, when one of the guys stuck 30 notes into my hand. By today's standards it doesn't sound too much for putting my good looks at risk, but I'm talking 1960 here. What a result. Thirty lovely one-pound notes, a bundle I'd never held in my life before. When you consider a good joiner or a plumber was taking home about £20 a week, I had nothing to complain about. The two fellas didn't tell me what they'd earned out of me and I didn't ask, but we shook hands, without spitting into palms, thank fuck, with the promise that there'd be more fights in the future if I was up for it.

Apart from a couple of lumps sticking through my hair and a red mark on my forehead, I was unmarked, so I could show my face to my parents just as I had after the battle with Denton. I slipped Ma 20 quid of my wages and had to suffer rib-crushing hugs and sloppy kisses and to hear that I was a 'good boy to his mammy' – bless her. It was a great feeling to please my Ma after all she'd done for me over the years and to contribute to the housekeeping – even though she thought I'd been shovelling tarmac all day.

With a few quid on my hip I started to get out on the town more than I might've done. Being young and stupid, me and my mates got into trouble every which way we could think of. Well, that is to say, we didn't deliberately set out looking for trouble but what else are high spirits going to lead to at that age? At least I've never been a drinker and, while I can imagine my Irish ancestors turning in their graves as I say it, it was a fucking good thing otherwise God knows how I would've ended up. I was irresponsible enough sober. Anything for a laugh, that was me, but anything stronger than a nice cup of tea never appealed to me.

As it was, the word 'tearaway' fitted me like a glove. I'm not talking about vandalism, thieving or mugging because, back then, fucking nuisances that we might've been, we still had respect for property and older people. Among ourselves though, no stunt was outside our boundaries and I was at the centre of everything. I mean, when it was suggested it would be a great crack to drive a motor bike into the local Corn Exchange, who was first in line to give it a go? Yeah, Paddy the lunatic. No sooner the dare than I've grabbed a bike off of one of the guys, kicked it over and gone ripping up about a dozen stone steps, through the double doors, down some more steps and out onto the main floor. I'll point out there wasn't a meeting or anything going on at the time but plenty of staff were wandering about. I've done three circuits of the hall, filling the place up with the stink of exhaust fumes, finished with a wheelie that left skid marks on the polished floor, then up the steps again and out into the street, to the cheers and whistles of my mates. I'd had the sense to pull a scarf over my face, but even so I'm sure Old Bill had a fair idea who the culprit was, though I never got any comeback from it.

As for cars, I didn't own one myself at the time but that never stopped me borrowing one every now and then, to scream around the streets of Abingdon and Oxford – no licence, no insurance. Later on, when I was old enough to drive legally and had a motor of my own, I still drove around without any legal documents at all. Doesn't work today, but, back then, the label from a Guinness bottle looked remarkably like a tax disc, at least from a distance. We all stuck one of them in the holder on the windscreen or failing that, a scribbled note stating, 'Tax in the post.'

When you consider I got sent down for something that wasn't what it looked like and something I didn't start, I seemed to lead a charmed life after that. I was pulled plenty of times by the law, mostly for motoring offences and brawling in the town, but nothing to get me sent down. It was crazy. There was I going off with the travelling lads for a bit of knuckles, picking up a decent bit of scratch then handing it over to the government in fines. I must've had a file two inches thick down the local police station, but luck of the Irish, as they say, nobody thought I should be taken off the streets for a good long stretch.

Meanwhile, good earners though they were, the bare knuckle fights weren't regular enough to be called a living. I had to think about getting a job so that Ma and Da didn't think I was wasting my life away.

CHAPTER TWO
The Barn

What was holding me back as a young man, more than being a bit of a tearaway, was my lack of education. I'd left school without even one piece of paper showing an exam result. I had the ability of a small child when it came to the three 'R's. And I had no concept of anything that was going on in the world apart from what concerned my everyday life in that little patch called Abingdon.

I make myself sound a right thick twat and, in fairness to myself, I shouldn't. When it came down to street level I could be sharp as a knife. Look at my fighting record. I could work out strategies in a blink of an eye, weigh up odds as quick and when it came to money I could work out any equation.

I weighed up my skills – very fit, strong, good fighter, almost illiterate and magic with a shovel. None of them put me in the frame for sales manager, bank clerk or tune-up specialist, whatever that meant. I tore up the jobs pages and set out on a tour of building sites looking for an opening as a labourer. Skills needed: strong back, strong shoulders and at least half a brain – right up my street.

Eventually I got fixed up as a general labourer on a building site and boy is there any better training for a fighter than that? One minute I'd be digging a trench, the next passing up 20-foot lengths of timber to the roofers or unloading tons of cement and carrying a bag on each shoulder for 20 yards. If I thought I was fit when I started, by the time a month had passed any trace of fat – and there wasn't much to start with – had turned to muscle.

Just as well, because those two mates of mine had put up a challenge on my behalf against some gypsy wild man who, according to them, was the nearest thing to a gorilla outside a zoo. Thanks for the vote of confidence guys.

Though I'm a Catholic by birth, a very lapsed one, Mamma used to read to me from the Bible as a change from *Boxing News* and to make sure I didn't grow up completely godless. The story of David and Goliath sprang to mind as the fight loomed. A consolation for me was that the little guy won; we'd see.

This fight was to take place at Appleby, probably the oldest and best-known of all the horse fairs. It meant a good long drive because it was up in Cumbria, over 200 miles away. This time we went in style in a very tasty Ford Capri. Folded up in the back, because these motors were semi-sports jobs, I never even considered commenting on the tangle of electrics hanging out of the ignition – an obvious sign of hot-wiring. Say no more.

The atmosphere at Appleby was much the same as a lot of the other fairs at which I'd fought, except on a bigger scale. Everything about it screamed money or ego. Not as many scrap vans or lorries as mainly new Range Rovers and expensive trailers were parked all over the place. I got the impression that travellers feel that showing what you're worth is what you are.

I was due to meet King Kong at about 2pm, so to pass the time I wandered around, sticking my nose in out of the way places and watching a few battles. A lot of these fights struck me as not much more than playground brawls, especially among the younger fellas. A lot of mouth, bravado and dancing around, without much damage. On the other hand some of the fights amongst the older guys were pretty bloody. You get two grown men knocking the bollocks out of each other and I can tell you, it ain't for the squeamish. If you couldn't stand blood, busted jaws and broken teeth, you wouldn't want to be watching.

Two o'clock came round and I made my way to where I'd been told the match was gonna be, pushing my way through a crowd about fifty strong, just in time to see some battered-looking guy being dragged away by his feet.

As I'm standing looking, the crowd parted opposite me and this big traveller, stripped to the waist, appeared shouting, 'Where's the fucker? Where's the fucker?' I guessed I was the fucker he was looking for, so, not seeing any point in hanging about, I pulled off my jacket and stepped forward.

I don't exaggerate when I say his arms were bigger than my thighs. Paddy, old son, this one don't look too easy.

This fella wanted it over and done with and me spark out as soon as. Without a nod or a kiss-my-arse, he came roaring at me like a fucking bull. I dodged out of his way and ducked under a fist as big as a leg of lamb. His rush carried him past me and I managed to slip a good belt to the top of his spine. He swung round and kicked me in the leg and it went dead. Ducking and weaving, I managed to keep out of his way until the feeling came back. I got the idea that he wasn't too skilful and relied on steam-rollering his opponent until he wore them down for the kill.

The problem for me was that I couldn't deliver one of my knockout punches because those slabs of meat he had for arms made the perfect shield. Only thing I could do was force him to drop his guard and that meant I had to keep jab-jabbing away at

23

his arm muscles. I'm not bragging when I say that you know when you get one of my best punches, and every blow I landed on his upper arm made him flinch.

So I was in and out – I'd go bang, bang on each arm, then I would back-peddle out of his reach. I could see the numbing effect it was having. My punches were making his arms heavy and they were dropping slightly. Seemed like David was taking the piss out of Goliath.

Then I went for him, slipped on a stone and only by flicking my head away avoided my face being hit full on by one of his huge fists. It brushed my cheek, ripped into my ear and blood ran down my neck and shoulders. At least he didn't spoil my good looks. My ear hurt like buggery and I hate to say it, but for a split second I lost my temper with the big bastard, something I very rarely do. Anger made me misjudge what he was going to do and I left myself open to a punch full in the face. It broke my nose and sent me sprawling backwards. I was straight back up again, blood everywhere and my nose on fire.

Now I was fucking mad, but, after my little lapse of judgement, I stayed cool and focused on getting those arms down. Taking a leaf out of the book of my schoolboy hero Rocky Marciano, I bobbed, weaved and rolled into every punch with all my power. I never let up for a moment and slowly but surely those arms dropped. Every time they did I drove a pile driver through his open guard, bang on target.

Finally, he reeled away from a very tasty knock to the forehead and dropped his arms by his side, giving me the perfect opening. I practically jumped in the air as I put everything I had into a straight arm, a bone-crunching blow to the point of his chin – it was all over. And just as well because I was bleeding like a pig and my hands were swollen up like balloons.

My mates led me to a trailer belonging to a friend of theirs and set about cleaning me up. There was nothing to do with my hands except soak them in cold water. The blood washed off easy but the bad part was having my ear lobe stitched back into shape with a needle and black thread and my nose roughly squashed around like a piece of putty until it looked something like a nose should. During a fight, with adrenaline pumping, you don't feel too much pain. Afterwards was a different story, and I was squealing like a pig.

I'd been lucky when it came to getting marked up in a fight. Plenty of sore ribs and bruises where they didn't show, but that day, looking like I did, there was no way I could get away with telling Ma that I'd been working. I could've lied and said I'd tripped over a wheelbarrow but I'd never been a liar. I stretched or bent the truth slightly, but I couldn't bear to lie to my parents, so after Mamma's shock wore off when she saw my mashed face, I told her I'd taken up boxing and left it at that. She wasn't happy about it but would've been less happy if I'd added 'bare knuckle' to the word boxing.

It's always been a regret of mine that I wasn't able to take up the noble art, as they call it, properly. The study of the sport had been an obsession of mine since I was a little kid and to have joined the ranks of my heroes would've been a dream come true. I know without any doubt that I could've been a champion. Out in the public eye, my name mentioned among the greats and the bonus of plenty of money that I could've used to repay the enormous debt I owed my parents for the sacrifices they'd made for all the family. It wasn't meant to be though.

I achieved champion status in the years to come but unfortunately it was in the darker side of the sport, where illegal fights had to be kept secret and the money by comparison was shit.

I carried on my life much the same month after month, year after year. Grafting my nuts off and picking up fights whenever they were offered. In the back of my mind, though, I always felt that there had to be more to life than what I was getting out of it. I think we're all the same when we're young: some sort of belief that things will change and fame and fortune will come knocking some day. Doesn't happen too often, and those dreams fade as the years creep up on you, but in my own case I couldn't have imagined in my wildest dreams where my life was heading.

An image that always stuck in my mind was a minor thing from my first setting foot on the pavements of Abingdon. I was five years old and fresh from Ireland, so every sight and sound was completely different from anything I'd been used to. I was standing holding Mamma's hand when I caught sight of a strange-looking man. Strange to me because his slanting eyes and complexion was like nothing I'd seen before. I wasn't to know but he was Chinese and I couldn't take my eyes off him.

Mamma eventually gave me a nudge, whispering for me not to be so rude. The man noticed this, gave me a smile, ruffled my hair and walked away. By a strange coincidence this man was related to the girl I'd eventually marry.

Sure, I was a wild young man in those days, but what turned me away from brawling and getting myself into trouble, was meeting this girl. If she hadn't set me on the straight and narrow, God only knows where I'd be today.

Abingdon isn't exactly London or New York, so our paths had crossed over the years. But I never had the nerve to approach her because she was so beautiful and I was frightened of rejection. Me, frightened? I put myself up against some of the toughest guys in the country and here was me afraid of asking a girl out.

I'd been with girls before, in fact, I had my fair share of them, but with Sandra it was different. Right from the start we fell in love. Her father was the son of an Abingdon girl who had married

26

a World War I Chinese interpreter with the unmistakable surname of Chung.

Well after years of plucking up courage I did eventually ask her out when we were both 20. I took her to the local dance hall which, as you will have gathered by now, was the focal point for us youngsters. What happened that night could've spoiled our relationship before it had even started.

With a good result from one of my fights I had bought myself an old banger of a motor. Triumph Mayflower; the bollocks. It was a big old bus, built like a tank and it would definitely impress my date. I picked her up, drove to the dance hall, and parked right outside like I owned the place.

The *News of the World* had already named Abingdon as 'the most trouble-torn town in England' and they came to this conclusion because of the fighting and aggro that went on between local lads and the Paras from the town's RAF training camp.

That night, the dance hall was packed more than it usually was because word was out that these Paras were coming mob-handed for a rumble and they were all a bad bunch of bastards.

I didn't want to get involved because of Sandra being a nice, respectable girl from a well-respected family. I didn't want her getting the impression that I was going to cause trouble and knock our brand new relationship on the head.

As the evening progressed, Paras started to drift in, and 20 minutes later the first scuffle broke out over in the corner. That seemed to pass off with a bit of shoving and pushing but then … Bosh! It kicked off for real and I could see some of my mates in the thick of it and not doing too well.

My instinct was to dive straight in and help my pals, but my first concern was for Sandra's safety, so I made sure she was well out of any danger by placing her in one of the balcony seats, apologised for leaving her, promised she'd be okay and dived into the fray.

27

I could see one of my mates getting knocked on his arse by a big fucker who was obviously the ringleader. Having put my mate and a few other guys down, he stood in the middle of the floor, stripped to the waist and shouting, 'C'mon you bunch of c**ts, who else wants some?'

Now I wasn't one for giving free shows – remember, a good lump of my earnings comes from fighting for money and I certainly didn't need to show that I was hard. The whole town knew that already – this fight was purely personal with that twat attacking my mates.

I was pulling off my shirt as I walked towards him and he just stood waiting with a smirk on his face: this guy didn't know me at all. Most of the local boys did though and, guessing what was about to happen, disentangled themselves from the various fights that were going on and started to form a big ring round the two of us.

As we circled round each other, I could tell he wasn't just another mug like the rest of his mob. He looked like a fighter and he moved like a fighter and, like me, had tell-tale puffy eyes and scar tissue above the lids.

Round and round we went, sizing each other up, both of us throwing out jabs to test the water. We were both looking for an opening.

It was my intention to back him into a corner, slip under his jabs and catch him with a few hard belts to the body. Then I noticed that every time he threw a jab out he dropped his right hand, leaving his chin exposed. I waited, suckering him into a jab, slipped under it and came up over the top to connect with a right and left to the jaw. He went out like a light. With him sprawled out on his back the place erupted into an uproar of screaming, shouting and brawls that kicked back into action again.

Next thing, the Old Bill was pouring through the doors, hitting out with truncheons in all directions. It seemed they directed the

28

worst of their attacks against the local lads and as those that got out of the place a bit smartish passed the word on, trouble spread through the town like wildfire. It escalated into a full scale riot. Later, police reinforcements came from nearby towns like Didcot and Wantage. Military police from the RAF camp showed up.

By the time all this happened, me and Sandra were well out of it because I'd slipped her out of a side exit with the idea of jumping in my motor and getting her home. Good job I wasn't the getaway driver for a bank job because my Mayflower was wedged between two police vans. There was nothing for it but to take drastic action.

I told Sandra to wait outside the car while I made room for our getaway. I beckoned her to the car and she got in and held on tight – no seat belts back then. Like I said, this car was built like a tank, so, revving the bollocks out of the engine, I stuck it in first gear and crashed forward. I went straight into reverse and backed up with a crashing sound of crumpled metal. Fortunately, the law had enough on their hands inside the dance hall, so with a dozen manoeuvres like that I managed to create enough space to drive out without being stopped. As I swung away from between the two vans, I was spotted by a squad car coming out of a side road. It was obvious what I'd been up to because one van was skewed up on the pavement and the other looked like it had been in a head-on collision.

I took off in a cloud of smoke from my spinning tyres. Tank or not, my motor had taken a beating and the driver's door, buckled out of shape, kept falling open. I got Sandra to lean round me and hold the door closed every time I took a left hand bend while I concentrated on losing the squad car.

I knew Abingdon like the back of my hand and I can only guess that the driver following had been drafted in from somewhere else because eventually I was on my own. Now what? First things first, I had to get Sandra out of the situation (although, straight and respectable as she was, I think she was enjoying the excitement of it all).

As I got closer to an area known as the wharf I made my mind up about what needed to be done. I pulled up, told Sandra to stand just inside an alleyway and said I'd only be two minutes. She didn't question me. The wharf had a slope from the road running straight into the Thames and, yeah, you've guessed it, my lovely old Mayflower was gonna sleep with the fishes. It only took seconds to get the car rolling down the slope and about as long again to disappear under the water. Being red hot after my manic journey through the streets, a plume of steam went up into the air about 30 feet; then it was gone.

Now the two of us were just another courting couple walking home from a date. Pity we were on the wrong side of town because now we had a long walk ahead of us. It wasn't wasted time though, because we got to know each other better during that walk than we might've done any other way.

If you think that love at first sight is a load of romantic bollocks and fades as quick as it arrives, let me point out that me and Sandra are still together after 44 years and we still feel the same about each other as we did on that first date.

Something that did worry me with her that night, was wondering how she would react when she found out how I earned an extra crust. Funnily enough she resolved that problem before the evening was over. We weren't too far from her place when she came out with, 'I hate violence Paddy.'

My heart sank and I thought here we go, I'm getting the elbow. Then she said, 'When you were fighting that big bully you looked just like boxer ... Are you?' Now or never Pads me ol' son, so I told her I was, sort of.

When she looked puzzled and questioned the sort of, I explained that I had the occasional fight as a bare knuckle boxer, which meant we didn't wear boxing gloves. I went into a bit of detail but I could see it was going right over her head 'cos all she came back with was, 'Oh … Ok.'

Much later on in our relationship she realised that boxing proper and bare-knuckle fights are worlds apart. The first time she saw my ripped, bloody and swollen face she took it bad. Though, once she had stopped crying and saw that most of the damage was superficial, she very, very reluctantly accepted that it was something I had to do.

In a way, years previous, I'd had a similar response from my Ma when after a severe fight I couldn't pretend that I'd fallen over some bricks on site or walked into a door and the truth came out. She hated the idea that her baby was giving and taking horrible violence. Da was different. Concerned in front of my Ma, out of her sight he was secretly proud and often told me, 'Paddy, give it your best son, that'll be good enough.'

My brothers knew what I was doing and they were chuffed that their wee brother was such a tough little bastard. My sisters were kept in the dark about the whole thing, 'cos being girls they would've told the world. So as far as they were concerned I got myself into a helluva lot of ordinary fights and the rest of the family never put them right.

Considering how successful I was in the game I guess it's odd that not one of my family were ever allowed to watch me fight.

A couple of years earlier, around 1962, I'd been approached by a man who was to become my best friend and mentor. Tommy Heard was a war hero, manager, promoter and matchmaker. He'd heard about my reputation as a fighter and had seen me in action a number of times. He thought I would be ideal for regular fights at The Barn, a notorious venue for some of the bloodiest bare knuckle fights.

When I agreed to give it a go, I never imagined that at the end of 18 years – a long, tough and potentially damaging 18 years – I'd become Bare Knuckle Boxing Middleweight Champion of the World.

It's been something like 28 years since I gave up 'knuckles' and retired, but I admit that I do give an occasional nostalgic thought back to those good old days when I fought in that rammed-tight barn or way out in a muddy field in some makeshift ring with only a single rope. All I ever really got out of it was a battered face that reminds me of those days every time I look in a mirror. Sometimes I go through my cardboard box of old photographs and look at pictures of myself before I started street fighting. I had no scars and no broken nose. Over the years my face has been changed out of all recognition. I must have been fucking crazy earning a living like that.

My advice to any young fella today is not even to think about fighting on the cobbles. That fighting is nothing like boxing proper – it's brutal and bloody and, at the end of the day, entertainment for bloodthirsty morons who would like nothing better than to see one of the fighters sprawled out dead. As a fighter, I know the choice was my own, but, really, we were modern-day gladiators, and to my mind we were only a very short step up from cock-and dog-fighting or badger-baiting – all illegal.

It was only once I'd given the game up that that I realised how dangerous it was: if I'd known then what I know now, I wouldn't have done it. Still, I did do it and if we all had the power of hindsight none of us would do half the things we do.

But back then, when I stepped through the doors of the Barn where the fights were put on, it felt as if I was walking into some kind of time warp. Every step took me backwards in time – into the 18th century.

These particular illegal fights took place on alternate Sundays, out in the wilds of the Hendon countryside, packed with up to three hundred bloodthirsty spectators, many drunk as skunks and all shouting and cursing as they turned up to lay bets on knuckles like myself.

There was no thrill or glamour in it for me. I was there simply because I had to be there in order to provide for my family. If I'd had a choice then that barn would've been the very last place on earth I'd be on a Sunday afternoon. Yet at the time, I'll admit that scrapping for a few quid seemed enjoyable enough and let's face it, it's the only thing I was any good at. At least it was organised.

In the far corner of the barn there would be two tarpaulin-sheeted frames, where the fighters would go to have the hands covered with the only protection we were allowed. This would be six feet of cotton bandage on each fist, wrapped around the wrist as support. The knuckles were covered by the crepe, wound between the base of the fingers. It wasn't much, but then it wasn't a boxing match and we were supposed to be using our fists – and if the tape slackened or came off during a fight, we were expected to carry on without. Taping-up was supervised to make sure that knuckle dusters or other foreign bodies (like glass crushed into the glue) couldn't be hidden underneath. It was hard, but everyone knew – though they would never say – that the punters turned out to see blood, broken bones and torn faces and they were going to get what they paid for.

At first the fights consisted of no more than three rounds, each of which lasted three minutes. The rules were simple: no eye-gouging, throat-punching, knees-in-the-bollocks, kicking, hitting below the belt or biting. Most of the decent fighters stuck to the rules but there were a few who simply ignored them, as I was to find out soon enough, seeing guys with an ear missing. I remember meeting up with one poor sod who had half his nose bitten off and I almost had the same thing done to me. But I'll come back to that later …

Most of the fighters thought the Marquis of Queensberry was a pub and most of the others didn't give a toss for rules: they were just a bunch of out-and-out street-fighters. We would never consider throwing a fight to make money out of a bet. The organisers (who I'll point out were not Boy Scout leaders by a long shot) warned us clearly what the consequences would be.

Every single punter was vetted before he could be accepted as a regular. These people were something of a clan. It was a tight-knit circle: only the privileged were admitted and allowed to place bets.

The ring was a roped stand, built so that it could be dismantled in no time if there was a police raid. Lookouts surrounded the barn, but I never experienced a raid, even though the noise coming from the crowd was enough to take the roof off.

After my first couple of battles, Tommy asked if I'd turn up and fight on a monthly basis and, for the sake of the extra dough, that's what I did; then I'd collect my purse and fuck off for home. I'd never hang around that place any longer than I had to. A lot of the guys stayed on to watch fights so as they could get an idea of the different styles. I didn't give a shit who I'd be fighting next – it was all just money to me. All I needed to know was whether they were smokers, 'cos they would be gasping for breath after two rounds, southpaws or just straightforward orthodox.

As time went on I found I was being pitched in with some of the meanest and toughest fighters on the circuit. They didn't give a toss for the rules: they had their own. But no one ever forced me into those fights. I knew what to expect, and I knew how to dish it out as well as the others. I knew I was a favourite with the organisers and the punters, but the feeling wasn't mutual. I regarded it as my trade, or a job I had to do. I just couldn't wait to get out of the gaff, because those sadistic punters sickened me.

The only person who dreaded the thought of me fighting more was Sandra. She was always worried about me getting cut up and banged around, but I'd always say to her, 'This ain't nothin',

Above left: Mamma and Dadda on their first wedding anniversary

Above right: My dear parents, half a century later, on their fiftieth wedding anniversary.

Below left: The main street in Ederney, Co. Fermanagh. Although I spent most of my life in Abingdon, Ederney has always felt like my true home.

Below right: Me as a cute little toddler. Needless to say, I've changed a fair bit since then!

Above: Moneyvriece Public Elementary School photo, 1949. I'm the podgy little fella third from the left in the second row. My big sister, Roisin, is the one standing behind me wearing a light pullover.

Below left: Here I am with Mamma and Roisin – this was taken not long after we moved to England.

Below right: Mamma and me on a day-trip to the seaside. I always was a 'mamma's boy'!

The greatest day of my life! The day Sandra became my darling wife.
Doesn't she look beautiful?

Our honeymoon.

Above: Me and Sandra at the top of the Monument, Pudding Lane, where the Great Fire of London started.

Below: Sandra, with Tower Bridge offering a nice background.

A promotional shot for the Abingdon Boxing Club, an amateur boxing club I founded in 1968 to try and give the local kids the opportunity I never had.

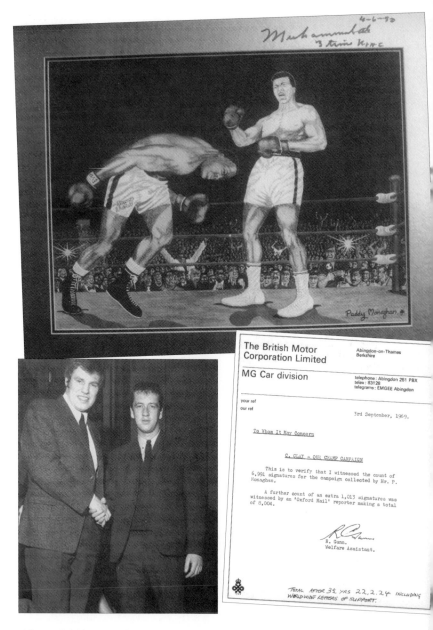

Above: My impression of Muhammad Ali beating Sonny Liston.

Below left: Me and Billy Walker, London's 'Golden Boy', Abingdon, 1971.

Below right: This was early on in the campaign. Over the next few years I got many more signatures on the petition!

Above: With Ali outside the Hilton hotel.

Below: My gorgeous wife Sandra with four of our kids (*left to right*): Belinda, Clare, Saydee and Tyrone.

Above: Muhammad Ali and the late Jack Lynch, former Prime Minister of the Republic of Ireland, Dublin, July 1972.

Below: One day, out of the blue, Muhammad turned up at my rundown little council house in the ragged end of town. As you can see, I was totally speechless.

you should see the other poor bastard.' Looking back on it all now, I realise that I must have put her through hell.

There were a lot of nights that if somebody had dropped a bomb on the place, London crime would've been wiped out because it was a favourite meeting place for a lot of the top faces. Reggie and Ronnie Kray were regulars and I was chuffed to fuck the night Reggie came up, shook hands with me and told me I had his money riding on my back. Years later, when I retired from the game, the twins got one of their friends, Laurie O'Leary, to organise the presentation of a gold watch to me and I took it as great show of respect towards me. It wasn't only villains who turned up though – more than one top copper was pointed out to me, rubbing shoulders with the guys he was supposed to be nicking. Ah, well: a place like that was a great leveller.

You might still think there's a lot of romantic mystery surrounding bare-knuckle fighting, possibly because of hundreds of years of history and people thinking of Gentleman Jim Corbett and fighters like him who fought for hours and hours. Believe me, there was no magic or romance from where I was standing. Think about it. Would you put yourself up for getting a broken nose, busted hand bones or a cut that went to the bone if I offered you a couple of hundred quid? Course you wouldn't, probably not even if I offered 500 quid. But that's what I did it for. Luckily, as the fights got harder, the money got better.

By the time I met Sandra, looking at the fight record Tommy painstakingly kept, I had had roughly 40 fights at the Barn in a two-year period and I won every one them. The first 26 or so were against guys from all over Britain, but then I started to see opponents include fighters from Germany, France, Romania and from as far away as Canada. They travelled a long way to get properly fucked by 'The Rough Diamond' as I was often called. I seemed to have been fortunate not to have had any layoffs due to injuries but, shortly after meeting Sandra, I got one bastard that put me out of the ring for over five months. I'll come back to that later.

So, the night of the Abingdon riot, I walked and talked the new love in my life back home to her parents and let her break the news that she'd met a new fella. Being as straight and conventional as they come, her mum and dad weren't too pleased to find out their daughter was getting mixed up with a brawling Irishman: particularly as this Irishman had a bit of a local reputation as a tearaway. Sandra didn't need to tell her parents this as her dad had already heard the local gossip. They did their best to nip our romance in the bud by confining Sandra to the house of an evening. Looking back, you can't blame them for trying. But we got round this by meeting in secret every lunch hour and taking days off work to do nothing worse than ride around Oxford on the bus.

Eventually I proposed to her and she accepted. So, diving straight in, I asked her to marry me the following May and she said, 'I'd marry you tomorrow if you wanted me to.'

'Okay,' I told her. 'Tomorrow we'll become officially engaged and I'll get you an engagement ring, but tonight I'm going to see your parents to do the old-fashioned thing and ask for their consent.'

Later that evening we went to her house, I was introduced and without messing around I got straight to the point and told her mum and dad that Sandra and me were in love and wanted to get married. Sandra's mother didn't approve at first, but her father seemed to take it okay. He was a bit tasty with his mitts himself, but he was a great guy with a heart of gold. Sandra's mother is a lovely and very understanding lady. Once they both saw that Sandra and me were deeply and totally in love, they gave their full consent to our marriage. We got engaged the next day.

We were married at the Roman Catholic church in Abingdon on 8 May, 1965 and it seemed to me as if the whole town turned out for us. A lot of old friends came and from among them I was pleased to see some well-known faces from London and several fighters I'd been up against on the cobbles. By turning up at my wedding reception, those fellas showed a respect that is only shared by fighters.

In the years before I met Sandra, my inability to read and write had left me completely ignorant of the world around me. Boxing was a part of my life; it was about the only subject I knew anything about. I didn't care about what was going on in the world other than what had a bearing on me. You might think that was a pretty selfish attitude but I'll say before anybody else does that in hindsight it was down to pure ignorance. I didn't know anything about history, geography, proper books or of any standard school stuff that other kids soaked up naturally and I was happy to let things stay that way.

One Saturday, roughly about the same time I took up fighting in the Barn, my attitude to learning changed completely. I was 18 and I was watching Cassius Clay boxing Alejandro Lavorante on TV. I'd followed Clay's progress from the time he'd won a gold medal at the Rome Olympics back in 1960, when he was only 17. Since then it had become almost a full-time job for my mother to read out loud to me all the news about this exciting young boxer. What he was doing was so different from the fighting game I'd got used to that I have to admit I was a bit envious I'd never had the chance to show what I could do in the legal boxing world.

As I watched him knock the bollocks out of Lavorante, two things impressed me. First, everything he did was wrong according to the textbooks, and second, what he did wrong it seemed to me he did perfectly. He displayed boxing skills and an ability that had never been seen before. After seeing him box on

TV that afternoon, something changed in me. I wanted to be able to read all I could about him and not have to rely upon my ma to do it. Cassius Clay had inspired me and, because of that man, all of a sudden I was desperate to learn how to read. If you want to imagine how difficult this was for me, try learning Chinese. That'll give you some idea of what an uphill struggle I set myself.

First off, I got hold of some kid's ABC books. You know, one page taken up with giant A and a picture of an apple. Twenty-six letters to learn – absolute piece of piss. But believe me, it wasn't. If you're having a bit of a chuckle at my expense, feel free. But remember, you probably learned the same thing at about four or five years old and never gave that bit of learning a second's thought. Lucky you.

After a long time, with Ma helping out, I got the hang of what the alphabet looked like and could painfully write out each letter. Next step was to work out the meanings when these letters were strung together in words. Don't forget, my goal was to be able to pick up a paper or boxing magazine and read all about Cassius Clay 'the king' of the boxing world, so I really did work my nuts off.

Whenever my mates called round for me to go out and have a laugh and a tear-up, I'd make all kinds of excuses – my ribs were too sore from a previous fight or I'd had a kick in the knee so was resting it up. Any old bollocks, so I didn't have to admit that all I wanted to do at that time was shut myself in my room and study those kids' books.

The only people who knew what I was doing were my mother and father. Mamma encouraged me a lot by listening to me and pointing out how to break long words into little bits or – as I found when I was slightly more educated – syllables. Dadda was a great encouragement to me as well, but in a different way. Every now and then he'd simply only have to ask: 'How's your reading coming on, son?' And that was all I needed to try that bit harder.

Time went by and come the day when I picked up my first Enid Blyton book I could've shouted to the world: that's how big a step forward it was for me. Talk about a small step for mankind and all that, to me it was a giant leap. Every night after work, I'd go straight upstairs and get stuck into the *Famous Five*. Okay, I had my finger slowly sliding across the page under each word, but I was enjoying the freedom of reading for myself. Trouble was, until a long time after when I got into books more suited to my age, I thought every book started with 'Once upon a time' and finished with 'lived happily ever after.' Never mind that though, I did it. I actually did what I set out to do. I could read the English language. Not brilliantly, in fact, slowly and not as good as an eight-year-old, but to me it opened up a world I'd been ignorant of for many, many years.

I was encouraged by my mother and father and was motivated by the young boxer I saw on the TV screen. The more I watched his fights, the more I became convinced that he would be the next Heavyweight Champion of the World. About a year later, I read – yes, I read myself – that Cassius Clay was coming over to England to fight the British Champion, Henry Cooper.

I must have been one of the very first to buy a ticket, because I got one just as soon as they became available to the public. When Clay arrived in London prior to the fight, I made it my business to find out where he would be training. It was a long shot, but I had it in my mind that it would be great if I got the chance to shake his hand and to wish him the best of luck, in person. That would be something to remember and treasure for the rest of my life.

I found out Cassius was training at the TA (Territorial Army) Centre Gym in Wood Lane, in Shepherds Bush. I took a day off from my job of hoddying bricks on a building site, got a train to Paddington, then went the rest of the way by bus to Shepherds

Bush – with my fingers crossed all the way. I was gutted to find I'd been given the wrong time and he'd just finished his training session. Christ knows how many people were waiting outside the door just to see him, but guess who was stuck right at the back of the crowd? Yep, Paddy the unlucky bastard who now had about as much chance of shaking his hand as winning the pools. I stood on tiptoes, craning my head up hoping for a decent look at the guy I'd cheered so many times on the box.

Suddenly I got a very strange feeling that we'd met somewhere before, a feeling at that time in my life I didn't have a clue about but now know is called déjà vu. It was about as likely that I'd seen him before as I had met the Queen or the Pope. I had to tell myself to get a fucking grip.

Clay moved through the crowd, laughing, joking and signing autographs. Then, for no reason that I could see, he stopped meeting and greeting and, looking this way and that, seemed to be looking for something. Then he locked eyes with me and walked straight towards me with a big smile and his hand stretched out.

I automatically put my own hand out and he gripped it saying, 'Hi man, how you doin'?'

As he spoke to me I could almost see the cogs in his brain going round because he had this puzzled look on his face. Me? I was struck dumb for the moment and that's a joke, because it was well known that not only had I kissed the blarney stone I'd practically ridden the bloody thing. Still holding my hand he said, 'Don't ah know you?' What's your name?'

'Paddy,' I said, 'Paddy Monaghan, and, no, we've never met.'

'You sure, man? Ya seem kinda familiar.'

I wished I could've said we'd met before just to take that look off his face, but that wasn't an option, so I just said, 'No, champ, this is the one and only time we've met and probably the last.'

The guys in his team called him back to his limo and, as he

40

headed off to make his way through the crowd, he turned, saying, 'Okay, Paddy. Ah'll see ya.'

As the car drove off, he waved to the crowd but I could see his head moving from side to side, again as if he was looking for someone. Then he caught sight of me and fixed his eyes on me for a few seconds, just long enough for us both to nod at each other, and then he was gone.

I'll never forget that first time I met the man who was then known to everyone as Cassius Clay. I'd achieved more than I'd expected that day. We were both only youngsters: I was 19 and he was 21. Not only had I been privileged to meet the man and shake his hand but he'd spoken to me and asked my name. Yeah – I felt ten feet tall.

On my way home on the train I ran every second of that strange meeting over and over in my head. Why should he have made his way through the crowd to greet me in particular and why did it strike him and me that we had met before? This was a question I repeatedly asked myself and never came up with an answer. Perhaps he had mistaken me for someone else. Yeah, that would be it.

I want to say here that I regard myself as a very ordinary man. He made my day and I have total respect for him. It has been said that some people idolise Muhammad Ali and worship him. I don't hold with that at all. I think that any person who worships another human has got some sort of screw loose and they ain't me.

I don't idolise Muhammad Ali. I don't worship Muhammad Ali or anyone else in this world – he isn't a god. But he's a great man in my opinion and I respect him as one fighter for another.

Well, when I got back home to Abingdon I went round to all my mates, telling them that I'd met him and that I'd spoken to him. They were all buzzing round asking questions, until one of them said: 'Hey, Paddy, where's his autograph?'

I stood back, closed my eyes and all I could say was, 'Oh shit.'

Only then did it strike me that I'd completely forgotten to get his autograph. Well, that's fucked it, I thought. I had the chance to get it the same as everyone else in that crowd and I go and forget to ask. My mates called me a right arsehole and without a word of doubt they were dead right.

CHAPTER THREE

Fierce Fights and Family Life

It was 18 June, 1963 and I was off to catch a train to London again. The day of the big fight had eventually arrived.

I spent a few hours walking round, then in the early evening I jumped onto a bus to Wembley Stadium. I'd never seen such a large crowd of people in my life. I had only been able to afford to buy one of the cheapest tickets and from where I was you would have needed a pair of powerful binoculars to see the ring and I'm not kidding.

Anyway, the fight itself is history now and for years after people got sick of watching the endless replays on TV. Henry Cooper putting young Cassius Clay on his arse at the end of the fourth round is what people remember. Cooper did himself proud that night, no doubt about it. The punch that dropped Clay was a beauty and it was unfortunate for him that it came only just before the bell to end the round. Clay had just been careless for a moment. That's why Cooper caught him with a good left hook and if that fourth round had only been about a minute or two old, Henry might have won by a knockout.

What we don't often see is what Cassius did to Henry when he came out for the following round. Before the fight he predicted that he would win in the fifth and that's exactly what he did.

Henry Cooper got a return fight with Ali two or three years later, but he couldn't manage to land that great left hook for a second time. Another great performance from Henry, but he couldn't handle the cuts in the sixth round. Both Ali and Cooper earned my respects that day.

He had come a long way – and not just in terms of the number of miles between Louisville and London. Back in the early 1960s, racism was worse than anything we can imagine today, particularly in America. There were loads of people hoping for the shit to be knocked out of this upstart. They all wanted someone to button the 'Louisville Lip'.

Right from the start, Clay deliberately set out to make his mark, not only as a fighter but as a showman. He later told me his big-mouthed campaign was copied from an old wrestler he'd seen on TV called Gorgeous George. I never did see this guy myself but from what Muhammad told me, George invented the approach to the game. I mean, today, every wrestler or bad-boy cage fighter comes down to the ring in a blaze of colour, accompanied by blaring music and wearing showy gear and often sporting dyed, long blond hair – the whole nine yards. Imagine the reaction back in 1947. Nothing like it had ever been seen before. Though he was married and as straight as a die, George camped it up until he got noticed by the whole of America. James Brown, among a lot of others, copied his style to create a sensation.

Of course, nobody could say Ali camped it up but he knew a great publicity stunt when he saw it. 'Ah am the greatest' was his catch phrase and he became world-famous for naming the round in which he'd put his opponent down in poetry, as he called it. In Cooper's case it was: 'It ain't no jive – he falls in five.' In this case he got it right all round – it definitely weren't 'no jive'.

In fact most of the time he was spot on. He predicted and then devastated Archie Moore in the fourth round. But he couldn't get away from the fact that three months before that Cooper fight, he'd slipped up with Doug Jones. Give him his due, he didn't make any excuses. Years later he told me that he took Jones too lightly, missed his prediction for a six-round knockout and he won the fight on points. He was booed from the ring but every one of those hecklers would talk about him and pay to see him fight again and that's just what he wanted. While the rest of the world was knocking this fella as arrogant, cocky and big-headed, my admiration for him as a boxer and respect for him as a man was growing fast. And that was only going to increase in the second month of 1964. At the start of the month, fearsome Sonny Liston was the Heavyweight Champion of the World, but on the 25th, all that was to change.

Leading up to the big fight between Clay and the title holder, all the self-appointed experts were hailing Liston as unbeatable. He was called 'the most dangerous unarmed man in the world'.

Many years later, Ali's closest friend, Howard Bingham, told me about what happened when he was with him in a Miami hotel room in the run-up to the clash. At the time Ali owned an enormous chrome bus. Painted in large letters right down both sides was, 'I Am The Greatest'.

'You know, Paddy,' Howard said to me, 'jes' right out of the blue he says to me: "C'mon Howard, let's you an' me take a drive to Denver an' rattle the big bear's cage."'

Then Howard said to me, 'Paddy, d'you know how far it is from Miami to Colorado?'

I didn't have a clue so just shook my head.

'Well, it's one helluva long drive, I can tell ya. In a straight line it's about 1200 to 1500 miles and by my reckoning that has to be from one end of your Great Britain to the other an' back again.

45

I didn't say anything. I was shovelling shit when the other kids were doing geography at school.

'Anyway, in the middle of the night we arrive in this bus right outside Sonny Liston's house. Then Muhammad tells me to go an' knock as loud as I can on his front door an' then move, like quick. Ali's stood out on Sonny's front lawn ... So I banged on the front door. Then, shit, man, I ran like hell back onto the bus. Soon after, Liston opens the door, an' Muhammad's out on that front lawn, raising both his hands in the air an' hollering out: "Ah am the greatest." Liston does some cussin' an' then goes back in an' slams the front door ... An' we drove back, laughin' all the way to Miami. Jeez, it was a long drive, I tell ya, but Ali had his fun.'

Many rated Liston as the most powerful heavyweight champ ever. And I'd go along with that. He had one big disadvantage though, and that was no fault of his own, he happened to be around at the wrong time. The same could be said for Frazier, Foreman and a few other fighters.

Liston was an ex-convict who they say was just as mean as he looked. He had for a number of years been known as the bad man of boxing. Suddenly, in the eyes of the public, he was turned into the goodie in the white hat while young Clay, who didn't have any sort of criminal record, was made out by the papers to be the baddie. Clay had dared to stand up and speak out to the world about how his people were treated and that's why the rednecks hated him.

In Abingdon, almost everybody agreed that Liston would win: Liston will knock the shit out of that big mouth ... Liston will knock him out in the first round ... I think I was one of the few who believed that Cassius could win. This was my honest, opinion and nothing to do with the fact that I had met him and shaken his hand. I believed he was going to be a Champion even before the Lavorante fight.

If I'd had any money I should've put it on my man because he

46

became the king by winning the fight dramatically. He stopped the 'unbeatable' Sonny Liston when he couldn't come out of his corner for the seventh round, claiming that he couldn't fight on because of a shoulder injury. Okay, I gave him the benefit of the doubt, but he was thoroughly beaten anyway. All the way through the contest, Liston was battered by his opponent and it looked like he couldn't do anything to save himself.

I picked up from the TV news that the following day he turned up at a hospital in Miami where he was kept for about four hours while a team of doctors examined his shoulder injury and patched up his cut and swollen cheek. When he eventually came out to face the crowd of reporters and general onlookers, his arm was in a sling and surgical plaster covered his face.

The verdict of the doctors was that because of his injuries he had been 'incapacitated and prevented from defending himself'. Now, I'm no medical man, but I do know a bit about boxing. That injury to the shoulder, if it was genuine, was probably caused by Liston's own power. By putting his usual tremendous force into a punch on a target that wasn't there, when the blow arrived, he would've wrenched the hell out of his shoulder. In a way, you could say that really it was Clay's reflexes that caused the injury. Apart from that, the whole world saw Sonny Liston take a right good hiding from the man who went into the ring a seven-to-one underdog. One of the reports I read in the paper was, 'The biggest upset since Sitting Bull slaughtered General Custer.'

Cassius first successfully defended his Championship in May 1965 and, as I promised Sandra, we got married on the 8th of that same month. It was also the time when Cassius Clay dropped what he called his slave name and became Muhammad Ali. This defence was a re-match with Sonny Liston and Muhammad knocked him out in just two minutes and thirty-five seconds in the very first round. That was the best wedding present anybody could've given me.

Going back to my own career (if you can even glorify it as a career, it was a shabby affair compared to the glittering boxing of Ali), I was still taking on all comers at the Barn and beating them. I mentioned that I had a good long run without serious injury, apart from a damaged hand but that changed not too long after I got together with Sandra.

I was matched against a pretty tough character from Swansea, whose nickname of 'Mad Dog' was scarily accurate.

There were two things I never did at the Barn. I never turned up much earlier than was necessary – I would do a quick warm-up, get the hands bandaged, then out into the ring. I didn't need to watch other fighters having blood spilled or spilling it. I'd been fighting since I was five years old and quite honestly all I cared about was what I could earn. The other thing was that I never hung about afterwards. The only thing that kept me there longer than I had to was if I had a cut that needed treatment from Tommy's little bag of cure-all treatments. I'll throw in here that the treatment he considered the most effective was a mixture of axle grease and used tea leaves. Before the stitches were put in, he'd slap a load of that shit over the wound and for the next week or two any pillows and cushions that I touched were fucked for good because it never came off material. And yet I've often wondered why Tommy didn't sell the recipe to Boots the chemist because that stuff did the trick – fuck knows why.

So as usual I turned up and ten minutes later I faced Mad Dog. He looked a bit hazy because the cigarette smoke was thicker than an old-time London fog, but it was clear enough I was going to have my work cut out to get this fella to lie down. This was a gloved 'last man standing' bout and, as the name suggests, it would go on until one of us was spark out or too injured to carry on. Needless to say, Tommy had me training hard for this one. I became a regular at Charlie Shorey's gym at The Cottage pub in Carshalton, a place down the road from his gaff in Croydon.

We were pretty equal for eight very hard rounds. I knocked lumps out of him and he did the same to me. He seemed to absorb punishment that would've felled anybody else but no way was I going to let this Welshman spoil my unblemished record. By the ninth we were both getting tired. Tired? You're thinking – Fucking hell, you've only done nine rounds. But let me ask you, have you ever had a flare up? One of them where for 45 seconds you and some other guy have gone for each other? It's all over before it starts and you're left gasping for air and your legs like jelly. That's because initially you had a rush of adrenaline, then it's gone. Now think about doing the same for twenty to thirty minutes without letting up for a moment apart from a quick corner break. We were both getting tired, but him slightly more than me. Suddenly the opening I'd been waiting for showed itself and with a beautiful right I stretched him out on the canvas. Done and dusted; now it was time to go home for a nice cuppa.

While he was taking the count I headed for the corner where they pull my gloves off. I just said to Tommy, 'Another one for your record book,' when I saw his eyes opened wide as he looked over my shoulder and at the same moment, I felt a weight on by back, my head was turned and the next thing I know I've got this crazy Welsh c**t's teeth clamped on my nose.

I shoved him off me and, as I did, felt my nose tearing and a gush of blood swamping my chest. I didn't hesitate, but hit him so hard on the jaw his feet literally came off the canvas and he landed about five feet away, this time spark out – or dead for all I cared.

Back in what served as a dressing room, Tommy took one look at my ruined nose, shook his head and said, 'This is too much for the grease and tea leaves, I'll have to get you somewhere quick.' As well as the shock of seeing my nose hanging on by a thread, Tommy was very concerned that I get a tetanus injection to protect me from the Welsh c**t's bacteria.

Somewhere meant a trip into London to the bent doctor that patched up illegal fighters for cash, no questions asked. Give him his due, he put my nose back in one piece with fine stitching my Ma would've been proud of.

While he was cleaning the blood off, he asked if I had any other injuries and I told him I thought I'd broken my right hand because it throbbed like a bastard. He gently soaked it in warm water, then laughed out loud, which I thought was a bit unprofessional, even for a doctor who had been struck off. He got a little tin dish and a pair of tweezers and I heard a couple of little rattles in the dish which he stuck under my nose saying, 'Someone won't be smiling for a long time.' And there in the bottom of the dish were two yellowing, broken teeth that he'd extracted from my knuckles. After telling me that human teeth carry more deadly germs than a rat, he used my arse as a dartboard for, honest to God, what felt like twenty injections.

After that display of being a bad loser and a dirtier fighter than was acceptable, I heard that Mad Dog never fought again. Promoters won't touch a guy who has gone out of control, but the main reason – and this is only a rumour, honest – is a couple of fellas tracked him down in Wales and broke both his hands with an iron bar. As for me, I was fucked for the next six months when it came to fighting.

I was lucky in a way, because if something like that was going to happen it was best that it happened when it did. By January my nose was healed enough for me to train and spar again in order to take on Alan Brown from Govan – another win for me when the ref stopped the contest in the fifth. I managed to squeeze in three more bouts, fortunately without any further damage, before me and Sandra's big day. Didn't wanna walk down the aisle looking like a prize fighter, did I?

When Sandra and I got married she was five months pregnant, and I swear that I never knew a thing about it until the day after our wedding when she asked a question in that soft voice she had.

'Paddy, would you like us to have children?'

'Not much,' I said, 'I can't wait for the day. In fact I'm going to work on it day and night.'

That made her blush. Then in a sort of hesitating way she said, 'Paddy.'

'Yeah?'

'I don't think you'll have to wait too long.'

I guessed what was coming but pretended I didn't. 'What does that mean?'

'I'm five months pregnant.'

I was absolutely chuffed to buggery and showed it by picking her up – gently – and swinging her round until she squealed for me to stop. It was the greatest news I'd ever heard in my life … even greater than when I heard the news that Muhammad had beaten Liston for the title.

After Muhammad's win against Liston he went on to make his second defence of his title, this time against another former World Heavyweight Champion, Floyd Patterson. Ali stopped him without a lot of effort in 12 rounds in November 1965. His third defence was against the Canadian champ, George Chuvalo. Ali out-boxed and out-pointed him.

But around this time, boxing was shoved away to the back of my mind because all I could think of was my wife Sandra and October, when our baby was due.

We had no place of our own at the time and, as usual, no money to speak of, so we stayed with my parents. They both thought the world of Sandra and the feeling was mutual. I'd go running off to work, humping those bricks all day long and in the evenings we'd sit by the fireside, usually just Mamma, Sandra and me chatting about our future. My old man had a different idea of how to spend an evening – down the pub for a couple of pints.

October came round soon enough and the three of us were sitting round the fire as usual, me studying my books and the other two knitting for Britain, when Sandra's contractions started.

I'd always said that when the time came I'd be Mr Cool just like in the ring: cool and focused. Yeah right. When Ma told me to get down to the phone box and call the ambulance I could barely remember which corner it was on. I got through to the hospital and must have sounded like a dribbling idiot, mumbling and stuttering. The voice at the other end of the line told me to calm down and then asked, 'Is this her first baby?'

I've screamed down the phone, 'No, this is the father, Paddy Monaghan.'

I never did live that down because the receptionist passed it on to any nurse who would listen and the story went through the hospital.

The birth went perfectly apart from a little hiccup. I wasn't in the delivery room; dads didn't seem to do that back then like most do today. I didn't see, as Sandra did, the heart-stopping moment when she thought there was something wrong with her new baby's face. It was like he didn't have any distinct features, but in a flash the midwife peeled off a layer of membrane and said he was a lucky boy. Turned out this membrane is called a 'lucky cap' – the posh word is a 'caul' – and superstition says anybody born with it will never drown. Later Mamma told me I was born with one, a comfort to know should I ever get out of my depth.

Tyrone, as I had the father's privilege of naming him, weighed in at eight pounds and two ounces and I can't help repeating that it was the greatest day of my life. Only four other days were ever to be just as great for me: the births of my four beautiful daughters, Clare, Saydee, Belinda and Sarah.

The injury time I spent on the dole was beginning to outweigh any financial benefits I was getting from the fight game and too often I told myself I was fucking mad to carry on.

From the August before Tyrone was born, until June 1966, I was bolloxed by a hand injury.

I was cheered up by two announcements. The most important was Sandra telling me that she was carrying our second baby and it was due in December. The other was that Henry Cooper was to get a return fight with Ali, only this time the contest would be for the World Heavyweight Championship. The meeting was fixed for 21 May 1966, at Highbury Stadium in London.

This was the first world heavyweight title fight held in the UK and the first big fight for years that was not to be recorded for UK TV. It was to be shown on closed-circuit TV at cinemas all over Britain. That didn't mean a lot to me, personally, because I intended to be at Highbury to cheer my man on, just as I had done three years earlier in the far stand at the Wembley.

The tickets went on sale to the public and, not long after, the man himself arrived in London to help promote sales – hardly necessary – and to wind down his training preparations for his fourth title defence.

I wanted so much to take a day off from work and to go to one of the training sessions to meet him again, but with my family responsibilities I had to work all hours possible in order to feed them, clothe them and buy the essentials to furnish a home for which our names were on a waiting list. So though I was going to miss out on the opportunity of meeting Ali again, I had every intention of being there for the fight.

On the site I was working at I got chatting to a delivery driver who was in and out of London every five minutes. Bit of a Jack the Lad, he reckoned he could get me a ticket for the fight, cash up front. I dug deep, cut a few corners and managed to come up with the cash. Sorted.

Time was ticking away to the fight and I hadn't seen the driver for a while and started to get a bit worried. Then, with only days to go, from up on the scaffold I saw his van pull onto the site. You can't believe the relief I felt. I mean apart from being desperate to get to see the fight, I'd laid out money that quite honestly I couldn't afford. I shinned down the ladder, ran over to the van, pulled the door open with a 'Thank fuck you've turned up' and realised it wasn't the same guy. Yep, Paddy had been stitched up like a kipper. Turned out the fella had jacked the job in weeks ago and disappeared. By this time tickets were as rare as rocking horse shit, so I had no chance of getting in to Highbury. 'Luck of the Irish' my arse.

Small consolation for not being there was reading the reports of the fantastic fight. Ali won again, this time in the sixth, a round later than the previous meet. It came down to a stoppage due to cuts, but by all accounts Cooper did himself proud. But there was no clowning or relaxing from Ali this time: he did the job and left the ring unmarked. Sounds like a terrific fight I missed.

Apart from humping bricks all day and continuing to improve my reading and writing in the evenings, I spent much of my time playing with baby Tyrone and talking to Sandra about our dream of a home of our own and what we'd do in the future.

Almost every day Sandra would go into the council offices to remind them that we were living in overcrowded conditions in my parents' house, but it was always the same: 'You're on the waiting list. As soon as it is possible, your name will be brought up at one of the council meetings and you'll go on the short list.'

But she kept on bugging them and at times she was less than polite, which was out of character for her. She transformed from the lamb she usually was into a snarling tiger. God help any snotty official that didn't give her the time of day she expected. In the meantime, I carried on providing for my family as best as I could, which was through work, work and more work.

One day, sitting in the cement shed having a tea break with the guys, one of the brickies shoved a newspaper in front of me and said: 'Hey, Paddy your mate Ali's coming over here to fight Brian London.' If I'd had my way I'd have run out of the shed there and then to get myself a ticket, but I couldn't just walk out on the guys that were helping to put food on my table, so we agreed that if I could load up enough bricks for them to finish the day I could fuck off early. Tell you what, I moved so fast there must have been smoke coming off my boots. I'd done enough by two o'clock and a couple of hours later, still covered in dust and cement, I was in the queue for a ticket to the fight. I got one. Forget any bad luck I'd had so far, this time I was going to see Ali in the ring, in the flesh. I started counting down the days. Not once did my Sandra complain about me spending money we couldn't spare on tickets. A lot of women would've had the sulks for days, but not her. She knew what it meant to me and was happy for me.

With only days to go before the fight I had an accident that put me in hospital. I was shinning up a ladder with a hod full of bricks on my shoulder when a rung snapped. My leg went through the ladder and the weight of the bricks spun me round and snapped my leg. I hung upside down like a chicken in a butcher's shop window until my mates got me down. Tough as I like to think I am, I was screaming like a girl all the way down. That was me out of action for weeks and my chances of seeing Muhammad again out the window.

I was on the sick list with a broken leg and money was tighter than ever. The good news, and boy did I need some, was Sandra's efforts had paid off and we were offered a house with the condition that we decorated ourselves. Decorate it? I would have rebuilt it for the chance to start living a normal life in our own place.

While I was laying in a hospital bed with my leg in a cage the big fight came and went. Completely outclassed, Brian London was knocked cold in three rounds. Muhammad just opened up with a combination of punches after backing him into a corner.

Afterwards, the big heavyweight from Blackpool had nothing but compliments for the guy that had beaten him. London said, 'The only time I'd ever consider fighting that man again would be if he had a fifty-pound weight tied to each foot. I have no doubt whatsoever: Muhammad Ali is the greatest World Heavyweight Champion of all time.'

Six weeks after the fight, with my broken leg out of plaster and getting stronger every day, I turned up at the site ready to get stuck into work and start bringing some real money in, but, instead of being greeted like the prodigal son returning, I felt there was a bit of an atmosphere. A lot of shuffling feet and funny looks from the guys I'd worked with for so long. Turned out my job had been given to the brother-in-law of one of the brickies. Fair enough, I had been out of action for a while. What got me was that the same guy had visited me in hospital and swore my job would be waiting for me as soon as I was fit. Fuck them, I wasn't going to beg no matter how desperate I was, so I walked away in disgust.

Now I had to think about getting some decent work in before Christmas and with a bit of luck managed to get myself fixed up with a local firm, the MG car company. What was difficult was getting used to working inside after years of hoddying outside in all weathers, but I'd no choice and forced myself to adapt. Now

I had a new job, a new home and, most importantly, the baby was due very shortly.

The new home in Borough Walk was perfect. Once we got the key and turned up to view it, two funny things happened. Well, one funny haha and the other funny peculiar. Always an old-fashioned guy at heart, I stopped Sandra as she was about to walk in the front door, picked her up and carried her across the threshold like you're supposed to do. Only it wasn't as easy as it sounds. Remember, she was heavily pregnant and I'll put some stress on the 'heavily', because I had to struggle to get her up in my arms then stagger over the step with her screaming and laughing her head off. Once we got inside, and this is the funny peculiar, I got a very strange sensation of being watched. I reckon I'm about as un-spiritual as you can get but in that empty room with nobody apart from Sandra around, I actually shivered at whatever presence seemed to be there. I shrugged it off, but the weird feeling stuck with me for a long while and when Sandra commented that I seemed less than enthusiastic about the house, I said I was sorry, put a smile on and told her I was just knackered from my new job. Up at six every morning, I'd run all the way to the factory, then run home again at night to get down to painting and decorating ready for the arrival of the baby.

Though we were only tenants, like everybody else in the same situation, we looked on the place as our very own, but in fact nothing was our own. I'd furnished the place from top to bottom and put brand new carpets on every floor, but recklessly, or in the hope that the future would get us out of the financial mess we were in, everything, but everything was bought on the old never-never. We were so innocent. We never gave any thought to the fact that bills kept mounting up and weren't going to go away. Oh bollocks, let's enjoy Christmas and worry about things like that later.

Money aside, it was a great time in our lives. I had Sandra, our little toddling Tyrone and our newborn daughter Clare. I just couldn't have wished for anything more. It was the best Christmas we'd ever had.

Come New Year 1967, reality took over like it does for most people who've spent money on food and presents that should've been for the January bills that are guaranteed to pour through the letter box. The wages that I picked up every week with one hand had to be paid out with the other and that still left money owing. How could I have been so naive?

I got my priorities right. First, food on the table. Second, make sure the rent was paid because no way was I going to risk losing the home we'd waited so long for. After that it was descending scale of who got their money. Those hire purchase firms kept sending us reminders – and final reminders. My job at the factory was unloading tyres all day long from the delivery trucks, five days a week, so I did my best to get some overtime in other parts of the factory but I didn't have any luck.

During my dinner breaks I dodged into any building sites that weren't too far away and tried to get any sort of labouring work for Saturdays and Sundays. What I was hoping for was to get back on the hod. I know bumping bricks up a ladder all day is about the hardest physical job there is on any site, but I was good at it and it paid the best out of all the labouring work. Fortunately, after a couple of days of running around from site to site, I found a gang of sub-contract piece workers who gave me a start.

I didn't know any of them but what with the building game being a small world, they'd heard about my reputation for being a good hoddy. I was offered £8 a shift, which was top money for my line of work in those days. I started work back on the hod over the weekends and, as any hod-carrier will tell you after a long lay-off, it was murder trying to get back into the swing of it. That first Saturday, I really got stuck into it and lived up to my reputation as a good hoddy, but my hands had gone soft. In a nutshell, it was fucking murder. Was I glad to see the end of that day? Having already done five hard days at the factory I was tired even before I got on site, so that first night I got home I just collapsed into an armchair. There was a blister the size of a duck's egg on my shoulder and more little ones on the palms of my sore and bleeding hands, so I got Sandra to bring me a bowl of heavily salted water and bit on a handkerchief as I put my hands into it. I can't describe the pain and there was worse to come when I got into a salted bath.

As I lay back in that bath, I kept thinking that these fellas I was working for were the fastest brickies I'd ever come across. Instead of the usual two brickies to one hod carrier, I was expected to keep three of them going. I looked at my hands and my raw shoulder and wondered, 'What the fuck am I gonna be like in the morning?' Then I thought, 'Have I ever let anything beat me before? No. Am I ever going to let anything beat me? No.' So I told myself, 'Grit your teeth Paddy and get on with what you have to do for your family. Beat the pain: don't let it beat you.'

I just kept on, slogging my guts out, seven days a week. You could say that I had become a workaholic, but I saw it differently. There are plenty of people who work for work's sake, loving it and doing it because there's not much else in their lives that they enjoy. I was doing it for no other reason than to pay the bills. I mean, there's not too much job satisfaction in humping fucking great tyres around or endlessly loading bricks.

It was at this time of frantic work that we experienced the first of some very strange going ons in our house. One night when we finished our dinner, Sandra gave me a funny look and asked me: 'Paddy, why do you come downstairs during the night and turn all the pictures on the walls round?'

'What you on about, you know me, out like a light until that bloody alarm goes off?'

I got another funny look. 'Well you must walk in your sleep

then because when I got up this morning the pictures were all over the place.'

'Oh, it's probably 'cos the hooks behind the frames ain't level or something,' I said. 'Remind me to take a look at them later.' So we just brushed it off and the subject of the wonky pictures was forgotten.

While all this was happening for me, Muhammad Ali was busy too. My respect for him was matched by a real interest in everything he did, so I gathered as much information about him as I could from the papers and magazines. Up to that time, the World Boxing Association had their own 'Champion', big Ernie Terrell. Muhammad had upset the WBA over some contract dispute soon after he'd licked Sonny Liston. But now he wanted the title and he won it by unanimously out-pointing their claimant, on 6 February, 1967.

After this fight, Muhammad announced that he wanted to meet his three top contenders all on the one night. The papers shrugged it off as just a lot of talk and a publicity stunt. When he tried to get the challenge sanctioned, they began to feel differently. The boxing authorities wouldn't go along with the idea simply because nothing like that had ever been put forward before.

I don't suppose Ali ever thought his suggestion would come to anything and to be honest I think he was just showing the boxing world what he thought of any contenders willing to go up against him. Sensibly, why put on three big fights all on the same evening, at the same place and in front of the same crowd? There was three times the money to be made for everybody if Ali boxed his contenders separately and at intervals. In hindsight, I think Muhammad could've beaten the lot, one after another. We'll never know.

I'm a big believer in human rights. Ali was, and is, entitled to his views and religious beliefs, yet when he expressed them he was knocked back. Certain powerful people in politics and industry didn't like what he said. So when Ali spoke out, the rednecks, the Ku Klux Klan and other racist groups made an example of him.

In my language, he told the government to stick their oath up their arse when he was drafted into service with the forces. Muhammad was a devoted Muslim, 'Ah got no quarrel with them Vietcong,' was a reasonable explanation as far as he was concerned and, with the changing times, it's since been accepted that he was right. At the time he said, and I'm quoting from an old cutting, 'So now I have to make a decision. Step into a billion dollars and denounce my people or step into poverty and teach them the truth. Damn the money. Damn the Heavyweight Championship. Damn everything. I will die before I sell out my people for the white man's money.'

As a result, illegally, as far as I was concerned, Ali was stripped of his Championship and his licence to fight was taken away from him.

At the time too many people went along with this decision and I reckon in the back of their minds they had him down as some sort of coward. Although the sporting world had long recognised him as being an outstanding performer, his attitude hadn't made him too popular outside the black community. His fans saw him becoming the People's Champion outside of the ring as well as in. When he spoke out about the atrocities in Vietnam, even whites began to take notice, and he attracted a lot of sympathisers. Yet nobody was willing to fight in his corner when it came to his career.

Up to that point I had respected him as a boxer. Now I was beginning to respect him much, much more as a man. When those authorities gave Muhammad a hard time, the effect on me personally can't be put into words. Unknown to him, he'd inspired me to drag myself out of the ignorance I'd happily been

living in for years, so, right or wrong, I believe I owed him something, particularly when I felt he was being shat on.

Crazy as it must seem, living in a council house, piss-poor and
knocking myself out every day with hard labour, I came up with
the idea of putting my support behind a guy who had the world
at his feet. Our fighting careers were about as far apart as the
North and South Pole but that was neither here nor there. We
were both fighters and, laughable as you might think it, I felt I
should do something to raise awareness of the injustice of it all.

Hours after his refusal to go into the army, the WBA stripped
him of his title and took away his boxing licence. Both the New
York State Athletic Commission and the World Boxing Council
followed suit. Then they announced a series of elimination bouts
to find a new Heavyweight Champion.

Good on Ali, he stood his ground even when he was faced with
the possibility of being imprisoned for five years and a maximum
penalty of $10,000. Actually, he was stuck behind the door for a
few days and then released on bail, pending an appeal to the
Supreme Court. As it turned out, it took something like three-
and-a-half years before his case reached the high court.

I don't claim to know anything about the legal system, but I think
it's obvious that it was his right to be able to carry on making a
living in the sport while he was waiting for a result. It was a proper
case of a man being guilty until he was proved innocent.

That night, sitting nursing my blisters and cuts, I made up
my mind to somehow fight those bastards that were out to get
him. The kids went off to bed and later Sandra followed them,
after telling me, as if I didn't know, that I was working in the
morning, so not to be too late. Still I sat there lost in my own
thoughts of how the hell could I do something to make a
difference. Turn up at the White House and whisper down the
President's ear? Get a grip. Most of the time I didn't have the
bus fare for a trip into Oxford.

CHAPTER FOUR
The People's Champ

Muhammad Ali had been the inspiration behind me learning to read and write and when I decided to do something to support his cause, it hit me that I could use what had taken a lot of effort to learn.

I read somewhere that the pen is mightier than the sword: okay then, I would put that to the test. Yeah – I would organise a petition. I would promote a campaign called ALI IS OUR CHAMP. What that would mean and how I'd achieve it was something I still had to give a lot of thought to, but it was a start.

The next thing I remember was being shaken awake by Sandra. She had come down a few times in the night to get me to go up to bed but all she could get out of me was a mumbled, 'Be up in a minute.' After a while she gave up, chucked a couple of blankets over me and left me to it.

I was stiff, sore and my blisters were weeping and I had another day of bumping the hod in front of me, but as the dreamlike memory of what I'd made up my mind to do came flooding back, I felt I was ready for anything.

Even as I ran up and down the ladder that Sunday, my mind was ticking over with possibilities of where I'd go from there with my campaign. I'm a Monaghan and when I get my teeth into something there's no way I ever let go.

Every spare minute when I wasn't working I got myself out and about town collecting signatures to support my crusade. From that start in my defence of Ali, though it was sometimes clumsy, sometimes not thought out as well as it could have been, who would have guessed that my ordinary, uneventful life would completely change?

Most of those who signed my petition wished me the best of luck, though they probably thought my efforts would have about as much effect as pissing in the sea. Still, at the end of the day, they gave me their names and addresses, if for no other reason than to shut me up.

Later, when news of this reached the papers, it was too good a story for them to miss and I had loads of reporters leaving messages on my phone. In turn, I would send a message to them, saying where I would be collecting signatures at whichever particular evening. My campaign needed publicity, but I wasn't going to start collecting names just to be interviewed. If the reporters wanted to talk to me they were welcome, but they'd have to walk and talk at the same time, because I had to keep going.

Before long the campaign made headline news and what I was doing caused all sorts of reaction. Mainly along the lines of, 'Why would anybody spend his time fighting over the problems of a man living over three thousand miles away – a man he doesn't know and has only met for a couple of minutes?'

I got a large white sheet, painted on it the words 'ALI IS OUR CHAMP' in big black letters and stuck each end to a couple of broom handles. This would be my banner that I'd hold high above my head at every opportunity when I took myself into

London for rallies and one-man demonstrations. By the end of August 1967, the names and addresses on my petition numbered well over a thousand. I got every single one of the signature covered pages in my notebooks copied by a mate in the printing game and I took them along with my sheet banner and picketed the US Embassy in Grosvenor Square. Sounds crazy I know, but there was method to my madness.

First off, I walked up and down the road with my banner above my head, while two very large MPs standing just inside the embassy door watched me suspiciously. Pound to a piece of shit, I reckon they were expecting me to start throwing hand grenades. I just hoped they'd ask what my business was before they started shooting.

Eventually I think the suspense got too much for them and they came marching up to me, both put a hand on my shoulder and stood stock still in that position, saying nothing, just waiting for one of the staff to give them the okay.

The okay for what? I thought. Tell me to move on or beat the shit out of me?

I insisted that I be allowed to hand the petition to the ambassador personally and demanded none too politely to see the main guy. Them two fuckers still never said nothing, just stood stone-faced.

After a while another member of the Embassy staff came out, shook his head, waved his hand at the two MPs and nodded towards the door signalling for them to return to their posts. The three of them could have made their living as mime artists.

This official-looking guy looked me up and down and Cocky Bollocks here did the same to him. I'd been in the fight game too long to be intimidated by anybody. I must have passed whatever he was looking for because he took off back into the embassy and came out again almost immediately with another smartly-dressed guy, who, after giving me a sharp salute, handed me his card and introduced himself as the Chief Personal Attaché for the US Ambassador, Ronald Deutsch. This was the closest I could get to his boss, so I handed over a long letter that had taken me hours and hours to put together, 'For the attention of the President of the United States'. It asked that he order the boxing authorities to reverse the treatment they'd given Muhammad Ali while he was on bail. At the end I'd written that these same authorities thought they were above the law and that charges should be brought against them. Along with it I passed over a copy of the petition.

I wanted to be sure that my letter and petition would get to the President and I was gobsmacked when this guy treated me like some head of state. He stood to attention, raised his right hand and said, 'Sir, you have my word of honour that your petition and accompanying letter will be given to the President of the United States.'

Fuck me, Paddy, you didn't expect that.

I lost count of the number of demonstrations I did in the three-and-a-half years that Muhammad was locked out of the sport. I'd walk up Park Lane, down Park Lane, swinging my banner double-handed. I always carried plenty of paper for signatures and addresses of people who were willing to support the campaign. I went to Speakers' Corner no end of times and I'd spout on and on, calling out for justice. The crowds listened and my list of signatures grew as I somehow captured the imagination of the people. Tourists would stop at my soapbox at the top of Park Lane, and in Trafalgar Square, and congratulate me for what I was doing. I always pointed out that everything I was doing was for and about Muhammad Ali and in a sense nothing to do with myself; I definitely wasn't on some sort of ego trip. The news of my campaign spread to tourists' friends abroad and soon it was being talked about worldwide. Letters of support were coming in from people, saying that they'd been told by friends of what I was doing and I had their support. Every one of these letters got added to my petition.

My family didn't see very much of me at that time, but I knew I had their support and understanding.

Instead of being chucked in the bin as they had for a long time, all of a sudden my letters to newspapers and magazines were being accepted without argument. Publication of them was a big boost to my campaign, but I always made it clear that this was about human rights as much as it was about boxing.

By October 1967 there were over 8,000 signatures on the petition and photocopies were sent in batches to the World Boxing Association. Eventually, I got a brief letter from WBA Secretary Jay Edson that said he was pleased to hear from a boxing fan like me. What a wanker. He ignored every point I'd made and never once mentioned Muhammad Ali. Was the WBA made up of hypocrites or were they all just stupid?

During this time, on top of constantly campaigning, I was working seven days a week and still going away to train for my regular fights at the Barn. It knocked the bollocks out of me, but I never once considered giving up. Then again there's only so much your body can take before something gives. I'd come back from one of my demos and fell into the armchair completely wasted. I sort of half dozed off then came to because I needed to pee. I stood up and I felt a funny feeling of dizziness come over me followed by a frightening pain across my chest. Sweat was pouring off me and I just fell on my knees and put my forehead on the floor.

Yeah, of course, I was scared. I could take cuts, broken hands, bumps and bruises, but this was something I couldn't see and to be honest I thought I was gonna die right there on the floor with a heart attack. Sandra and the kids were all frightened by seeing their tough old man rolling on the floor moaning in pain. She rang the doctor and if it had been a heart attack I'd have been long dead by the time he turned up, moaning like fuck at being called out.

He felt my pulse, stuck a stethoscope on my chest and, while he was packing his bag for a quick exit, told me I had nothing but indigestion. I've had indigestion more times than I can count and though I wanted to believe him, I felt he was wrong. In the end, even though I was still in pain I told him to piss off because he was a waste of time. All that did was give me a bit of satisfaction and get me taken off his list.

After a while the pains in my chest settled down to a steady ache and to ease Sandra's mind I said I was okay and that perhaps the doctor had been right. In truth, I felt like shit, but at least it stopped her worrying. Next day I was still in pain and walked slowly to work instead of doing my boxing training routine of run, sprint, walk and sprint again. I'm no doctor but during the day I was very conscious that my heartbeat was all over the place and I didn't feel like talking or even getting up to my usual piss-taking fuck abouts like every other day.

We were unloading a full lorry load of big tyres one minute and the next I came to in a hospital bed, tubed and wired up, the whole nine yards. Turned out my blood pressure was through the roof and I had chronic exhaustion and that meant staying in hospital while they stabilised me and ran a load of tests.

Cut a long story short, the tests didn't show any more than the first diagnosis, so I was sent home with orders to take it very easy. I did for a while, but I've never been one for doing nothing so I got myself back to work as soon as I could. Perhaps too soon, because one day I was stacking tyres onto the racks in a well out of the way warehouse, and next thing I'm on my back looking up into the worried faces of two of my workmates. I guessed what had happened but those two boys didn't, so I told them one of the tyres had slipped and given me a bang on the head and that I was fine, so no need to report it. One thing I didn't want was the boss to know was that one of their workers was falling about all over the place in that dangerous environment. I didn't even mention it to Sandra when I got home.

The third, and more serious, attack came three weeks later. Same old story, out like a light, but this time I cut my chin and only the quick reaction of one of the guys stopped me being mangled up in one of the factory machines. As before, the first I knew was when woke up in the same hospital I'd been in two months previous.

A week later I got the results of much more extensive tests than I'd had months before and I've got to say it knocked me for six. I was an epileptic. Me. One of the fittest guys in Abingdon; it took a long time for it to sink in. Worse was to come.

The guy who was looking after me, Professor Ritchie Russell, got me in his office and broke the news to me that he'd had no option but to inform my employers at MG of my condition and stress that I was not fit or safe enough to work around heavy machinery. We'd had a great relationship up until then but to my shame I kicked off at him a bit saying, 'Thanks a fucking lot doc, you've managed to take away the job I've had for the last four years and dump me on the scrapheap.'

He said, 'I can understand your anger, Paddy, but by law I had no choice in the matter. Still, your firm may find you something behind a desk away from the shop floor.' I nearly burst out laughing though didn't because I felt so gutted. Me? Behind a desk? He was having a laugh. I was a labourer for fucks' sake and a labourer who was shit when it came to letters and numbers. Oh yeah, I could see MG treating me with sympathy.

I was right and they didn't. I was 26 with a medical condition that would frighten off any future employers and nothing for it but to accept a life on the dole. The only positive thing to come out of my stay in hospital was that everybody, from doctors to medical students, signed my petition. See, even when I was flat on my back I didn't let the chance pass of spreading the word.

After a short period of something close to depression, sitting around on my arse with nothing to do but think, I suddenly realised how pathetic I was being. Okay, I had this problem, but outwardly I was the same old Paddy I'd always been. I'd had a few attacks, or seizures as they're called, but fortunately Sandra was with me and knew what to do. What did piss me off was to hear people who happened to see me lying on the pavement saying, 'Look that fella's having a fit.' Fit, my fucking arse, that word hadn't been used to describe an attack for many years and then only in ignorance.

Anyway, I gave myself a good mental kick up the backside and told myself to live life to the full and, if I couldn't do a day's work, find other things to fill my days up.

One of the first things I did was start an amateur boxing club in Abingdon. I'd always had the idea in the back of my mind to give local kids the opportunity I never had and with the publicity my campaign was getting, it made it a lot easier for me to get a club started. It was also a good place for me to train, but I had to be careful to keep a low profile – I didn't want it coming to the attention of the Amateur Boxing Association (ABA) officials.

At first, it was suggested that it should be called the Paddy Monaghan Amateur Boxing Club, but I wouldn't have it. I've never been one for being up my own arse and I didn't want this club to look like an ego thing, so I insisted they named it after the town. I formed a committee and they got the club affiliated to the ABA.

It was generally known that I was a boxer. But my other life, in the Barn, was a very well-kept secret around town, and everywhere else come to that, due to the illegality of bare knuckle boxing.

After a lengthy lay-off, I gave Tommy a bell and told him I was fit enough to get back on the card at the Barn. I must've been fucking crazy but I wanted to carry on and better my unbroken record of wins and I needed some way of topping up the shit dole money. It was only one Sunday afternoon a month – what harm could that do?

Looking back, though my intentions were for the best, I was a selfish bastard when it came to Sandra's feelings. She cried, begged and pleaded for me not to go back to fighting, but I ignored her and did what I thought was best. What a twat. If it was the other way round, how would I have felt if the person I loved had a serious medical condition then went out every month to come home bloody, bruised and battered? Well, I know the answer to that and it puts her feelings into perspective, I can tell you. It didn't matter that I'd won my fight and had a few quid on the hip, Sandra would kneel beside my armchair, crying and gently touching my often wrecked face.

I pulled off my usual wins straight off, though I did have a sort of nagging worry in the back of my mind that any one of the head punches I took might set off a seizure. The doctor had explained the risks in detail but most of it, if not all, went straight over my head. I don't remember him saying that knocks to the head were the cause, so I stopped worrying about it.

A quick look at Tommy's well-kept record to jog my memory tells me that by that time I'd fought and won 60 contests; every one of them a challenge of ruthless violence and filled with bruises and blood. During one fight, I took a belt full on the eye. I carried on, but as the minutes ticked past I noticed that as I looked to my right all I could see was this vague lump and nothing else – a bit of a handicap when you need all-round vision for where the next punch might be coming from. End of the round I sat in the corner shaking my head as though that was gonna repair what damage there was. Tommy pulled my head back, stuck his face close to mine and said that he was going to stop the fight. I told him to fuck right off. Stop the fight and wreck my unbroken record? I'd rather go blind in that eye. Yeah, I know, pretty bloody stupid in hindsight, but my record meant everything to me.

The blow to my eye had made the lid fill up with blood until, believe me, it was the size of a small plum. In the short time I had sat on the stool, me and Tommy argued until, exasperated by my stubbornness, he grabbed up his little bag, dug out a new razor blade and with a quick slice cut into my eyelid. The blood shot halfway across the canvas and having had just enough time to apply adrenaline and a wipe of his special concoction, I was up and into my opponent. Dunno what we would've done without the old 1000 and 1. This was a mix of 1000% alcohol and 1% of adrenaline that was applied to any cut with a cotton pad. It stopped the bleeding in seconds and allowed you to carry on fighting. Usually it was used around the eyes or forehead, because with claret running into your eyes, you'd be constantly wiping or be blinded – which ain't much good when you got a fist flying at your face.

It wasn't all blood and guts battles at the Barn. I also had a period fighting at fairground booths. It wasn't a bad earner and was more about entertainment than actual fighting, though the punters didn't know it. I was known as a 'gee' and that means I was the bloke planted in the crowd to challenge the booth fighters. It was no good relying on local young fellas to make a genuine challenge.

I did this work with an old pal of mine – one of the best guys I'd ever met in the fight game: Ricky Porter, the Southern Area Welterweight Champion. He was a tasty boxer and if I remember right his last fight was on the under card to the Joe Frazier versus Joe Bugner fight in 1973. During his career he beat the

European Champion, Roger Menetrey, in a non-title fight and lost by only half a point to future World Champion, John H. Stracey. Ricky was one of that rare breed of fighters too good for their own good.

I had some good times with him over the years and plenty of laughs at the craziness of those booths. One time, when as usual we were acting out a fight in the booth, he got me in a clinch and whispered: 'Okay Paddy – I'm gonna go down now.' He stood back, expecting me to throw a punch, then dropped to the canvas like a bag of shit. Only trouble was, I hadn't had time to hit him. He got back up on his feet looking dazed and staggering about, with the crowd screaming, 'Fix! Fix!'

Ricky yelled back: 'No, it fucking ain't. That was a phantom punch.'

That fairground gee always helped me to get Christmas presents for the family because Jack Gage, the owner of the booth, gave me a fiver a night – and that was good money then – plus the money thrown in from the crowd when we gave them a good show.

But away from all that and my family, my main preoccupation was still the Ali campaign. That banner was becoming a routine sight round London. The one thing nobody seemed to ask was the obvious question of who gave the boxing authorities the right to do what they did to Ali? And why, it seemed to me, didn't anybody give a fuck or challenge these people except Paddy Monaghan?

The reporters who interviewed me didn't seem to want to know about the human rights issue and only touched on the subject of boxing and how I regarded Ali as the rightful Champion. I was depicted as a fight-crazy fanatic, but I was still getting lots of publicity. That was good, anyway.

The WBA and the New York State Athletic Commission set up a series of eliminating bouts to find a successor to Ali, though I reckoned that whoever ended up with the title would be wearing a cardboard crown they didn't deserve. Nobody in their right mind, if they had any sense or love of the sport, could accept the winner as a true Champion until he had defeated Muhammad in the ring. That's the only place where a title should be won or lost in my book. Eventually, it was 'Smoking' Joe Frazier who ended up wearing the cardboard crown. He stopped Buster Mathis in the eleventh round in Madison Square Gardens in New York.

About this time I came up with the phrase, 'Ali, the People's Champion'. It didn't exist before then, but eventually would be known and used throughout the world. Even Elvis Presley, a big fan of Ali's, presented him with a stunning dressing-gown with the title I'd thought up in gold sequins across the back. I believe that robe is now a bit of a showpiece and on display in some New York gallery or museum.

As often as I could, I'd shoot off up to London on my demo to collect more signatures. I'd unwrap my old banner and on my own would set off from the bottom of Park Lane. By the time I'd reached Marble Arch my banner would've attracted a crowd, all yelling: 'We want Ali. We want Ali.'

Some of them would even give me a break and take the banner so that I could rest my aching arms. By the time we reached Speakers' Corner in Hyde Park, you couldn't hear any other speakers that were there for the chants of 'Ali. Ali. Ali.'

I was chuffed to fuck that at last I was being taken seriously, that people didn't think I was some sort of nutcase or had taken too many punches to the head. Many people were taking my campaign seriously and letters were arriving from all over the world and in them all the message was the same: 'Muhammad Ali is the People's Champ.'

One of the countries I heard from most was my place of birth across the Irish Sea. The supporters there of the ALI IS OUR CHAMP campaign knew that I was one of them. Dublin

THE PEOPLE'S CHAMP

University sent a very long list of signatures, with addresses of the undergraduates. That was a great help and particularly encouraging. Thanks, Dublin.

But not every letter I got from abroad patted me on the back for what I was doing. I got a threatening letter, typed on headed paper, from the Ku Klux Klan. It was posted from a town in Georgia and read:

WARNING – YOU.
Drop it, you nigger-loving son of a bitch.
WARNING – YOU.

That was the exact wording and at the bottom of the page it was signed, KKK, with the number 3 typed beside it.

There was space left at the bottom of the page, so I gave whoever had sent it a typical Paddy Monaghan reply: 'Fuck you'.

Then I signed it and sent it back.

Apart from the rare piece of shit like that, I was getting so much mail in support that the postman on his bike couldn't handle it and the Post Office made arrangements for our mail to be dropped off in a sack. Then Sandra had to go through the whole lot, checking which was our personal correspondence.

After the final batch of signatures and addresses had been sent off to Phoenix – grand total now 22,224 – something happened at last. I can't take full credit for it, but I think my campaign definitely helped. And no-one in the world was happier than I when I heard the news.

The Governor of the State of Georgia was a man called Lester Maddox, though he was known by a lot of less polite names by many people who didn't go along with his racist speeches about the black population. He was up for re-election and, like most politicians, he was quite prepared to kiss ass, no matter what colour it was, to get a vote. Until then, whenever he'd spoken of

75

Muhammad Ali, his speeches were something along the lines of: 'That black so-and-so will never get my permission to box again in my state.' But now Maddox was sucking up to the voters, and in particular, the growing number of black voters. In a massive turnaround he gave his blessing to a fight between Ali and the white contender, Jerry Quarry.

Howard Hughes didn't like it and J Edgar Hoover didn't like it, and whatever they didn't like, Richard Nixon didn't like. But all Maddox wanted was to keep himself in the governor's mansion.

In June 1971, Ali was found innocent by seven Supreme Court judges and still, all these years later, the boxing authorities have never even commented on what led them to change their attitude and grant Muhammad a boxing licence again.

Though I know that Muhammad Ali has forgiven them now, I still feel that a public enquiry should be held and I've still got 22,224 people throughout the world waiting for the explanation. If they broke any of the constitutional laws of the United States of America, and I believe they did, then there should be federal charges made against the people responsible.

When my last batch of names had been signed, witnessed and sent off, I was convinced that any petition with the opinions of such a lot of people couldn't be ignored. In fact, I've been told by an somebody at the US Embassy that it did 'set off some rumblings in the high corridors of power'.

On 14 September, 1970, Muhammad Ali was granted a licence to box in Georgia and my three-and-a-half years of slogging, demonstrating, collecting names, flying here and rushing there and damaging my health, were now finally over and with a winning result ... although Ali still had to await his appeal to the Supreme Court.

Jerry Quarry, the man selected as Ali's comeback opponent, was no pushover. Muhammad could've chosen someone a bit softer to get back into the swing of things after so long but he dived straight in the deep end and took on one of the few white heavyweights.

The date set for the fight was 26 October, 1970. Shit, I thought, that gives my man only six weeks' training time after being off so long. They should give Ali more time to prepare. The venue was at Atlanta, Georgia – and yeah, that rings a bell. Atlanta: that was the name of the town I got the Ku Klux Klan letter from.

Muhammad Ali beat Jerry Quarry in three rounds, but at no time was he really tested. He was the superior boxer and he stopped his man with a badly-cut brow.

Next in line was the number two contender for the official title, Oscar Bonavena, who was a really hard man – an immensely strong fighter who packed a wallop and who seemed to soak up any punishment thrown at him.

I didn't like the match because I was worried about Muhammad's timing, his coordination, his distance and his pacing. To get rid of all that ring-rust these things need to be sharpened and honed in less dangerous fights. The Quarry fight had done nothing for him because they hadn't been in the ring together long enough.

But I have to say, all those people who said that Ali didn't need warm-up fights were right. In December, Bonavena came out of his corner like a bull and as the pair swapped blows Ali was seen to be beating Bonavena at his own game.

This time he didn't 'float like a butterfly, sting like a bee'. He floated like a tiger and stung like a cobra. He came down off his toes, he stalked his man, he spread his legs and planted his feet. He hit. What a fight that was. Bonavena went forward all the time, but Ali dominated him. It was a 15 rounder and it looked as if the battle would go to a point's decision with the Argentinean too strong to be stopped. But in the very last round, Muhammad really opened up. He dropped his opponent to the canvas no fewer than three times. Under NYSAC (New York State Athletic Commission) rules, that meant that the ref had to stop the fight and class it as a knockout win. Bonavena was beaten inside the distance for the first time in his life. It was one of Muhammad Ali's finest performances.

My man was not scheduled to fight again until 8 March, 1971. This time it was to be the big one and versus the official – to me the cardboard – Champion, Joe Frazier. For the first time in boxing history, two unbeaten men would clash for the World's Heavyweight Championship title.

Both men were Olympic Games gold medal winners and both superb boxers. Soon after the Bonavena fight the build-up began. Some named it 'The Fight'. Others called it 'The Battle of the Century'. I named the coming contest 'The Official Champion vs The People's Champion'.

With everybody planning and buying for Christmas, things were a bit different in the Monaghan household. This was going to be the first time we wouldn't be having turkey or all the trimmings, because with no fights there was no spare money, so we'd be settling for the cheapest supermarket chicken. And I remember that the thing which really choked me most of all was Christmas Day itself, when all my neighbours' kids were outdoors, showing what Father Christmas had brought for them. I went out and sold my only cherished possession: a small, bronze, limited edition figure of the great Jack Johnson. Then I went straight into a toy-shop and got some things for the kids and a new dress for Sandra.

Soon we were into 1971, and before I knew it came the day of 'The Fight of the Century'. No other sporting occasion in history had ever captured the attention of the world as this one had. As an 'official' Champion, Joe Frazier was one of the all-time greats.

He was like a machine. Some of you youngsters might think that Mike Tyson is awesome. I'll tell you, compared with Joe Frazier, he's just ordinary.

Johnson, Louis, Liston, Frazier, Foreman – yeah they were all great, but if it's proof you want it's proof you'll get. Ali is the finest Champion who ever lived. In fact in my opinion, there's no heavyweight who can come second. That distinction goes to a middleweight, 'Sugar' Ray Robinson. But watch Ali's contests and take a look at his record. He licked three of the big fellas I mentioned above and I feel sure he could have beaten the other two.

Leading up to that first battle between Ali and Joe Frazier, I had that same nagging thought – I wished Muhammad had got himself sorted with two or three more warm-up fights. It wasn't a doubt, but I wished he'd made it a bit easier on himself. Here he was, about to tackle this phenomenal puncher and he'd only boxed 18 rounds for real since his return to the ring. It was four years since he fought Zora Folley and I didn't think he was ready yet. But apart from that one wish that he'd taken more time to prepare himself for the big one, I was confident that he would beat Joe Frazier.

And those tossers, who had always hated him and had hoped for his comeuppance, now had their moment of glory. Muhammad Ali was judged to have lost on points to Frazier over 15 rounds. I've watched that fight loads of times since and I still think that Ali won, apart from being knocked down in the last round. I think that knockdown must have swayed the judges in the close battle.

He got up pretty quick, taking a count of three, because he couldn't afford to waste time, but I think that the left hook Frazier landed on Ali's jaw that night would've been the end of the fight if it had connected with any normal heavyweight's chin. But Muhammad Ali was never a normal heavyweight.

Okay, I know that people think I'm biased, but I'm not blind and I know a fair bit about boxing. There are plenty of other people who agree with me in thinking that Ali had slightly the better of things that evening: I'm not just one in a million. But Joe got the verdict this time.

After that first meeting between the two guys, I got shitloads of mail from Ali's fans from all over the world. With practically nothing else to do, I'd just sit down and reply to as many letters as possible.

But before I settled down to that job, on the day after the fight, I started writing to every national newspaper in the country, as well as to the *New York Daily News* and a host of boxing magazines. Some published my letters and some didn't, and in the case of those who didn't I'd write to them again until they did.

It wasn't until after that first fight of Ali's with Joe Frazier that I realised that what I'd started four years previously, was, in fact, a Muhammad Ali Fan Club. His enormous numbers of fans were still writing to me long after Muhammad was given his licence back and my campaign had finished. I asked Sandra to get me some large writing pads and started to make a list of all those names and addresses of people who had written and were still writing to me. I was hearing from fans from as far away as the United States, Canada, Australia, New Zealand and, surprisingly, from places where they had been taught our language, like, Russia, China and Japan.

On some of the envelopes there wouldn't even be an address. Just, 'Paddy Monaghan, Muhammad Ali Fan Club, England,' yet they all arrived at my door. Yeah, Ali might have lost the verdict to Joe Frazier, but he was still the People's Champion.

It was my intention to hang onto all these letters and pass them all over to Muhammad himself when, hopefully, I got the chance to see him on his next visit to this country. Then I read that Muhammad's manager, Herbert Muhammad, was making a visit to London and made up my mind to try and see him.

I played detective, found out all the details I needed, then when Herbert arrived, I went to his hotel in London, introduced myself and explained to him: 'Look, this is just some of the mail I've received from Muhammad Ali's fans, so would it be possible for you to arrange for me to see him and to pass this lot over to him personally, whenever he comes to England again?'

At first he'd seemed a bit wary, perhaps wondering what my scam was, but soon he started showing real interest and was diving his hands into the sack, fishing out letters and studying the postmarks. Finally he said, 'Sure you can get to see Muhammad Ali next time he comes here. He'll be delighted, and before you go I think you'd better write down your name and address for me.'

I did what he said, handed it over and that was that as far as I was concerned. He folded the paper and put it in the top pocket of his jacket. Apart from shaking hands and swapping goodbyes when I left, nothing more was said. I didn't tell him a thing about what I'd been doing during Ali's three-and-a-half-year lay-off.

Then, one morning in May, not long after I had met Herbert in London, a letter arrived for me from Philadelphia. It was addressed simply: 'Paddy'. Sandra was doing the housework when it arrived, I remember. As I opened it, thinking it was just another letter from a fan, I was taken aback with complete surprise when I saw the printed lettering at the top of the page. The letter was in Ali's own scrawled longhand:

Memo from Muhammad Ali

Paddy, keep up the good work. I will see you when I'm in England. Good luck.

Muhammad Ali

I just sat there staring at that piece of paper, for I don't know how long, until Sandra's voice brought me out of the sort of daze I was in by saying, 'Paddy, why are you staring at that letter? What's wrong?'

I didn't speak. I just shook my head, tapping the letter and indicating to her to come and read it as it lay there on the table. I remember her being confused, initially, and then the letter started to quiver in her hands. Only Sandra could possibly have had even a close idea of what that little note meant to me. I still cherish it to this very day.

CHAPTER FIVE

Meeting Muhammad

Unknowingly, as founder of the Muhammad Ali Fan Club, I had become a spokesman for all the people who had contacted me over the years. They would ask me to hit back at the journalists who saw Joe Frazier as a convincing winner. So I did hit back. In a standard letter to the doubters I'd challenge the use of the words 'convincing winner'.

I was now in a unique position. With my loyalty to Ali fans as well as to the man himself, I realised only too well by now just how those supporters throughout the world were feeling about Joe Frazier and the decision.

When Frazier arrived in London on 14 June, 1971, with his pop group called The Knockouts, I made sure I was at Heathrow Airport to meet him, and not as one of his fans. What I was to do next was for all Ali's fans throughout the world.

Everything went wrong for Joe right from the start. As he came out from customs, I stepped forward, two broomsticks holding my old banner screaming out the message, 'ALI IS OUR CHAMP'. It obviously caught Frazier's eye. He didn't look very happy.

He gave me a glare intended to intimidate the shit out of me, then between clenched teeth he hissed at me, 'What's this, man? Ah don' fuckin' believe it.'

In a temper, he threw his hand baggage and it bounced off a wall across the hall. The place was packed with passengers and it went dead quiet. Nobody could believe what was going on. Everybody seemed shocked.

I broke the silence with, 'Welcome to England. When you get back to America, tell Howard Hughes, Hoover and Nixon that you're just their champ – and that Muhammad Ali is the people's champion.'

In case you think I'm a very polished speaker with snappy comments on the tip of my tongue, I've got to admit I'd rehearsed those words over and over in my mind since I got up that morning.

The look in his eyes was frightening and if I hadn't been a guy who was used to going up against big, ugly bastards, I reckon I would've needed a change of underwear. He was actually snarling when he said, 'Put that fuckin' thing down.'

'No, fuck you.'

Then he bent forward, put his forehead against mine and said again, 'Put that thing down, you bastard. 'Cos ah'm gonna nail you if you don't.' The situation was very tense, but there was no way I was going to drop my banner. My confrontation was having an even bigger effect on him than I thought it would.

Things had developed into a battle of wills between us. We were nose to nose, head to head and he was shoving me backwards. But I just held my banner even firmer and higher. Frazier's temper was deteriorating by the second and I was thinking that any minute he was going to try and take my head off my shoulders. If he took a swing at me and it connected I could say goodnight sweetheart to Paddy but, for what it was worth, I would've done my best to put up a fight against him.

My first move would have been to hit him over the head with the two broom handles. Yep, I'm up against one of the most fearsome fighters in the world and I'm going to smack him on the head with two-inch diameter broom handles. I got myself ready because I could see he was getting wound up for an attack, regardless of all the people that were watching the display. I'll never forget those eyes filled with hate and fury. His cursing and swearing could be heard by every tourist in that packed terminal.

I wasn't going to thank the Lord for what I was about to receive, but I was prepared to be thankful for small mercies – I wasn't going to back down from any man in this world, even if that man was Joe Frazier.

Before it got even uglier, we were pulled apart by members of his pop group and the airport police. And the only time I lowered that banner was when one of his team kicked out and caught me on the leg. I swung round and caught the cowardly bastard back with a lovely old-fashioned right hander. That was it. That was the signal for them all, except Joe, to get stuck in, punching and kicking me from every angle: I made sure that a couple of them went down first.

Then the airport police jumped in to save me. They pulled the group off me and I got up, bloodied and bruised. That bunch of pricks, thinking I'd been arrested, looked across at me, grinning and smirking as I stood between the coppers. I wasn't done yet and wiped their smiles off by shouting at them, 'The Knockouts! You lot ain't knockouts – yer a bunch of fuckin' dropouts.'

As the airport police let go of my arms, I lashed out at the group before I was grabbed again and dragged out of the building with Frazier screaming out, 'Ah want you so bad, ah kin taste you. Ali kin wait – ah want you now, man.'

A crowd of officials restrained him. His group had mobbed me, but I'm glad to say that Frazier didn't touch me. The scandal of a World Heavyweight Champion striking a geezer my size on arriving in the country would have ruined his reputation. He could have lost his boxing licence and I admit that I took advantage of the situation.

Passing through the door, I shouted over my shoulder a repeat of my little speech that had wound Frazier up in the first place, referring to Hughes, Hoover and Nixon. The two policemen who'd escorted me outside the terminal building asked if I wanted to press charges against the members of Frazier's pop group.

'Shit no, that ain't my style.'

Then I saw a famous face coming towards me. It was Michael Oliver, the ITN interviewer, who was one of the witnesses of my confrontation with Frazier. He wanted to question me, but the two cops, with tight grips on my arms, had other ideas.

All Oliver had time to tell me was that his job was to escort Frazier to the TV room for an interview. He jotted down my name and telephone number and muttered that he'd contact me in the afternoon.

'I'll call you later,' he promised.

Escorting Joe to the TV room, eh? I had my own couple of escorts and if they were going to interview me it certainly wasn't going to be in a TV room.

Finally, the two coppers got me into a small room where, believe it or not, they actually cleaned me up like a couple of nurses, dabbing away at the cuts on my face with cotton wool and clearing away the blood. The cuts were fuck-all but as my nose was bleeding all down my front, it looked a lot worse than it really was. I had a fat lip, cuts inside my mouth, a few bruises and some swellings on my face. That was all and probably a lot less than I picked up once a month at the Barn. The real pain was coming from my ribs and legs, in particular my shin bones. I'd collected one or two boots in the balls as well. I was beginning to feel sick. Those bastards were experts in the art of kicking: they knew just which parts of the body to aim at.

The two coppers told me that the clear-up wasn't part of their job. All they'd been ordered to do was to usher me out of the terminal building.

'Then why are you cleaning me up?' I asked.

"Cos, me old son,' they said sarcastically, 'We'd like to be your managers.'

Then they reminded me again that I was well within my rights to press charges. 'We saw them attack you first – and although you were provoking Joe Frazier, you weren't provoking any of them.'

'No way,' I told them. 'That's something that I'd never do to anyone.'

'Okay, son, that's up to you ... now on yer way.'

During my train ride home, I had time to think. It gave me great personal satisfaction to know that I'd just done the ultimate for all of Ali's fans. I'd done more than they would have expected, but nothing more than what I'd expected of myself. That was how my mind worked in those days.

Sandra was waiting for me. 'Thank God you're home. Where have you been? What's happened? Look at your face.' She didn't give me a chance to get a word in.

'Sandra, just sit down ... Take it easy, I'm fine. I'm okay ... Nothing's wrong. In fact – I've had a very good day.'

Before I had finished telling her what had happened, she was on her feet.

'Do you realise that your life was at risk?'

'Sandra, my life is at risk every day. You know that.'

'Yes, but ... if he'd hit you, he could have killed you.'

'Nah ... it would take more than Joe Frazier to do that.'

'Paddy. He could have taken your head clean off your shoulders with one punch. Then what would you do?'

'Then I would have picked it up, thrown it at him and then walked back home with it under my arm.'

'Oh, you're such an odd bugger.'

'I know. People have been telling me that all my life.'

Later on that afternoon, Michael Oliver did in fact phone me, wanting to know why I had confronted Joe Frazier, who was so furious that he'd refused to be interviewed afterwards. It had taken a lot of persistence and friendly persuasion to get him to sit before the camera.

Oliver went on to express his 'deep regret that no TV camera had been on hand at the scene of action to record an incident the like of which will never be seen again. I was amazed at your stand. I had to see it to believe it and I congratulate you.'

I grabbed a sheet of notepaper and jotted down what he said. I'm quoting from that bit of paper that I've still got:

'Joe Frazier told me – off camera – that he was about to "nail your coffin". You came that close to death.'

Later on, I stretched out on the settee to watch the six o'clock ITN bulletin. A photo of me confronting Frazier flashed onscreen, my hands high, holding up the large banner. It made TV headlines. In a later interview about the incident, Frazier answered Michael Oliver's questions cocky as you like.

'Wha – wha – whaddya mean? That weren't nuttin'… It was jes' one big set-up. Aw – you know what ah mean, man.'

But Oliver wouldn't let it go at that and pressed more questions at Frazier, making the big man scowl and twist in his chair like he had pins sticking up his arse.

'Aw – whu – dat guy wuz jes' part of some big organisation,' he kept repeating himself. 'You know what ah mean, man.'

Oliver carried on pushing even though he knew he could only press so far, as Frazier wasn't just sitting on pins, he was beginning to look like he had a sword stuck up his arse.

'What do you mean by some big organisation?'

'Ah – duh – well – ah knowed it was jes' planned.'

Oliver didn't say nothing else. Apart from the pins and that sword up his arse, Joe now had a thorn in his side and had to save face.

'Yeh – uh – ah'm tellin' ya, man,' he blustered on, 'dat guy – he was – oh, part of some big organisation that lost a lotta money on duh fight ... Dat's all it boils down to. Uh – he didn't worry me none, though. Aw – you know what ah mean, man.'

So that was it: some big organisation. One man?

Hughes, Hoover and Nixon probably never got my message, but sure as hell Joe Frazier did and I know it's a day he'll never forget.

A couple of weeks after this, two mean-looking and thick-set debt collectors turned up on our doorstep, banging the knocker enough to wake the dead. I hadn't paid anything off the arrears, or even the arrears on the arrears, 'cos I'd had no spare cash for ages.

I answered the door and the stockier one said, 'Mr Monaghan, you haven't been paying anything to our company for the last couple of months and you're going to have to, or else.'

Or else? You c**t, 'What do you mean, "or else"? If that's a threat, pal, I hope your firm pays sick money 'cos you'll need it. I ain't got no money, so you can't have it. Now I'm just thinking, if I was lucky enough to have a job and I was at work right now, I reckon you would be terrorising my wife for money behind my back and I don't like the thought of that at all. So a word to the wise, come back in a month and I'll see if I can spare a couple of quid but for now, get off my fucking doorstep or I'll put you on your back.'

I went to close the door but the big fella put his foot inside, and shouldered his way into the passage, saying to his mate, 'C'mon, let's get some of this gear outa here,' – meaning our furniture.

If this twat had done his homework he would've come mob-handed to try and walk into my home. As it was, he thought that because he was twice my size, I'd roll over – what a mistake. I lashed out with a right-hander and followed with all I could put into a left hook. He was hurt and dazed, but he was supposed to have gone down. He should have been off his feet and he wasn't. I knew that if he got hold of me I'd never match him for strength and I wasn't going to give him the chance to charge at me, so I kicked him hard in the bollocks and he doubled up. Only trouble was he was still on his feet, until I sent in another right hand. He dropped like the sack of shit he was.

He lay out on the path groaning, so I said to his mate, who had decided it was a good move to stand by the gate, 'Hey you, move this sack of shit away from my door.' What with the shouting that had gone on a few neighbours were standing out on the pavement wondering what was going on.

'Paddy, what was that all about? Who were they?'

'Oh, just a coupla Jehovah's Witnesses.' That made them talk among themselves.

Back indoors Sandra was looking very worried. 'Oh Paddy, what happens if they get the police onto you?'

'They won't, because what they're doing is illegal, anyway. They can't just barge into people's homes and take away their furniture.'

'But, Paddy, they do, you read about it in the papers all the time.'

'I know they do. They'll do anything, if people stand by and let them. These two were just a couple of cowboys employed by finance companies to do the dirty work. So don't be worrying about them getting the police onto me ... Anyway, even if they did, they know what the consequences would be if they grassed me up to the Old Bill.'

'Maybe you shouldn't have hit him like that.'

'What – hit him? If I'd had a gun I'd have shot the bastard. I was fighting to protect my home, you and the children. No-one walks over that step unless I invite them, 'cos no-one walks over me, you, or the kids. Right?' After that we didn't hear no more from that particular finance company and didn't see those two fat bastards ever again either.

Meanwhile, Muhammad Ali was to fight against his old sparring-partner, Jimmy Ellis, who had grown up with him in Louisville, Kentucky. Neither man really wanted this contest, but it had to be done in order to establish which of the pair was the top contender for the official world title and because it was for the North American Boxing Federation Championship.

Both Jimmy and Muhammad, who had been brilliant amateurs, were now no longer fighting for little tin trophies as they had done in the past. They were seasoned professionals who looked on boxing as a business and a very lucrative one at that. Close friendships had to be forgotten in that situation.

Ellis was a former holder of the heavyweight title and an outstanding boxer, though naturally overshadowed by Ali. You didn't have to be psychic to work out what the result was going to be. On 26 July, 1971, in Texas, Ellis was completely outclassed and was knocked out in the 12th round. With that piece of business over, the friendship carried on like it had been before.

A month before that, on 28 June, Ali had scored the victory of his life. Sticking two fingers up to all those people who had knocked him for his religious and political beliefs and cheered like fuck when he lost his championship and boxing licence, seven Supreme Court judges voted unanimously that Muhammad Ali was innocent of all charges made against him in 1967. It had taken four years and three months for these judges to overrule the boxing bodies. Why did it take so long?

One thing that made me laugh was that the judges went out of their way to have a go at those people who'd gone after Ali. Now the judges were saying exactly the same things that I had been kicking up about. They made it quite clear that this was not a boxing issue and what had been done was undemocratic. But I'd like to know why those people were allowed to get away with it in the first place and for such a long time.

It was on the morning of 11 October, 1971, that Muhammad Ali was scheduled to visit London again. This time he was on a short promotional tour for Ovaltine. And this time my visit to London Airport at Heathrow was to be a very different and much more pleasant occasion than my last.

I took with me an extra-large sack of mail – bigger than the one I had shown Muhammad's manager a few months earlier. At the airport I was just one of a crowd. These weren't tourists: they weren't travelling to or coming from anywhere. They had all turned out to meet, or at least see, Muhammad Ali.

The atmosphere was really something else. These people waited with cameras, pens and paper at the ready, eager to get photos of the man and get his autograph. I just wanted to hand over that sack of fan mail and to get to shake his hand – no more, no less – and then to make my way home.

Despite the size of the crowd, I was determined to do what I'd set out to do, just as I had with Joe Frazier. But this time there would be no confrontation. I was determined to get his autograph otherwise I'd never live it down with my mates.

I leant against one of the walls and looked round at the faces in the crowded terminal. Ali wasn't due for a while yet but already these people were excited: young and old, male and female. There were parents there who were more excited than their own children.

By comparison, I guessed I was the calmest and quietest

person in the place. Personally I thought that they were all out of their minds, but I didn't feel superior, just different. If any of them knew what I had been up to for so many years, I expect they would have considered me just as mad.

A man and a woman ran to the spot where they'd worked out Ali would make his entrance. In their rush to get the best spot, they bumped into a very elderly Asian-looking man, knocking him clean off his feet and sending his stick flying. They never even stopped to help him up or apologise, ignorant bastards. Surprisingly, when you think us British are usually pretty polite and helpful, nobody was bothering about the old fella. I could see he couldn't get up on his own, so I ran over to him and helped him, saying, 'You okay, mate?'

In broken English he told me he wasn't hurt, just a little bit shaken up. He seemed more worried about his stick than anything else. I found it under a seat and gave it to him. Clasping his hands together he said, 'God bless you for your kindness.'

With the old man leaning on me, I slowly walked him over to the nearest row of seats. Every seat was taken, so I explained to a young guy sitting on the end what had happened and asked him if he'd let the old man sit down.

'Piss off,' he said. 'Took me a half hour to get this seat.'

I grabbed him by the hair, put my face down to his ear and very quietly said, 'Get your fuckin' arse up now or I'll rip your fucking head off.' He moved sharpish and I sat the old man down, telling him to stay where he was until the crowd had thinned out.

I picked up my sack of letters and I'm thinking, I've heard of Beatlemania, but that's nothing compared with this. It's Ali-mania. The magic of the man was at work among the crowd long, long, before he was seen. And suddenly, the deafening screams of young girls and women broke out, loud enough to bring planes down. Then I could hear the men, with their chants.

'Ah-lee! Ah-lee! Ah-lee!'

93

I couldn't see him because of the enormous crowd pushing forward, but I grabbed my sack and, with a lot more consideration than people had shown earlier, I forced myself through the crowd to the front. There he was – larger than life – the man I owed big time, the man I'd fought for all those years.

As he strolled down the opposite side of the barrier, he raised his arms high in the air. He was waving and grinning all over his face as he greeted the screaming crowd. Unlike Frazier, he didn't have dozens of hangers-on and definitely no pop group at his heels; he just had one man at his side. The crowd had gone wild. They were trying to climb over each other to get to him, with no thought at all for those who were being hurt in the process.

'Hi, there, everybody,' he said, with his familiar smile. His next words echoed my own thoughts: 'Hey, there's little children an' old folks here. Ah want you all to be very careful – ah don't want anyone to get hurt. So stop pushin' an' shovin', will ya? Ah'll get to meet y'all.'

Then, as he reached the end of the railed-off barrier, I unrolled a piece of red carpet that I'd carried all the way from Abingdon. He stopped, he looked down, his eyes widened and then he walked back just so he could walk along my red carpet. This started off an explosion of cheering and clapping.

When he reached where I was standing, I put my hand out and said to him, 'Hi champ, I'm Paddy Monaghan.'

'So you're Paddy Monaghan.' He shook my hand like a pump. 'Ah been hearin' your name a lot back home an' about some of the good work ya been doin'.'

I needed to cut any thanks short to save myself embarrassment, so I handed over the enormous sack of mail to him and told him every one was from admirers.

He said: 'Yuh mean to say that all these are from mah fans who've written to you?'

I was dead proud but all I could get out was a simple, 'Yep.'

94

Right at that moment, I noticed the old foreign-looking gent, who I'd helped a bit earlier on, stood there smiling and looking up at Muhammad and me. How he got through that mob I'll never know. He glanced at Ali and with his arms outstretched and the walking stick dangling from his wrist, he embraced Muhammad as his fellow Muslim.

'As-salaam-alaikum,' he said.

'Alaikum-salaam,' said Ali.

I have always been puzzled by what happened next. The old man reached out for my hand and placed it into Ali's. Then he cupped our hands together and wrapped them in his own. For a few seconds he closed his eyes and muttered a few foreign words. Then, with a smile, he simply stood back, nodded to us both, held firmly onto his walking-stick and with shuffles instead of steps he moved his way through the hysterical crowd. Apart from Ali himself, nobody in that airport that morning impressed me as much as that old man.

So, I'd accomplished what I'd set out to do that day. I'd managed to get to shake the great man's hand and to pass all the mail over to him. That's all I'd ever wanted. It was mission completed and I had a memory of a couple of minutes that I could hold onto for the rest of my life: simple as that.

As I said my goodbyes to him and turned to squeeze my way through the mob and start my journey back home, he said loudly, 'Hey, Paddy, what you talkin' about, man? Goodbye? This is jes' the beginnin'. Ah want you to come with me to mah hotel.'

I did a double take, 'You're joking. What, me?'

'No, man, ah is serious. You the only Paddy around here, ain't you? C'mon, but stay close, an' don't be gettin' lost in the crowd.'

I grabbed up the sack of letters and stuck close. The police had been called in to reinforce airport security in an effort to control the crowds. As we weaved our way through, two lines of policemen formed chains by linking arms to hold back the people. The way I felt at that moment I haven't the skill to put into words. It would never have surprised me if Sandra started shaking my shoulder and telling me it was time to get up for work. Surreal is the only word that comes into my head.

Ali reached out to touch the outstretched hands and signed as many autographs as he could for the young, the not-so-young, the men, the women and the screaming young girls, who, I suppose, couldn't help being impressed by his good looks. They jumped up and down, biting their fingers. And the men both young and old alike, were trying to drown the sound of the screaming females with the deafening chants of 'Ah-lee! Ah-lee! Ah-lee!'

A security guard immediately blocked my path into the VIP lounge. 'Sorry, but you can't go in.'

'It's okay,' Ali said, 'Ah asked him to come. He's with me. C'mon, Paddy.'

Inside, Muhammad gave a press conference, promising everybody in the place, with his usual modesty, that whenever he fought Joe Frazier again, 'Ah'm gonna whup him good.'

After the conference, it was, 'C'mon Paddy, you're comin' with me.' We headed off to his car.

There was I, Paddy Monaghan, unemployed labourer, dressed in clobber bought from a jumble sale and with holes in my shoes, sitting beside Muhammad Ali. Where I come from, we only ever see a Rolls Royce on the television or at the pictures and there was me lounging back on the posh leather seats like it was something I did every day. It was all front though because inside my stomach was churning with nerves and excitement: wait until my family hear about this! Instead of being alone with my thoughts in some grimy train carriage on the way home, I was being chauffeured in style towards the Royal Lancaster Hotel.

During the journey I did more thinking than talking. I had to pinch myself to believe that this was really happening. I thought, 'When I tell my mates about this they'll think I'm talking shit.' Anyway, I didn't care who believed me, 'cos I knew it was happening and I didn't need to broadcast it to the world.

My feelings about what was happening were difficult to explain. A lot of people might think – Oh yeah, Mr Swanky bollocks thinks he's something special 'cos he's spent a bit of time with Muhammad Ali the famous boxer. That's why he did all that campaigning shit, just so he could make himself look good.

They'd be closer to the truth if they said the Pope was a Protestant. Get real, how could anybody think that I would put myself through the kicks, ridicule and knockbacks that I went through for years, on the flimsy chance of meeting the man himself? I must admit that as my campaign grew, I did get a sort of recognition, but I never looked for it or expected it.

I was 27 years old and, believe it or not, I'd never been inside a hotel before. Hotels were for the very posh and I'd only ever seen them from outside. I'm the sort of guy who accepts people for what they are and never even considers that what they've got should make them better or worse than me. I just hoped the staff and guests felt the same way. There's Ali, suited and booted, tall and good-looking and the world at his feet. Then there's your man Paddy, tidy enough for Abingdon, but my down-at-heel shoes and denim jacket didn't quite fit in with the luxury of the Royal Lancaster. Remember, I was carrying a sack of mail on my back so I must've looked like a delivery fella who'd come in the front instead of the tradesman's entrance at the back.

We were escorted up a flight of stairs and it might have been my imagination but the sideways look I was getting from the guy who led us seemed to ask, 'Who the fuck are you?'

As soon as we got inside the suite, Muhammad threw himself on the bed, reached for the phone and ordered two meals to be sent up straight away. As he was doing it, he put his hand over the mouthpiece and asked if I was hungry. When I said my belly thought my throat was cut, he burst out laughing and was still giggling when he put the phone down, saying, 'It's sure gonna take some time to get used to your English expressions, Paddy.'

What did he expect? 'One is rather peckish, Mr Ali?' Fuck off. I didn't know what airs and graces were, so there was no chance of putting any on. Anyway, I was me and nothing could change that. At the same time I was finding that Muhammad was just another guy once he was out of the limelight. Okay, our colour was different, our backgrounds were miles apart, he was an exceptional boxer and loaded, but we had the same kind of piss-taking humour and in no time it seemed like I'd known him for ages. Over our meal of steak, something that wasn't on our menu very often at home, we laughed and joked about all kinds of subjects.

Eventually he asked me, 'What kind of job you got, Paddy?'

That was a fucking awkward question. I've just met the guy and no way did I want to start telling him my sob story of a Joe Palooka bare knuckle fighter with no fights for ages ... So I lied.

'Oh, I work in a car factory in Abingdon.'

'Is the pay good?'

'Oh, yeah. Very good, me an' my family are doing very well.'

'Tell me,' he said, 'have you really been doin' all those things ah been hearin' 'bout you back home?'

'Well, Muhammad, I don't know what you've heard, but yeah, I've been doing quite a bit.' He didn't make any comment, just sat looking at me and shaking his head. I took that to mean he was surprised and pleased that somebody would put themselves to such efforts with no thought of some financial gain.

We must have spent about three hours in that suite and we really hit it off. I felt that he liked me and the feeling was mutual.

Then his phone rang and soon after visitors started to arrive, one after the other. A proper mixed bunch they turned out to be.

Most of them had some sort of financial interest in mind. They ranged from some of the top boxing promoters down to the sharks and parasites of the fight game. There were a few genuine well-wishers as well who didn't seem to want anything from him at all.

I began to feel like an intruder and slightly uncomfortable among all these people who were way outside the world I was used to. I think Muhammad picked up on that because he kept turning to me and involving me in the conversation. Even so, I was beginning to think it was time I made my excuses and left.

I had come to accept that this opportunity to meet the man whose career I'd followed for years, was a one-off, that it would be my only chance to spend time with him and, to be honest, what I'd had so far was so well beyond anything I could've hoped for. I reckoned that a man as busy as he was, a man regarded as being the most famous person in the world, would give me a polite brush-off, without being unkind. How wrong I was.

When I stood up and said it was time I made my way home, he jumped up, grasped my hand and said to a guy he'd been talking to, 'Quick, gimme a pen, I need to write sumthin' down.' He scribbled away for a couple of minutes then handed me the piece of paper. He'd written when he would be in London after he'd finished promoting Ovaltine and asked me to ring the hotel on those dates – ''Cos Paddy, ah wanna see you agin.'

He asked me to thank all those fans who had written to him and said he'd make arrangements for the sack to be flown to his home, after assuring me that he would reply to as many letters as possible. He was a man of his word, because over a period of time I got loads more letters from people thanking me for passing on their mail to him.

His last words as we said our goodbyes were: 'Yuh know I'm over here for a promotional tour for Ovaltine?'

'Yeah Muhammad, I know that, what about it?'

'Well, just what is this stuff, Ovaltine?'

I told him it was a popular milky bedtime drink in England. I didn't tell him I thought it tasted like shite or that even though I hated the stuff it hadn't stopped me pestering Mamma for me to join the Ovaltineys, the promotional fan club, back when I was about five. I can still remember the words to the club's theme song that was played on the radio... But perhaps I'm giving away too much now.

His short tour lasted three days and I was to see him a couple of more times before he went back to the States. The more we saw of each other the better we seemed to get on. He invited me along with him to a packed Royal Albert Hall, where he rounded off the evening's professional boxing with a clowning exhibition session with Cliff Field, Graham Sines and a good mate of mine, 'Gypsy' Johnny Frankham. Ali told me that he was very impressed by Johnny.

You will guess that it would take the combined talents of Shakespeare, Dickens and Hemingway or, in my case, Enid Blyton to describe my feelings when Ali wrote down his home telephone number and asked me to ring three weeks later to finalise arrangements for me to visit him in the United States of America.

When I returned home to Abingdon that time and told Sandra I'd been invited to the States she was really pleased for me and so were my parents. I arranged for her and the kids to stay with my mother and father. Then it was just a matter of waiting.

Apart from my days away training and my few short stays in hospital, this was going to be the first time I had ever been away from home for any length of time, so it was something of an occasion. December came, we had another very quiet Christmas, and the time arrived for me to get myself ready for the trip.

Sandra and Mamma started fussing: I must make sure I do this and make sure I do that and remember to take my pills. Packing wasn't too tricky. The clothes I owned would've fitted into a carrier bag and they were mostly clean underwear, toothpaste and shaving gear. That was just about it.

Mamma made Seamus, one of my older brothers, lend me a couple of his shirts and he lent me a pair of his shoes as well because the only ones that I had were filled with cardboard to cover the holes in the soles.

Seamus had the family trait of piss-taker and came out with, 'When people see you and Ali coming, you know what they're gonna say?'

'What?'

He answered with a take-off of Ali and his poems, 'Here's the champ/but what's he doing with that tramp?'

Okay, it was a joke, but I couldn't help thinking that there was a lot of truth in what he said. Maybe I'd be an embarrassment to Ali? Still, I wasn't in a position to go shooting off to Burtons for half a dozen suits, so people were going to have to take me as I was and have always been.

I phoned Muhammad at the time he'd suggested and he told me that he'd made all the arrangements and that my ticket would be waiting for me at the check-in desk on 17 February, 1972, and that was about ten days away.

I had a job to do the following day. Tommy had booked me in to take on a fighter from Grimsby named Gordon Moore. A good strong knuckles, but with the state of mind I was in about the coming trip, I felt confident enough to take on Joe Frazier (without broom handles). One thing I didn't want to happen was to pick up a broken hand, ribs, nose or anything more serious. There was always a good chance of that, but I didn't fancy turning up in the States for that trip of a lifetime looking like I'd been in a car crash. With that in the back of my mind, I climbed into the ring and bosh ... I KO'd Moore in the first round: lovely job, coat back on and home. A nice quick little earner, timed just right – well done Tommy.

As the countdown started towards the 17th, I think I must've driven Sandra almost round the bend with my talking about what was to come. I'll tell you something, that lovely wife of mine was a saint amongst women. Not once, not for the tiniest second did she ever pull a face or a sulk about me going away and leaving her with the responsibility of looking after the kids on the most limited budget you could imagine. I suppose that's one of the many reasons why I've always loved her.

CHAPTER SIX
My First Time Across the Pond

Having worked so hard for Ali without thought of reward, a handshake and a signature all I wanted, it was amazing to think that I was going to travel all the way to the USA and see Muhammad in his own country. He had been so good to me, just offering me the trip out of nowhere. I was determined to make the very best of it.

The day came and I got myself a lift to the airport, but once I'd picked up my ticket I found myself walking round like a bloody idiot, without a clue of what to do or where to go. I was lost and it was like being in a maze. Pretty obvious I wasn't cut out to be a jetsetter.

I'd never done fear or nervousness in my life. When you choose the path I had, those two emotions would be a proper handicap. So I was surprised to find out that I wasn't as cool, calm and collected as I always thought I was. Sitting on the plane I realised that I had a fear of flying. I was as confident as you like when I climbed up the steps, even managed a few jokes with the hostesses, but as those engines turned over and as we started to shoot off down the runway, my stomach was in Seamus's shoes.

Every muscle in my body was tensed and I was sweating. I looked around and almost everybody was relaxed, probably because this was just another trip to them. To me though, the jet was carrying me into a different world. I was flying into an adventure and lifestyle as different from anything I could imagine from my simple working class life in Abingdon.

Sitting next to me was a friendly, middle-aged American couple who politely introduced themselves and we got chatting. It was just what I needed because it took me mind off the fact I was 35,000 feet off the ground. They asked me questions about England and I asked them the same about America. Then came the question that always seems to get asked, as if what you do is what you are.

'So what line are you in?'

I'd never heard that expression before. 'What do you mean what line?'

'You know, what do you do in the line of work? What's your job?'

'I've got no work. I'm an unemployed labourer.' (I never did like telling strangers that I was a bare knuckle boxer).

'Oh, I see ... so you have relatives in the US who are bringing you over?'

'I've got relatives in America, yes, but they're not bringing me over.'

He paused for a bit and I could see he was trying to work out what I was all about.

'I hope you don't mind my asking this, but how on earth can an unemployed labourer afford to visit the States?'

'Oh, I've been invited over by Muhammad Ali'

'Oh. I see '

The guy leant across his seat and whispered something to his wife and I'm bloody sure Mamma would've had something to say about cutting somebody out by whispering in their company – rude bastard. I realised that in future I should keep the truth to myself, otherwise I'd be laying myself open for people to think I was some sort of retard living in a fantasy world. The both of them seemed to shrink away from me as though any minute I might attack them, take over the plane and order it to fly to Cuba.

The last thing they both said to me and both at the same time was, 'Oh, really?' and for the rest of the long flight all I got from them was nervous smiles and stupid giggles. It got on my tits in the end, so I was well pleased when the plane touched down in Philadelphia some time in the late afternoon, US time.

After clearing customs, a big, black fella was there to meet me with a bone-crushing handshake and a deep, husky voice: 'Welcome to America, Paddy.'

As an employee of Muhammad's, he'd been asked to give me a message.

'Mr Ali says he regrets not being able to meet you personally, but he's been called away at the last minute to Pittsburgh on business.'

During the drive in Muhammad's big limousine, the driver mentioned that he'd heard about my campaign for justice for Ali. He gave me the third degree in a very polite way all the way to New Jersey, showing a lot of interest in what I'd done back in England. It seemed that to him, the idea of a white man and a very insignificant one like me, sticking up for a black guy, no matter how famous he was, took a lot of thought for him to get his head around.

Eventually we reached New Jersey and pulled into Muhammad's drive. His house was a big villa, surrounded by iron railings and set among a load of trees. To one side of the house there were three garages and I could see his blue mobile home bus and a vintage Oldsmobile.

I was greeted in the friendliest way possible by his wife, Belinda and his mamma, who was there to help Belinda look after the three little children. The fourth child was expected the following month. What struck me straight away was how much his mother reminded me of my own. She was a warm and lovely lady and she spoke about her two sons with obvious affection for both of them. The resemblance between Ali and his mother was uncanny.

The house was like something I'd only ever seen at the pictures and I thought: fuck me ... what a gaff. It made the Royal Lancaster look like a Salvation Army shelter. Ali's mamma and Belinda must have thought I was very naive and I was, as I sat there and gawked like some country boy at my surroundings. The room was decorated with antiques and beautiful curtains and carpets that Sandra would've died for. Every wall in the living room had book cases filled with what looked like, to my ignorant eyes, very expensive books. In one corner of the massive room was a gleaming grand piano.

Pointing at this piano, for something to say really, I asked her, 'Does Muhammad play?'

She gave a big laugh and put her finger to her lips, 'Shh... He thinks he can but all he does is bang away enough to drive anybody crazy. But what is nice and it keeps him off it, is that every now and then he employs a proper pianist to play for him. He just loves pop music y'know, rock'n'roll an' all that, but don't ever ask him to play that piano.'

'Why's that?' I said,

''Cos Paddy, an' he know it, he drives me to distrac'shun with his hollerin' an' screechin' tryin' to be like that Little Richard.'

I felt as welcome as if they were family, the exact way my own Ma treated every visitor, whether friend or stranger. Belinda was in the kitchen getting a meal and the mother, obviously concerned that I must've been tired after my long journey, called through to her daughter-in-law saying, 'Belinda honey, does Gee-Gee know that Paddy's arrived?'

She called back, 'Yes, Momma, he knows. He's travelling home tonight.'

'Excuse me,' I said, 'But who's Gee-Gee?'

Momma giggled like a girl, 'Oh, that's just mah pet name for him, 'cos when he was a li'l baby in his crib, all we'd get outa him was "Gee-gee" an' it's been ma name for him ever since. Y'know what that silly boy o' mine said when he won the Golden Gloves? He says, when he was layin' in his crib he was tryin' to tell us what he was aimin' for – y'know? GG ... Golden Gloves.'

Then she pointed to her gold front tooth, 'He done that while ah was tendin' him in his crib, prob'ly trainin' for what was to come.'

After a meal of 'good soul food cooking', as Momma put it, Belinda drove me to a hotel that was only a short distance away. I'm sure Muhammad had got enough on his plate, but it was nice to know that he'd taken the trouble to book me in, over the phone, before he left Pittsburgh. He'd even left a message at the reception desk saying that he'd call for me at 8am the next day.

So I collected the key to my room, along with the message. Bear in mind that, apart from Ali's visit to London four months earlier, this was the first time I'd ever been in a hotel, and I'd never slept in one. I knew nothing at all about the services you could get at the press of a button, like early morning calls. So when I got shown to a very plush room, I was so knackered all I wanted to do was to get my head down. First I needed to set the alarm. The last thing I wanted was to oversleep.

I don't know how long I spent looking for an alarm clock, so I stood in the middle of the room, scratching my backside and thought, Ali will be calling for me at 8am, so I want to get up at 7, take a bath and be ready for him when he turns up. Look at this room, I thought, it's like a fucking palace. It's got everything you can think of, except a simple bloody alarm clock.

In the end I gave up looking, knelt down, said my usual night prayers and crashed out on the softest bed I'd ever slept in.

I was jerked awake at about 8 o'clock the next morning, wondering where the fuck that ringing was coming from and for that matter, where I was. Slowly I worked it out and picked up the phone.

'Yeh – uh – hullo.'

There was no mistaking the voice on the other end of the line.

'Hey, Paddy.'

'That you, Muhammad?'

'Nah, it's [Russian leader] Khrushchev callin' to see if you'd like room service.'

'How you doing, Muhammad?'

We had a bit of a craic and a few laughs and he said, 'Ah called you several times durin' the night, but ah guess you wus in deep sleep.' He was absolutely spot on there.

'Where you calling from?'

'Mah home, an' ah'll meet you in the lobby of the hotel in 'bout twenty minutes. Ah came all the way back from Pittsburgh during the night, an' we headin' back there this mornin'.'

'You mean you drove from Pittsburgh just to pick me up?'

'Yeah, man – ain't that somethin'?'

'Cor strewth.'

'Cor what? What's that mean?'

'Nothing, mate. I'll tell you later.'

'Paddy.'

'Yeah?'

'Ah'm contracted to box a series of exhibition bouts an' other appearances an' ah'd like you to come along with me. That way we can have some fun an' it'll give you a chance to see America. We'll have an opportunity to get to know each other. How's that sound?'

'Yeah, that sounds great, Muhammad.'

'Right on. Ah'll pick you up in twenty minutes.' Twenty minutes? I was ready in five.

With me standing on the sidewalk – yeah, picking up the lingo already – bang on time, he rolled up in a huge black Cadillac and greeted me with a hug and his usual playful, threatening fist. This was no show: he was genuinely pleased to see me again. My own feelings? Well I'll just have to fall back on my usual, there are no words to describe them; at least, not with my vocabulary, anyway.

'Paddeee Monaghan – mah main man.'

He was full of fun and laughed and joked all the way to the airport. He was a complete nutcase when it came to driving; toe to the floor, or foot on the gas, wherever we went.

In three hectic weeks we went all over the place and grew to like each other more. I saw a lot of his beautiful country and met too many of his countrymen to count. I found most of them were sound as a pound. Yeah, no doubt about it, I really took to America and its people.

I was getting a taste of life that was different from anything I'd known back in England. Yet wherever we went and whoever we met, Sandra and the children were never out of my mind.

Here I was in the United States as a guest of Muhammad Ali, travelling with him every day and being privileged to work with him as his corner man during exhibition bouts. I met celebrity movie stars, pop stars and sports stars, stayed in posh hotels and was driven in posh cars ... Soon I'd be back in Abingdon, thumbing a lift to London to watch him fight on closed circuit TV at the Hammersmith Odeon, then thumbing a lift back home. The whole thing seemed more like fiction than fact. I was travelling with Muhammad Ali.

Forget all that shit about him as the cocky, boasting loudmouth who called himself 'The Greatest' at every opportunity. That wasn't the real man. The real Ali is quiet, thoughtful, considerate and the most genuine guy I could wish to call a friend.

What struck me was that I could sense in him a real sympathy with working class people. And just as noticeable was their response to him. Everywhere we went; his schedule in each big city would include personal appearances at posh banquets and even posher functions in his honour. Yet away from all that I saw a side of him that the world never knew.

He would visit the ghettoes and talk to the junkies, the drunks and the dropouts. He'd give them hope and he'd put smiles on their faces. It didn't matter how unwashed or scruffy they were. It didn't matter that some of these people were what a lot of people might call the dregs of society, he made time to have a word.

These unfortunate people – and I say that even though most of their troubles were self-inflicted – would crowd round him. None of them begged or showed aggression because of what he had. All they wanted was to talk to him.

'Hey man … you Muhammad Ali, ain'cha?'

Putting his hands on their shoulders, he'd say to them, 'Yeh, man. Ah'm Muhammad Ali.'

Sometimes as many as 20 or 30 of these people were trying reach out to touch his arms, his hands, or his face, to make sure that they weren't dreaming and he didn't reel back in disgust or push them away.

'You the greatest man.'

He'd say, 'You wanna make me happy?'

'Yeah, Muhammad, yeah … anything, man, jus' name it.'

'Then kick the habit, brothers. Kick it.'

Being by his side all the time, I saw that although the haves of this world appreciated his support at posh functions, the have-nots appreciated him even more.

But he also undoubtedly enjoyed being a celebrity. We were being driven through some small town and someone had given Ali a big, brown paper bag full of sweets and chocolate. He noticed several young couples coming out of a store with their children. He said to the driver, 'Hey, stop the car.' We got out, he brought the bag with him, then said 'Hi folks' to the couples who looked liked like they'd been hit with a brick. Even in a typical little American hick town you didn't have to be a fan of the fight game to know who the man was.

Within minutes people seemed to come from nowhere and flock around him for autographs. He signed every bit of paper that was stuck under his nose then turned to the children and started digging sweets out of the bag and handing them around until they ran out. Now, I knew none of these people wanted to see Abingdon's top bare knuckle fighter, so as always at times like that, I stood back out of the limelight and just observed people's reactions and eavesdropped on conversations.

I watched and listened to two old men who were talking quite close to me.

'Hey, Mac, ah gotta see this tuh believe it – an' ah still don't. That is who ah think it is, ain't it?'

'Yeah ... Who'd have ever thought he was like that? Ah neva use' to like him, but ... hey, got a camera?'

'Whadda yuh tawkin' 'bout? We never brought no camera with us. So whadda yuh tawkin' 'bout man?'

'Then ah'm gonna buy one quick.'

The old fella took off and came back just as quick with a cheap camera in his hand. He fumbled and fucked around, managed to put a roll of film in it, then called out: 'Hey, Muhammad that was mah li'l grandson yuh jes' give that candy to. D'ya mind if ah jes' take a picture of yuh holdin' him in yo' arm?'

'No problem, sir. Give him here.'

And the old guy who had said moments ago to his pal that he hadn't liked Muhammad, was now clicking away like mad. Then he asked Muhammad if it was okay if he got a photo of the two of them shaking hands.

'Sure. Go ahead.'

'Oh, an' kin ah have yo' autograph, Muhammad?'

'Sure you can.'

His pal reminded him: 'Thowt yuh said yuh didn't like him.'

'Shit.' He said. 'Yuh gone hearin' things, y'ol' fool. Ah've always said he wus the greatest. You knowed that.'

Muhammad had the patience of a saint in situations like that.

Another time, we happened to slow down outside a primary school in Philadelphia and he said to the driver, 'Quick, pull over man, we jus' gonna be a minute or two.'

He looked at me, grinning all over his face and said, 'C'mon Paddy. Let's you an' me say "Howdy" to the kids.' I was getting used to this sort of thing by now so didn't show any surprise at all. Sometimes he was like a kid himself.

This was those good old days before weird shit started happening with guns and killing in schools, so there was no armed guards patrolling the playground. We just walked through the gates and in through the main door. He was actually tiptoeing when he led me along a deserted corridor, before opening one of the classroom doors, stepping inside and with a raised fist and in that mock aggressive voice, he said to all the kids, 'Ah'm lookin' for trouble.'

I'll never forget the pandemonium those four words caused. The screams of excitement – which included those of the lady teacher – brought a very worried-looking headmaster into the class, followed by what seemed like the whole school. Muhammad apologised for upsetting the lessons but he knew as well as everyone did that lessons were the last thing on anybody's mind. He didn't do those sorts of stunts for his own ego, he knew his presence was enough to bring a lot of fun and happiness.

The class was full and the hallway outside was packed and all you could see was a sea of faces and waving arms. I think the headmaster was too stunned to use his authority to call for quiet so, as he'd been the cause of it all, Muhammad raised his hand and gave a very firm order: 'Now listen all you children. You gotta stay cool. Calm down, 'cos ah don't want any of you getting' hurt. So if you can't control yourselves, then ah'm leavin'. An' do you want me to leave?'

Back came a roar of, 'No!'

He shook hands, in turn, with all the teachers and picked up many of the children, before asking them all to listen very carefully: 'Ah've got a few words ah wanna say t'all o' yuh.' He told them to work hard, for education was one of the important necessities of life, to be honest and never ever think about taking drugs.

If it wasn't schools and ghettoes we ended up in, it would be some road sweeper or down-and-out who would get his attention on the spur of the moment. He did this sort of thing all the time. He'd just stop his car and stroll over to greet groups of people and it didn't matter who they were.

I soon realised that he just loved to make people happy. Okay, not all of what he did was altruistic, I know, and here I'll contradict myself and say perhaps there was a touch of ego, but so what. He's human, like the rest of us, and I'd say a lot more human than most.

If you want a contrast, I remember seeing Ronald Reagan and Ali turning up at the same time to enter the Gresham Hotel in Dublin for the weigh-in for the Al 'Blue' Lewis fight. Surrounded by a load of bodyguards Reagan was tight-lipped and sullen; or in Abingdon speak, he had a face like a smacked arse. You can bet your life that if he'd got an election coming up he would've been smiling like a fucking Cheshire cat. Muhammad made himself completely accessible to the public no matter who they were. He had a permanent smile on his face and he was humble and grateful to be in the position he was.

He had a wicked sense of humour though and one time when we were driving through a small southern town he caught sight of what he'd call a typical redneck standing on the pavement. A guy well overweight and dressed in jeans, work boots and tartan shirt. He pulled up beside him, wound the window down and said, 'Hey man, ah hear tawk in this town that you gonna whup mah black ass. Well here ah am!' I will never, ever forget the look on that man's face as Muhammad burst out laughing and screeched off in a cloud of dust.

At first, without knowing him as a person, I wasn't aware of just how great this guy's strength of character was or how his appeal touched everybody: man, woman, old or very young. Don't get me wrong, I wasn't carried away by the fact that he'd stooped low enough to become friends with me. I'm a very strong-minded person and my feet are always solidly on the ground. I've already mentioned that I never have and never will have it in my nature to idolise Muhammad Ali, or anyone else. As I found out, he's a man just the same as you and me.

We'd chat, laugh and generally fuck about and play jokes on each other, just like any couple of mates might do. I'd be myself and it was the same with him. Yeah, sure, I knew he was different but at the same time he knew I was different as well.

So many people come out with: 'Oh, Muhammad, I think you're the greatest' or 'I've seen all your fights, I'm your biggest fan.' He never got any of that crap from me.

In fact, when we'd joke around, I'd say things to him like, 'Hey mate – know what?'

'What?'

'You're full of shit.'

Or sometimes I'd tie his shoelaces together when he'd be dozing in a hotel room. Things like that.

The man is about as genuine and sincere as anyone can get. For example, three days after arriving in the States, we were speeding along, as usual, in his Lamborghini. He was off to see his business people in Philadelphia. The weather was below freezing and the snow was coming down so hard you could hardly see in front. Muhammad was flooring it and laughing at me because he knew I'd be almost shitting myself at that speed in those conditions. Luckily, although he loved speed, he wasn't stupidly reckless and always had his eyes on the road. Just as well, because at the last minute a dark figure loomed out of the driving snow. It was a guy thumbing a lift. Bugger, that took me back to the way I usually travelled back home.

Muhammad swung around the guy, pulled up a little way past, and wound his window down. The guy, who we could see was navy, ran up to the car, and as he was bending down to the low window, he's already expressing his gratitude. 'Thank ya, sir, thank ya, I thawt I was gonna die out ... Oh, mah God. Ah jus' don't believe this.'

'Where you headin' for?' asked Muhammad.

'Oh – ah – oh, Virginia.'

'Well, I'm only goin' as far as Philly but if you kin squeeze yersel' an' thet bag in the back, yur welcome to a ride as far as we goin'. Be car'ful you don' stand on ma brother Paddy's hair, he's Irish, ya know.' The guy didn't know whether to laugh or not at this bit of piss-taking at the length of my hair, or the comment I was Irish that supposedly explained my hippy look. Me, a bastard hippy? Anyway the fella got in the motor and we skidded off. Looking up into the mirror, Muhammad asked the guy, 'Tell me, buddy, why you hitchin' a ride in weather like this?'

The sailor was obviously as nervous as fuck being in the car with Ali and could hardly stammer out the words that he'd lost his pass and couldn't afford the fare home. Yep, this guy seems like my American counterpart.

I could see he was fidgeting around in the back and after a while plucked up the courage to say, 'Ah – ah – Mr Ali ... sir, could ah trouble you fer your autograph please? Otherwise ma family an' buddies ain't never gonna believe this.'

'Well, ma friend, tha's a little bit difficult.' And he went quiet long enough for the guy to think, Oh fuck, I've overstepped this man's generosity. Then Muhammad burst out laughing, 'It's a li'l difficult 'cos ah'm doing one helluva speed on this icy road an' if ah start signing mah name, well you ain't neva gonna git to Virginia. Ah think it best ah wait 'til ah stop.'

In Philadelphia, Ali made a diversion and drove right into the bus station. He got out, shook the fella's hand and slipped him some cash saying, 'There's your bus fare back to your folks in Virginia.' We drove off with thanks ringing in our ears.

This was the kind of genuine care for other people that I used to hear preached about at church when I was a kid. Really, they were just words, and they went in one ear and out the other as the ramblings of a doddering old priest. I don't think I ever saw anything like that being put into practice – until then.

As we headed for the freeway the look on my face must've given away what I was thinking because Muhammad said, 'Paddy, I ain't always bin in the position I am today an', who knows, one day ah may lose it all, so if ah kin help any person in trouble while I can, then ah'm happy to do it. Jus' remember, consideration hurts no one.'

Travelling with him was an experience. I'm one of the very few people who have spent time with him on the road and I tell you – it's something else. Didn't matter where it was, in a car, in the air, or on the streets, the very sight of him never failed to cause excitement.

For example, we might be driving along in a car and he'd warn me: 'Hey, Paddy, watch these people's faces.' Then he'd lean out of the window and yell: 'Ah am the greatest!' He'd cause traffic to come to a halt, he'd cause cars to turn in mid-street; drivers would leave their vehicles in the middle of the road and shout out, 'Ah–lee! Ah–lee! Ah–lee!' He loved it and so did I. It was a great craic. There would be pointing fingers and speechless faces when he parked up and got out to greet everyone.

There was a time when an old man was watching Ali's charm at work. Then, with a big smile on his face he said, 'Ah confess ah never liked you after that trouble with the draft, Mr Ali, 'cos ah believed what ah'd read in the papers. That impression is different from the one you givin' here now. So can ah shake your hand?'

Ali respected the man's honesty. He put his arm round the old fella's shoulder, shook his hand and said: 'Sometimes it's better to read between the lines.'

Everywhere we went I saw nothing but respect for my friend. He didn't put himself on a pedestal and he never put on a phoney act. I can think of too many celebrities who have a fraction of his talent and could learn a lesson from him. Big names that are so far up their own arse they make me sick. When he walked among the people, what they saw was what they got. There was always pressure on him to be here, there and everywhere else all at once but he never showed any signs of being harassed. After flying through different time zones, he'd hardly ever show signs of jet lag or tiredness like I did. In private, he'd tell me that at times he felt too exhausted to carry on, 'But ah just shakes it off. Ah'm used to it by now.'

Apart from his public appearances, he had to make lots of business trips which allowed for hardly any sleep, but he'd cope.

I'd be absolutely wasted, and could hardly get up in the mornings, but often, when I forced myself to get up, I'd find out from one of the hotel staff that he was up at 5am and off to some business meeting. He'd leave messages scribbled on a notepad by my bed letting me know what time he'd be back. In his usual style there'd be a PS at the end: 'You snore louder than a hog.'

And you know what? Too many times I'd find he'd superglued my comb to the window sill, or stuffed a piece of chocolate cake in my shoe. He never got away with it though; I'd been pulling stunts on my mates all my life and was an expert. Were we childish or what? Yeah, course we were and that's what made the whole experience of sharing road trips together such a lot of fun.

CHAPTER SEVEN

Posh Cars and Movie Stars

I got to see a lot of America travelling around with Muhammad Ali – and I liked what I saw. I loved the country and its people. Oklahoma City, for example, was typical of every big city we visited. A massive crowd was waiting at the airport and after the usual handshakes and autographs we were escorted to a chauffeur-driven limousine and whisked off in a Presidential-style motorcade. The streets were crammed with what seemed to me to be the entire city and every one of them chanting, 'Ah–lee! Ah–lee! Ah–lee!' almost drowning out the car horns.

Imagine if, back then, Ali decided to run for a state governor or even put his name up for President. I tell you, he'd have been voted in by most of America. Years ago, if the public had been told that an actor called Ronald Reagan, who as a kid I can remember in cowboy films, would ever become the President of the United States, people would've laughed their nuts off. Same goes for Mr Terminator, Arnold Schwarzenegger, who became the Governor of California. So the thought isn't so strange.

With the crowd-pulling power that Muhammad Ali had, you'd have thought he would need an army of minders. But he wouldn't hear of it. The nearest thing to a bodyguard he had was an ex-cop who was an occasional presence. This man's name was Pat Patterson and he was a tough-looking guy with a warm and friendly personality underneath. He had a great relationship with Ali's fans.

I watched Pat lots of times as he did the job he was paid to do. He was an expert, especially when large crowds become hysterical and, believe me, that often happened. He'd move in, using discretion more than muscle, and calm everybody down without any trouble. The last time I heard anything of Pat, he was working for Madonna, Michael Jackson and other high profile stars.

Muhammad and me were often stopped by traffic cops over the years. I have two main fears: flying and being in a car with Muhammad Ali when he's at the wheel. He knew it, too. I'd ask him to slow down, but that was an invitation to put his foot down. It stood to reason that eventually the law would catch up with him. After we'd been stopped no end of times, we worked out a double act to get out of trouble.

The first time we were stopped, he pretended he was really worried, saying: 'Gee, Paddy, what we gonna do now? We both done for, man. They shoot first in this state an' ask questions later.' The speed cop casually walked towards us but his stern look changed in the blink of an eye as he recognised who he intended to book.

Ali winked at me before turning to the cop. 'Hi, there, officer.' he said. 'Hey, that sure is some fancy motorcycle you got there. An' ah bet it's a high-powered one, too. Yeah? Ah noticed you was goin' pretty fast back there.'

'B-b-but Mr Ali ...'

'Yeah that machine sure is somethin' else. Ah ain't never seen one this close up before, same as ah never seen one o'you officers close up before. Ah like that uniform. Looks real sharp, goes well with that nice motorcycle.'

'But Mr Ali you were speeding ba ...'

'Oh, was ah? ... No, ain't never seen one o' you officers close up before, with those fancy uniforms and them great lookin' motorcycle. Why, ah'm jes' gonna have to buy me one like that ... Hey, Paddy. You have any motorcycles like that over in England?'

'No, mate,' I said, dropping into the sort of cockney language Americans seem to think all English people speak. 'We ain't got nuffink like that.'

Then the frustrated cop got in a word or two. 'Champ, you were speeding.'

'Oh, was ah? Here – meet a friend of mine Paddy Monaghan. He's over here on a visit from England.'

'Cor blimey,' I said, before the cop could say anything. 'Wish I 'ad a camera wiv me to take a photo of that motorbike, they'd like to see it back 'ome.'

'Yeah, Paddy. An' do the police officers back in England wear such nice, sharp uniforms like this officer's wearin'?'

'No, mate. Compared with this our officers got no sense of dress at all.'

That cop was either very flattered or very confused after all this fast-talking bollocks and gave up on the ticket. Instead of writing anything himself in his standard police notebook, he handed it over to Muhammad and asked for his autograph. Then he shook hands and mumbled that his duty obliged him to request that in future he should observe the speed limits.

But Ali's wit and boyish charm didn't always work. I remember some twat of a speed officer who didn't look old enough to shave, let alone ride a motorbike: 'Could I have your name and take a look at your driving license?' He gave Muhammad a ticket. Where had he been all his life? Or was he conning us?

Ali said to me one time, 'Paddy, ya know how some folks collect stamps or tin badges or autographs?'

'Yeah, what's that got to do with anything?'

'Well ah'm wut you might call a ticket collector.'

On the night of my 28th birthday, we went to New York together. I'd mentioned that I'd like to see Broadway, so he took me and gave me a tour of the sights, finishing with a fantastic show. What I didn't know at the time was that he was supposed to be in Oklahoma City that same day. I found out 24 hours later, when we arrived in Oklahoma and read local press reports that Muhammad had unfortunately arrived a day late because he had been delayed by an important business meeting.

'Hey, you never went to no important business meeting yesterday.'

'Shh, that big Irish mouth of yours is gonna git me in trouble.'

By this time, and I don't know why it took him so long, he'd noticed that I'd been wearing the same clothes every day since I'd arrived. We were relaxing in our hotel room and he said to me: 'Paddy, why didn't you bring more clothes with you?'

I just shrugged. I didn't tell him that those clothes were practically all I had in my wardrobe, so I just said, 'Didn't think I'd be here this long.'

'Now c'mon my friend, you don' hev to give me no bull. In London last year you told me that you had a good job, yet ah've read some press clips 'bout you, all sayin' you unemployed, man. Now, who's right, you or them?' I thought. Well, it's the only lie I've ever told him and he's gonna find out sooner or later.

'The press reports are right,' I said. 'I ain't got a job.'

He just smiled, picked up the phone and asked some bloke to take me along to a local mall and get me kitted out. So that I didn't get the chance to save him some money and buy a couple of cheap bits of clothes, he wrote out a note of what this fella should make sure I got: Two quality suits, two pairs of slacks, five shirts, three pairs of shoes to match the suits and a selection of underwear.

I was a bit embarrassed by his generosity but no question once I got some of that gear on my back I felt like the dog's danglers. But again, I have to point out that I never, ever asked Muhammad for a handout.

If I had ever shown myself up to be a scrounging ponce our friendship would never have lasted as long, in fact it wouldn't have lasted at all. He was a guy who would give his last cent away without question, so it would've been the easiest thing in the world to have milked him and made a fast buck, like many others did. But being no mug, it wouldn't have taken him very long to have seen what was going on and he'd have dropped me like a sack of shit.

Over the years, I've seen a lot of fly-by-nights come into Ali's circle and I've seen them leave very quickly once he sussed out their game plan. But as far as Muhammad and I are concerned, it's a long time since I came onto the scene and he knows I'm not going anywhere.

A lot of times I helped out between rounds in his exhibition bouts. They were only exhibitions to him, but to me – oh shit – I felt about ten feet tall, to be actually working in his corner. Afterwards, he'd entertain the crowd with his jokes and poetry, promising that he'd whup that Joe Frazier in their next match: "Cos that man he's jes' too ugly to be the champ.' Then he'd introduce me from the centre of the ring and tell everybody about my showdown with Joe Frazier at London Airport.

'Paddy stuck with me when everybody else in the world said Ali would never box again. When they all said ah was finished,

Paddy fought for me in his own way, an' he was by mah side while the world wrote me off. An' he's by mah side now ah'm back ... Yeah, he'll be by mah side always, when ah regain the Heavyweight Championship of the World. Thank yuh Paddy.' These quotes were reported wherever we went in the States. After giving me this fantastic pat on the back, he'd hand me the microphone. 'Here, Paddy, say a few words.'

The first time this happened we were in Pittsburgh. I took the mike and my first thought was, Oh, fuck. Muhammad had caught me completely by surprise and he knew it. If only Sandra could've seen me. I thanked those way up in the back rows right down to the famous faces at the ringside for the welcome they gave me. The only audiences I'd ever been used to speaking to before had been the small crowds of people who turned up during my campaign days at Speaker's Corner, so talk about being chucked in the deep end.

All I wanted to do was get that microphone out of my hand. I reached out to pass it back to Ali, but he'd have none of it. 'No, Paddy, no, jes' say a few more words to the people.' He'd got me cornered. There he was, with both arms along the top rope and pointing for me to stand on my own in the middle of the ring. He'd really sprung one on me and there was no way out of it. I just had to speak to that crowd. So there I was, standing in the middle of the ring and left to make some sort of speech to thousands of people, with Muhammad Ali standing by, listening and looking on.

Once I got going, I felt fine. I even managed to throw in a bit of humour. But after several minutes I made to hand him back the microphone thinking, Shit, what a relief. He didn't take the mike but leaned forward and spoke into it to the audience, 'Ah dunno 'bout you folks, but ah'm really enjoyin' this. Do ya wanna hear more from mah friend?' I was hoping they'd start shouting get 'im off but no such luck and the shouts of 'Yeah!' were deafening. Clowning it up, he said, 'Hey, ah didn't hear that, I said d'ya wanna hear more from Paddy?'

'Yeah – yeah! More – more!' they screamed at the top of their lungs.

'Paddy, you hear that? They want more.'

So I had to carry on for another few minutes. I told them how much I loved their country and I thanked Ali for bringing me over. Then I wound up by saying to them all: 'If any of you out there visit England in the future, here's my address,' gave it out to them and told them they'd always be welcome at my home in Abingdon. Afterwards I thought, 'Shit, that'll cost a bomb in tea and biscuits if they all turn up.' Then came another burst of applause as I handed the mike back to Muhammad. I got out of that ring like my arse was on fire. He told me later that he'd enjoyed hearing me talk to the crowd and that he was very impressed by the tremendous response I'd got.

'Do the crowds give you that sort of reception back in England?' he asked me.

'Shit, no. I wouldn't even get invited to speak in a public toilet back home.'

He shook his head with a puzzled look, muttering, 'No kiddin'? No kiddin'?'

At exhibition bouts, after the speeches, there would be a rush for Muhammad's autograph and then they turned to me for mine. I must have written on enough sheets to paper the wall of a small living room. The first time this happened, Ali and me were standing back to back. He leaned his head over his shoulder and said into my ear, 'Hey, Paddy you famous now.'

Yeah, I thought to myself. I'm a household name in my own house. Just who the hell would have thought that anyone would want my autograph? As I was talking to that large audience and signing my name, I was thinking, If only my mates from the Barn and building sites back home could see me now.

There were times when we visited colleges and high schools and he'd always invite me to speak after his lectures. We went to posh dinners and banquets in his honour and met some of the most famous people in the world and, every time, without exception, I got: 'C'mon up here an' say a few words, Paddy.' At press conferences and on live TV and radio chat shows I'd be shaking hands and standing shoulder to shoulder with the rich and famous.

Every few days it seemed like I was surrounded by stars that my family and mates could only see in magazines or on TV, but I kept my feet on the ground and didn't let any of it go to my head. Of course I talked and mixed politely enough, but I was always aware that none of these people were really my part of the world.

The only down-to-earth person among the lot of them was Muhammad himself. He'd come from a simple background like me and he knew how I was feeling. He'd had years of this showbiz carry-on and he was used to it. I found a lot of the events a bit of a strain. I'm not knocking it, I felt very privileged just to be in the same room as most of these celebrities. Occasionally, we'd have a cracking night and I suppose what made the difference was who was in the place.

One of these good nights was a birthday party at the Inverary Golf Club in Florida, in honour of the comedian Jackie Gleason. As Muhammad's guest, I was treated like royalty and made very aware of how far away I was from my council house when we walked into the banqueting hall to a steady applause that grew and grew into a storm.

I found myself sandwiched between Muhammad and movie legend Mickey Rooney. The place was packed with celebrities from stage, screen and radio and politicians and businessmen. Mickey Rooney was to my left and, although he didn't know me from Adam, he was very friendly. As we ate, I was caught in the crossfire of the banter between Rooney and Muhammad, who was on good form. He was full of fun and he kidded Rooney no end about me. When Rooney left the table to go for a pee, Ali whispered to me, 'Would ya believe, Paddy, that li'l guy has screwed just about every fox in Hollywood? Ah ain't jokin', he's had 'bout ten wives who cost him a fortune in alimony.'

'You gotta be kidding,' I said. 'He ain't no oil painting.'

Rooney came back from the loo, sat down between us and straight away said that he was Ali's biggest fan.

Muhammad whispered to me: 'Biggest? He's only five-feet-two an' that's with his high-heeled boots on.'

Rooney turned to me and asked the question that everybody I met seemed to ask, 'So young Paddy, what line are you in?'

Now, I'm an ordinary fella and I don't put on airs and graces for anyone, probably, like I said, 'cos I ain't got any. So I told him straight, 'I'm not in any line at the moment.' As I said earlier, I didn't think it was appropriate to be telling strangers that I was a bare knuckle boxer.

He looked at me, sort of puzzled. 'Oh, right. What, ya sold your company or you livin' on a big, fat inheritance?' I got to love the American way of bluntness or fucking nosiness, depending on how you looked at it.

'No, none of those things. What makes you think that?'

'Jus' look around you son. Ev'ry one of these people here have made a pile, either honestly or dishonestly, with or without talent, so c'mon, you can tell me what line of business you're in. You ain't working for the British government are ya?' I can't imagine anybody looking less like James Bond than me, so I didn't even answer that question.

I dropped my voice down to a whisper and said, 'Well, I can tell you what line I *was* in.' He leaned right up close to me, like he was expecting to hear some big secret.

'I was on the end of a line of labourers unloading car

tyres in a factory back in England and before that I was a hod carrier.'

'You shittin' me? What's that?'

'That's a bricklayer's labourer, that's what, and for the past two years I've been unemployed. That's what line I'm in, the dole line.'

'You're one secretive son of a bitch but I'm gonna get the truth out of you one way or another.'

We finished the meal, left the table and went our separate ways for a while. A bit later I saw Rooney heading straight for me and he was grinning all over his face.

'Gee, Paddy, you sure know how to tell 'em. What gets me is how you looked so serious when you came out with that builder's labourer shit. Now I'm wise to you, so cut it out and give me a few tips.' Now it was my turn to look puzzled but not for long because right behind him was Muhammad and he gave me a wink. The penny dropped, he was up to his old tricks.

'What's the champ told you?' I said.

'That you're a stockbroker who came here from London, and that you know just about everything that's going on in Wall Street.'

'Listen, Mickey,' I said, 'I had to borrow a suit, this shirt, these shoes and even my haircut was paid for by money borrowed from my mother. If it wasn't for the generosity of the big guy over there I wouldn't be here at all.'

I could tell by his expression that he wasn't convinced and guessed he wasn't going to give up. What rescued me was speech time and it was Muhammad's turn at the mike. You could have heard a pin drop as he got to his feet and, once he'd finished, as usual he asked me to say a few words. By this time, I'd done a few of those speeches and they were a lot less scary.

As we were getting ready to leave, Mickey Rooney, convinced that the stockbroker story was the true, pushed through the crowd towards us.

'Paddy, gimme a bit of the action and I'll cut you in on a percentage of the action.' Ali butted in and told him that I was sworn to secrecy, so Mickey pressed his card into my hand and said: 'This is my personal number. Please get in touch.'

We were now into March, 1972, and Muhammad began preparing for his fight against Mac Foster in Tokyo. It was to be the first contest between two foreign boxers ever staged in Japan. Before he started training, he took me to meet the legendary Dundee brothers, Angelo and Chris, and they turned out to be my kind of people.

He'd laugh and joke with Chris, calling him Groucho because he walked just like the Marx brother and always had a cigar in his mouth. Sometimes I'd nearly piss myself with laughing as he imitated that walk, saying: 'Here comes the head, the ass follows.'

The next day, at the famous Fifth Street Gym in Miami, he began his preliminary work for the Mac Foster fight. I was introduced to the other fighters and trainers and the young Japanese promoter Yoshio Kou. After chatting to him for a while, Muhammad told him that I would be travelling with him to Tokyo. Fucking hell. This was the first I'd heard of it. Yoshio Kou nodded his head, shook my hand and told me, 'We will be happy to welcome you to Japan; no problem.'

Ali told me to ring home any time I wanted but, in all those weeks I'd made only two short calls to Sandra because I didn't want to seem like I was taking the piss by running up an expensive phone bill. Neither here or there that he could afford it, no way would I ever take advantage of his hospitality. Instead, I just sent postcards home every day without fail. This time I asked him if I could phone back home and let Sandra know about Japan.

'Why you ask a dumb question like that for man? Sure, go

ahead an' ring.' So I called Sandra from the hotel and I introduced her to Muhammad on the line.

He chatted to her for a while and then asked her, 'What's the children's names, an' their ages? Put them on.' Whenever he's talking to children his face lights up.

Then he handed me back the phone, saying: 'Here, Sandra's still on the line.'

I eventually got to tell her that Muhammad had invited me to go with him to his next fight in Tokyo the following month. She was delighted for me, bless her. And she said that she was going to send me some more tablets to the hotel. As she talked, I sensed something in her voice that told me she was holding something back. After you've been married to someone for a long time you get to know them better than you know yourself.

'Sandra, something's wrong. I can tell by your voice, come on tell me, what's the problem.'

'Nothing really Paddy, it's just – er – just that...'

'Just what?'

'Two days ago a man and a woman called asking strange questions. They said they were representatives of some government department.'

'What for? What government department?'

'Well, they both identified themselves as investigators and it was the woman who did all the talking. She asked to see you and I told them you weren't here. Then she said that some person who must remain anonymous had informed them that Mr Monaghan had gone off to visit America with the intention of trying to get to see Muhammad Ali.'

'Why didn't you tell them that it was Muhammad who brought me over here and that I'm touring the States with him?'

'That's just what I did tell them and they said they can't and won't accept that. I told them we've got nothing to hide.'

'So what's it all about, then?'

'Don't know. But then this woman asked to see our benefit payment book and then asked me to sign a form saying that this was our only income.'

'Have you still got the payment book?'

'Oh, yes, but when they walked off the woman said we'd be hearing from them again in the very near future.'

'Right, Sandra,' I said. 'Give the kids a big kiss from me and my love to Mamma and Dadda, I'll be coming home as soon as possible.'

Muhammad was in the shower as I hung up the phone. I could hear him singing 'La Bamba' and his mamma was right – whatever he thought, his singing voice was shite. Although I must admit, I did always enjoy his renditions of 'Stand By Me'. I threw myself into the armchair with the one thought in my mind, that there was no way I could go to Tokyo, as much as I wanted to. Being at home with my wife and kids was all I could think about. I'd got a pretty good idea of what all that investigator crap was all about but no idea of what might happen. I was choked at the thought of this trip being knocked on the head, but how could I justify swanning round America, having the time of my life, while my missus was getting all kinds of shit that I should be dealing with? Ah, well, that's life. I told myself I should be thankful for what I'd experienced, not complain that it had finally come to an end.

When Ali finally came out of the bathroom, he said 'Right, Paddy, let's go for a drive, an' ah'll show you along some of the Florida coastline.'

I put on a front with: 'Okay, let's go.'

As we drove along the coast he would stop every now and then and talk to groups of people. I'd laugh at him as he did a terrible and exaggerated copy of my accent. He'd slow down, then holler out: 'Watcha, mait 'ow's it going'? D'ya 'appen to know where we kin git a decent cuppa char 'round 'ere?' Or, 'Oi, mait, where's duh nearest pie, mash, an' licker shop? Ain't they got no fish an' chip shops in these parts?' His was the worst impression of a cockney I'd heard since I took the kids to see *Mary Poppins*.

Back in our room I wondered how to tell him that I wouldn't be going to Japan with him. Oh, bollocks, the only way to get it over with was to come right out with it.

'Muhammad,' I said.

'What?'

'I ain't gonna be able to go to Tokyo with you.'

'Sure you are, you heard me tell that promoter.'

'Yeh, I know, but I've gotta get back home instead.'

'But you jes' spoke to your wife earlier ... Is everything okay back home?'

'Oh yeah,' I lied. 'No problems at all. It's just that this has been my first time away from the family and I'm a bit homesick.'

He just sat there for a few seconds, looking at me kind of puzzled. Then said, 'Whassa matter Paddy? Yuh tellin' me yuh don't wanna come with me to Tokyo for mah fight?'

'Yeah,' I said, "course I do, but ... I just got to get home instead. When you brought me over here I thought it'd only be for a couple of days.'

'Yeah, so did ah but that was before you got here. How long you bin here now?'

'Over three weeks.'

'Mah. How time flies.'

This was his way of saying, that if we hadn't got on so well as we had I'd have been sent off back home after a day or two. I could tell that he enjoyed my company and no question, I enjoyed and appreciated his. And now, here I was, telling him I had to go now. That hurt enough, but what hurt more was having to give some stupid excuse about being homesick.

'Okay, Paddy, it's up to you. When yuh wanna go?'

'Soon as possible mate, soon as possible.'

Ali got on the phone to Angelo and asked him to arrange for me to get home on the next possible flight out of Miami. Then he handed me the phone. 'Here, Paddy. Talk to Angie.'

I read out from my open ticket all the details needed to arrange my return flight. Angelo said, 'Paddy, can't you stay on a while longer? It's good for him having you around.'

'I want to, Angelo, but I can't.'

'Okay, Paddy. Stay put until I call you back.' Then it occurred to me that I'd better get my bags packed in case Angelo rang back saying that he'd got me booked on a flight I wasn't ready for. I had a sudden thought. I'd arrived in America with just the clothes I stood in and a change of underwear. Practically the only gear I had was my shaving gear. The only bag I had then was one very small suitcase to hold my few bits and pieces. Now I had suits, shirts, slacks – the works. I stood looking at all these clothes trying to figure out some way to carry them all home with me.

Muhammad had been unusually quiet since I'd told him that I couldn't stay any longer, so I said, 'Tell you what, mate.'

'What?'

'I'm right up shit creek here.'

'Watcha tawkin' 'bout?'

'How am I gonna get all these clothes back home?'

He headed to the wardrobe and pulled out his own extra-large canvas bag. 'Here, Paddy, take this, it's the very first thing ah bought myself after ah won the Olympic gold medal in Rome and when ah turned pro back in 1960. It's bin all around the world with me since.'

'Yeah, I've seen loads of photos of you with it.'

He unzipped it, took out all his own suits and clothes and said: 'Now here, you kin have it.' I packed all my own stuff into it, but it was so big there was still loads of room to spare. We chatted away for the next hour or two and, during our conversation, he asked me to ring him at his home, ten days after the Foster fight.

The phone rang. 'Paddy, it's Angelo ... Paddy, I can get you a return flight back to London tonight if you want it, but before you take down the details I wanna talk to you first. Now, they're gonna hold onto the booking for you. Now, listen, Paddy, I know Muhammad's in the room, so just answer me a simple yes or no. You got that?'

'Yes'

'Right. Now, Paddy, I've grown to know Muhammad pretty well over the years, an' to me he's family. I love that guy like he's my own, an' when he's happy then I'm happy. Now ... I notice he's happy having you around an' I've told you before you're good for Muhammad. Right?'

'If you say so, Angelo.'

'Now remember Paddy, keep it to just yes and no, 'cos you may not think so but he's listenin' to every word you say.'

'Oh, I know that.'

'Careful, ah said stick to yes or no, so be careful what you say now. I'm askin' you is there any way at all that you can stay on an' come with us to Tokyo?'

'No, Angelo, no.'

'Okay, Paddy, we can talk openly now. You'll be on tonight's flight. We all enjoyed having you here with us. You've got my office an' home phone numbers, so keep in touch.'

'I will,' I told him, 'and thanks for making me feel so welcome, I'm already looking forward to seeing you again.'

Then I handed the phone to Ali, 'cos he wanted to speak to Angelo again and during their conversation I heard him say: 'Nah, nah, no cab. Ah'm gonna drive Paddy to the airport mahself.'

He wrote down a couple of numbers where I could contact him at any time before the Mac Foster fight and he asked me again to ring him at his home ten days after the contest.

He pulled out two hundred dollar bills and tried to put them in my top pocket, but even though I didn't have a penny to scratch my arse with, I stepped back saying, 'Oi, mate ... no, no, no. Don't ever do that, not with me.'

He said, 'Ah knows that, Paddy, but it'll make me feel whole lot better if you'll take it ... Now, here...' and he placed the two hundred dollar bills in my shirt pocket.

'Do me a favour?' I said.

'Yeah, sure. Name it.'

I looked him in the eye as I said, 'Don't ever give me money again.'

'Why?'

''Cos you're me mate, that's why.'

He looked at me kind of puzzled at first. Then with a big grin he said, 'Ah understand what you mean, Paddy, ah understand.'

Soon it was time for us to get off to the airport. He parked the car where he wanted, right at the main entrance doors. He got out of the motor with me and walked right up to the check-in desk.

'Give mah love to your wife an' children,' he said, 'an' tell 'em that ah look forward tuh meetin' them all when ah come visit your home next time I'm in England.'

I thought nothing more of it at that time but it turned out that it wasn't just something to say, he really meant it. And after that, he visited my home every time he came to the UK, no matter which part he travelled to.

I thanked him for giving me the opportunity of seeing so much of his country and especially for the chance for the two of us getting to know each other and I said: 'Y'know something?'

'Whazzat?'

'This has been the best three-and-a-half weeks of my life.' Then over the intercom came the flight call.

'Hey, Paddy, that's your flight they callin.'

And then came those words, the highlight of my visit.

He put his hand round my shoulder and said, 'Paddy, ah want you to know that from now on you are mah brother an' a true friend an' ah value our friendship.' Then, as we gave each other a hug, 'You take care, mind … Bye for now, brother.'

I walked down the long corridor and I looked back over my shoulder to see him being surrounded by huge crowds asking for his autograph. And as I was about to turn the corner, I hollered back at him, 'All right, my bruvver?'

He hollered back, 'Oi'm all right, mate. Oi'm jest orf t'git me a nice cuppa char.'

As I walked down the corridors and onto the plane I had mixed feelings. I was desperate to see Sandra, the kids and my parents, but at the same time I had the strangest feeling of loneliness and sadness at saying goodbye to a guy I'd become so close to over the last three weeks.

Yeah, if I tell the truth, and this is what this book is all about, Mr Tough Guy, brawler, unbeaten bare-knuckle fighter, seemed to have got a bit of grit in his eye as he looked down on the disappearing lights of Miami.

Back to reality. Back to the lifestyle that I knew. And back to the cold, wet and windy English weather. Back as well to my home and my greatest love of all – Sandra and the children.

CHAPTER EIGHT

Back to Reality

My adventure in America was at an end. In just under a month I'd experienced things that I never expected to come across in my entire life. I'd met people from a different culture, made new friends – and got myself a brother in the process. Muhammad Ali had shown me real kindness but, more than that, we had become firm friends. Things could never be the same again.

Being in the States had been like dying and going to heaven, but I was back in England for not five minutes and I got nothing but hell.

Trouble greeted me from the moment I landed. I was made to fork out all of the $200 from Muhammad so that I could keep the clothes he'd bought me. I didn't know airport procedure, so I didn't have a clue as what to do and what not to do when going through Customs. I walked into the 'Nothing to Declare' section and got picked for a random baggage search.

They saw the brand new clothes, some still with the price tags on, and insisted that I paid duty on the lot. So that meant goodbye to all the money I had to my name. Thank fuck the pissing rain had stopped by the time I set off to back to Abingdon – thumbing a lift as usual.

And then more trouble. It was those government inspectors Sandra had mentioned on the phone. They were from the social, which was, apart from my monthly fight pay, the only source of income for my family since the doctors stopped me working. Sandra told me that they had been in touch again that same morning and had taken away my invalid payment book. I was knackered with jetlag, but I set off on foot again, this time to their offices in Oxford.

They were convinced that I'd paid for my trip to America. I kicked up holy fuck, telling them, 'Listen you mugs, I couldn't even afford the bus fare from Abingdon to get into this office today.' I tried everything I knew to convince them that it was Muhammad Ali who'd invited me and paid for the trip and all expenses, but it was like talking to a wall.

They thought I was bloody mental and said outright, 'We're sorry, but we just cannot accept that as the truth.' I got a lot of sneering remarks about my suit and my sun-tanned face, 'Did Mr Ali take you to Miami to get that tan? I suppose you expect us to believe that when he took you to Miami he bought you that expensive suit as well?'

'No,' I said, 'he bought it in Oklahoma.'

When I asked to speak to the manager, they told me to wait. Then different staff came out pointing and sniggering at me. At length this snotty-looking old bastard came out to give me another interview. Again I told the truth, but the old git just sneered at me.

He lowered his voice and said: 'Look, Mr Monaghan, you've taken up enough of our time today. I've read what you said to our staff in your statement.' He waved it in front of me. 'Do you really expect us, or anyone else for that matter, to take your fantasy story seriously?'

'I don't see why they shouldn't, it's the fucking truth.'

He stood up and marched off, so I shouted after him, 'Listen, you snotty old c**t, what do I have to do to convince you load of fuckers that I'm telling the truth?'

My language was the last straw and he shouted for someone to call the police. I didn't need that sort of aggravation right then, so I walked out making sure I almost knocked the door off its hinges.

I set off back home, depressed, knackered and freezing my nuts off in a light summer suit, hardly the best gear for the bitterly cold March wind. Paddy, my son, you're in deep shit once again.

It occurred to me then that as far as the social was concerned my story must've sounded like the ramblings of a madman. It was unlikely that Muhammad Ali, one of the most famous men on earth, would even piss on an 'unemployed nobody' – social's words – if I was going up in flames. As for inviting some illiterate scum to visit him in America, all expenses paid ... Beyond belief!

Suddenly, I had a brainwave. I should have thought of it straight away. Who better qualified to back me up than Muhammad Ali himself?

Later that evening I rang Muhammad as we'd agreed I'd do anyway.

'Paddy mah man. Ah'm glad yuh called. How was your flight?'

'Couldn't have been better, mate.'

We had a bit of chat about families and that sort of thing, then I casually dropped into the conversation: 'Oh yeah, I meant to ask you while I was with you for some sort of letter from you to let my local social office know that it was you who brought me over to the States as your guest. If it's not a problem, could you get it posted off to me in the next couple of days?'

'Shame ya forgot to ask me before you left but, hey, no

problem. In fact, ah can do better than that, ah'll git a cable off to you right now. Why, have you run into some kinda problem over there?'

''Course I ain't, they just told me it's only a matter of procedure and nothing to worry about at all.'

Fuck it; I hated myself for lying to my friend, but it was the only way to stop him feeling sorry for me and think I was tapping him for something. Stupid really, 'cos if he hadn't got to know me inside out over those three weeks, then he never would.

The next day I got a cable from him confirming that I was his friend, that he'd invited me to America as his guest and that he had taken care of all expenses. It was signed, 'from your friend and brother Muhammad Ali'.

To save time, I scrounged the bus fare from Dadda and travelled in style by bus into Oxford and went straight to the dole office. Did I enjoy the looks on all their faces when I handed over the cable? What do you think? Suddenly I went from worthless, workshy scum to something like visiting royalty, with people poking their heads round doors just to look at me. In the time it took for them to sign some papers, all my payments and back payments were okayed. To top it off, that nasty horrible git of a manager had the front to ask if he could keep the cable and frame it. I didn't kick up a fuss, I didn't make a fool of him in front of his staff, I just quietly told him to go and fuck himself and walked out.

Shit – was I pleased to get that sorted because there were no jobs to be got around that time. Well, jobs yeah, but nothing in my line of unskilled labourer. And what would make it even more difficult for me still was that everyone knew I was forced onto the the scrap heap by doctor's orders.

When me and the family went back to our own house after staying with my parents, laying among the usual pile of bills on the door mat was a card from the post office letting me know that there was a couple of sacks of mail for me and would I go and pick them up.

I got a mate of mine to shoot down and get the mail thinking, with nothing better to do and no work to fill my time up, it would be a good opportunity to get stuck into answering these letters from Ali's fans that had built up while I was away.

As I expected, the letters were all much the same. Everybody wanted to know how I got on in the States: Did I enjoy it? What was it like to travel around with the man himself? And so on. Considering that these letters looked like a small mountain when they were tipped out on the kitchen table, to even think about giving interesting answers to every one of them would've taken weeks and during that time another pile would build up. So what was the answer? My brainwaves were like leap years, they came at four year intervals, but when I got one they usually weren't too bad. I came up with the idea of putting together some sort of newsletter. That way, all it would take would be perhaps a week of writing, plus a hunt for a few pictures of the high spots of the tour.

A printer mate of mine had just started his own little business in town, so I got straight on the blower to him and asked for whatever advice he could give me and the biggy, how much would it cost? This printer didn't owe me any favours but he was a good pal and he came back with a very reasonable price. Well, reasonable if you've got a few quid on the hip. Out of the question, what with me being absolutely brassic – no change there.

The idea was too good to let go of for the sake of money. I came up with a scheme to ring the guy who'd bought that small figure of Jack Johnson. He was well into sports memorabilia and back then had said to me that if ever I wanted to sell some of my paintings and drawings he'd be interested.

I always had an interest and a skill with either a pencil or a paintbrush. I can't say I'm one of those people who can knock out a landscape or a perfect likeness, but, as a copier, I was pretty good. In fact, over the years I have often thought about where that skill could've taken me if those bastard teachers had shown the slightest interest in me.

Anyway, bottom line was, I had a few large paintings of various boxers – Ali in particular. There were two that I'd managed to get signed by Sonny Liston and two more signed by Rocky Marciano. I wanted to keep these paintings, especially the Liston ones, but what could I do with no other option for raising the money? I wasn't expecting a fortune for my work but I was definitely looking for a figure that would cover the printing costs.

I got in touch with the potential buyer and he was well up for a deal. He wanted to buy the lot, but I stuck to my guns and I told him, no, he'd have to settle for just one. I hoped he'd pick a Marciano, but he chose the Liston. I got a nice surprise when he offered me a figure much higher than the printing costs, so I was able to give my mate the go-ahead.

The newsletter was a cheap-looking thing, but it had photos of my visit so it was interesting for the fans. I wanted it to go out free, but the printer suggested I wouldn't be robbing anybody if I stuck on a cover price – pennies really, but I did.

I was getting loads of mail from ordinary people like myself, but quite a lot from well-known celebrities too. One of these was from the legendary George Best and that guy would've been a legend to me Irish or not. A reporter called John Roberts, of the *Manchester Guardian*, contacted me on George's behalf to invite me to his home just outside Manchester. He was a big fan of Ali's and he did little else but talk about Muhammad and ask questions about him. After our meeting, I got an invitation to visit his new nightclub, called Slack Alice, up in Manchester, but I couldn't make it. George wrote a letter for publication in the Ali fan club magazine and finished it with a poem he'd written in a friendly piss-take of Ali's style.

> When Ali says:
> 'Watch it.'
> if only for fun,
> then either take notice,
> get help,
> or just run.

I got a really nice letter from the footballer Bobby Moore for publication as well. In response, I offered both Bobby and George honorary membership of the Muhammad Ali Fan Club, which they accepted, stressing that they felt privileged.

After a while I had to give up the monthly magazine because the printing costs got too much for me, but I managed to carry on sending out a two-page monthly newsletter. What people loved and looked forward to was that Muhammad would send me messages for his fans and I'd put them in the newsletter.

Back in 1971 on one very warm evening towards the end of June, when Tyrone and Clare were upstairs asleep and little Saydee had dozed off on my knee, I suddenly felt a strange sensation. It was so hot I was sweating my knackers off and wiping the sweat off my face with a towel every few minutes, but it felt like my guts had turned to ice and a chill went right through to my spine. I'd only ever felt anything like it once in my life before and that was the cold night in '66, five years earlier, when I first stepped inside the house after we got the keys.

I didn't say nothing; Sandra was distracted watching TV. But I got a sensation that some kind of presence was in the room, just like I'd felt all those years ago. I knew it; I couldn't see what it was, but I knew it.

Sandra looked away from the television to say something to me, looked a bit puzzled and said, 'Paddy – look at your arms and shoulders – you've got goose pimples. Are you cold?'

'In this heat? You've gotta be joking me.'

It wasn't the cold that bothered me. It was the weird feeling of being watched by something that wasn't there that was putting the shits up me. I knew that this was something that I couldn't shove to the back of my mind.

I asked Sandra to bring me a blanket down when she put little Saydee to bed. Then, as she left the room, whatever it was that had given me goose bumps and frozen my insides, disappeared straight away, leaving me sweating again in the heat of that summer's night. I knew that if I said to Sandra, there and then, that there was something very wrong in that house, it would have frightened and worried her, so instead I asked her quite casually to go and visit the council offices the next day in order to apply for another place as soon as possible.

'Oh, I've already done that – ages ago, because two bedrooms are not enough for a growing family like ours.'

'Oh, fine,' I said and just left it at that.

Then, a good while later, not too long after I got back from America, we woke up one morning to find that the pictures on the walls were hanging all over the place. This had happened before. I remember once shortly after me, Sandra and the kids had celebrated Tyrone's second birthday, Sandra had said, 'Paddy, all those pictures in the room turned lop-sided again overnight and this time I've left them as I found them – have a look will you?'

They were hanging all over the place like before. I was just off to work so I told her I'd have a look later on. I later took each picture down one by one and couldn't find anything wrong with them at all. I didn't make much of it to Sandra but it started to play on my mind. This time some of them had even been taken off the walls and put on the floor, right under where they should've been. Rugs had been folded up neatly and laid on the settee, and trophies I'd picked up over the years were all shoved neatly onto one half of the sideboard. If that wasn't enough, the front and back doors were unlocked. I always made sure the doors were locked every night.

This time I went across the road and told Mamma all about these odd things that had been happening over the years. Good old Ma, she took that bit of news in her stride and simply suggested that I went to see the Roman Catholic priest at St Edmund's, in Abingdon. Me and Sandra went to see him together and I told him that I thought this was about the fifth time that it had happened since we'd first moved there, but Sandra chipped in with, 'No, Paddy, you're wrong, It's happened more than you think.'

Then she gave her side of it to the priest: 'Sometimes, Father, I'd washed all the dishes and put them on the draining board to dry overnight. In the morning I'd get up and find them all put into the sink again. Sorry for not telling you Paddy but I didn't want you worrying.' She'd known all along and while I'd been trying to play it down with her, she was trying to keep it from me.

The old priest gave what we'd said a bit of thought, then he said, 'Well, Mr and Mrs Monaghan, from what both of you have told me, I come to the conclusion that you have a poltergeist in your home.'

I didn't know the word but guessed its meaning, 'You're joking me, Father. So how do we get rid of the bastard?' He ignored my language, although he looked like I'd just slapped him.

'By exorcism,' he said. 'But I have neither the power nor the authority to conduct an exorcism.' This was getting fucking weird.

'What power and whose authority do you need, Father?'

'Even I don't know exactly what power is needed, but the authority has to come from the Vatican.'

'You mean ... from Rome?'

'Yes.'

I said, 'Now look, Father. I'm not asking for the Pope to come to my house all the way from Rome. All I want is for a priest who can do this exorcism thingy to kick whatever's messing with our gear out of our home.'

The priest gave us a lift home because, as he said, he wanted to consecrate the house with holy water. It didn't take long, 'cos the place was small. I walked him to his car and he told me that not all poltergeists were as harmless as the one in our house and that they liked to be surrounded by children and infants.

'But I have to add, your children are in no danger. You've been living here for the past seven years and no harm's been done, though I'm quite convinced from what you and your wife have told me that there is one of these spirits in your house – it's just one who seems to like causing mischief.'

'Look, Father, I've got to get my family out of this weird place. Our names have been on the council list for years but we've heard nothing. So would you write to those people about this ghost business?'

'Of course. I'll do that. I'll pop round and give it to you in the next few days.'

As he was about to leave, he asked me, 'Do you happen to know the name of anyone who died in this house?'

'I don't know, Father, I'll ask my neighbours. Why, would that make any difference?'

'Normally it would be of no significance whatsoever, but under these circumstances, yes, I would like to know. See if you can find out before I bring the letter around.'

So we asked all our neighbours if anyone had died in the

house and found out that an old man called Mr Parker had died in the downstairs room and that he was very regimental, very neat and tidy and everything had to be in its proper place. We moved the kids into our bedroom and we stayed that way until we changed house.

When the priest called around as he'd promised, I gave him all the stuff we'd found out about Mr Parker and he gave us the letter. Straight away Sandra made an appointment for us to go and see the housing manager. We told her about the strange goings-on and she raised her eyebrows like she thought, Oh yeah, this is a novel way of jumping the queue for a bigger house. She changed her tune when I stuck the priest's letter under her nose. After she read it there was a silence.

'Mr and Mrs Monaghan,' she said, at length. 'I'd like to ask you a favour. I'd appreciate it if you and your wife kept this business quiet. Because being a council dwelling, talk of this nature could scare off any future tenants and if you do talk, then you won't get that move.'

Sandra leant over that desk. 'Listen, we're going to tell everyone we can until we're rehoused, so do it or I'll spread it all over the local paper,' and she slammed her fist down on the woman's desk.

'Well young lady, if you think you can intimidate a council officer by rudeness and threats, I suggest you think again.'

Sandra leaned forward, 'You ain't seen nothing yet, you old bag and if you don't get us moved out of that haunted house you'll get more than threats.' Then, fuck me, she wiped everything off the desk with her arm.

I was gobsmacked by her aggressiveness, I mean, that's usually my game. I calmed her down and we left with her still mouthing off at the woman. We'd no sooner got home than the Old Bill was knocking on the door and a woman PC told Sandra to think herself lucky she wasn't being arrested for threatening behaviour and criminal damage. The housing manager was applying for a restrictive order.

'What's that?' asked Sandra.

'It means that you can't go within a hundred yards of the Council's offices.'

Apart from all this drama, I was still in regular touch with Muhammad. He told me that he'd accepted an offer to fight in 'your ancestors' country of Ireland.

'Here, hang on a minute' I said. 'It ain't just my ancestor's country, it's mine as well.'

'Nah – it ain't.'

'Yes, it is.'

'How come? You lived in England all yo' life.'

'That don't matter. I was born in Ireland and that makes me an Irishman. And proud of it too. That makes it my home country. Anyway, what about yourself, you're nearly as much Irish as I am.'

A little-known fact is that Muhammad's ancestors came from Ireland. I'll quote from notes I made from the *Irish Times*: Muhammad's mother, Odessa Grady Clay, was the great-granddaughter of Tom Morehead, a freed black slave and of John Grady from the Turnpike area of Ennis, whose son Abe had emigrated from Ireland to the States during the famine. Some time after he arrived in the US, Mr Grady married an African-American woman. Their son married an African-American woman as well and one of their children was Ali's mother Odessa Lee Grady, who married Cassius Marcellus Clay Snr in the 1930s and lived in Louisville, Kentucky, before their son Cassius Clay Jr was born in 1942.

When I found out about this, it made me think that perhaps this was why the both of us had such an affinity right from day one.

I asked him, 'Are you really going to fight in Ireland?'

'Yeah, man.'

'Whereabouts?'

'In Dublin.'

'When?'

'July.'

'Who you fighting?'

'Joe Frazier.'

'Come on, pal,' I said, 'don't take the piss.'

'Nutha one o'yo' crazy expressions. What's the hell does that mean?'

'It means you're shitting me.'

'Yeah, Paddy, I reckon ah am. Truth is ah'm gonna fight against Al Lewis.' Then he said, 'Hey, Dublin ain't far from you, is it?'

'No, it's only about an hour on the plane.'

'Well ain't that sumthin', Paddy. In that case ah want you to be there with me in mah corner, for you to walk right up there an' help out like ya did when you wus over here.'

'Bloody hell, I'd be chuffed.'

'Whazzat mean?'

'Oh – shit, don't start that again. It means I'm well pleased.'

Then he told me that he'd phone me to let me know when he'd be leaving the States, so that I could meet him at Dublin Airport.

'Okay, I'll be looking forward to hearing from you and I'll be seeing you in Dublin.'

Blimey, I was chuffed all right. My first job was to arrange for Sandra and the children to stay with my parents again while I was away and my next thought was, How the hell am I going to get over to Dublin? There ain't no bridge across the Irish Sea for me to thumb a lift on. Then I resigned myself to the fact that the only way I could get the money was to sell a signed painting of Rocky Marciano.

I was saved from parting with that painting literally by the bell – the phone that is. I got a call from a charter flight company asking if it would be possible for me to supply them with a list of names and addresses of British members of the fan club so that they could get in touch with them with details of a charter flight they were organising to Ireland for the Ali v Lewis fight. In return, I would get a plane ticket to Dublin, a place to stay and a ticket for the fight, as long as they could say I recommended them.

All I'd need was the flight, but I couldn't travel on the charter because that was going on the day before the fight. I had to get there before so I could meet Muhammad at Dublin Airport. I got the charter people to find me an earlier flight and book me in somewhere for just one night's accommodation.

Eventually I got myself settled in a hotel in Dublin. I'd just stretched out on my bed when the phone rang. It was some Irish newspaper reporter asking questions about Muhammad. I asked him how he knew who I was and where I was.

'Got the information from some agency, through the air charter company.'

I'd no sooner put the phone down than the bastard thing rang again. It was another reporter, asking the same questions and I gave him the same answers. In the end, I left the phone off the hook and got myself a couple of hour's kip.

Next morning I read in the newspaper headlines: PADDY MONAGHAN: THE FIRST OF ALI'S CAMP ARRIVES IN TOWN. They named the hotel I was staying in and a steady stream of people made enquiries at the desk about meeting me. Guess what? There I was, signing autographs again. I hadn't ever given it any thought, but I had as much of an ego as the next man and I lapped up the attention. If it made Ali's fans happy, then where was the harm?

Once I got inside the airport terminal I could hear the chants of 'Ah–lee! Ah–lee! Ah–lee!' When he finally came through into the main area, the shouts and cheers were as loud as I'd ever known them.

There he was, as always, with a big smile on his face and those arms in the air like he'd just taken a title. I could see him okay, but he couldn't see me through the packed crowd. He was looking this way and that and I guessed he was looking for me, so I squeezed my way through all the people and got to his side.

'Paddy, mah brutha.'

'Wotcha, pal,' I said and we gave each other a hug.

He'd brought along some of the people I'd met in America, including Howard Bingham, Herbert Muhammad and the brothers, Angelo and Chris Dundee. Ali made his way through the crowd, shaking hands and having a quick word with reporters. I was walking behind the group when he stopped and called out, 'C'mon, man, you gittin' too old to keep up? You ridin' alongside me.' And we headed off for the hotel we'd be staying at for the coming week.

It was another plush gaff called the Opperman Country Club, a couple of miles outside Dublin in beautiful countryside with views of the Wicklow Mountains. As the motor turned into the club entrance, we couldn't help noticing a guy sitting on his own, leaning back against a flagpole playing a guitar. Turned out he was Roc Brynner, son of the actor Yul Brynner. The staff and the manager welcomed Muhammad and in turn he introduced me to them and to the members of his staff who had followed up in other cars. Muhammad had arranged for me to have a big luxury suite, right next to his, all to myself. After I'd unpacked, my phone rang. It was Muhammad on the line.

'Hey, Paddy, you ain't met mah brother Rahaman yet, so come along to mah room.' Rahaman looked more like their father than Muhammad did. He seemed a great guy, with the same polite way of speaking as his famous brother. After he shook my hand, he said, 'You stood bah mah brother at a time when he most needed support. We won't forget that, Paddy. Nice to meet you.'

During the week, a senior official of the Irish Boxing Board of Control came out to the hotel in order to clear a few things up. 'Apart from Mr Dundee, do you have anyone else with you who will be working in your corner as a second?'

'Yeah,' said Ali. 'Mah friend, Paddy Monaghan.' The official turned to me and asked to see my second's licence.

I could rarely force myself to be polite or friendly to official types, so I just shrugged my shoulders, 'Ain't got one pal.' He was a rude fucker and spoke to me like I was a piece of shit.

'Well, then, you will not be working in Muhammad's corner.'

Ali chipped in, 'Well, ah says he will.'

'But, Mr Ali, as he hasn't got a licence it's impossible for Mr Monaghan to be in your corner. The Board just simply will not permit it.' (Apparently he'd heard of me and knew that I was a bare knuckle boxer).

Muhammad shot back with, 'Look, whenever you or your Board are in there doin' the fightin', then you kin say "Yes" or "No" to Paddy in your corner, licence or not. But this is mah fight, an' Paddy don't need no licence, 'cos he's mah friend. He's definitely gonna be in mah corner, you kin tell that to your Board.' This official pointed out that the Board would be unbending over such an attempt to rewrite the rules.

But Muhammad would have none of it. Before long, things were hotting up behind the scenes but the big fella stayed defiant as Board representatives visited the hotel in a steady stream and made phone calls. There would be no argument that I could be allowed to work in Ali's corner.

Officially, the promoter was Butty Sugrue, but behind the scenes it was Hal Conrad whose money was invested – a tall, skinny guy, who I got on with very well. He wasn't a happy bunny.

'Paddy, you know as well as anyone that obviously ah've gotta lot of money tied up in this fight ... Now, the Board ain't gonna back down an' as sure as fuck you know, an' ah know, that Muhammad ain't gonna back down, either. Ah'm sorta left in the middle if ya git what ah'm sayin'. This is a Catch 22 situation, an' somehow I gotta sort it out ... If ah don't, I'm in deep shit. Now, ah bin thinkin', an' the only way this problem is gonna be solved is through you.'

'How the hell can I solve it?' I asked him.

'Ah'll tell yuh, you gotta back down, by goin' along to Muhammad an' tellin' him you don't wanna be in his corner after all this fussin'.'

'No, Hal, I couldn't say that to him.'

'Paddy, name your price,'

'What do you mean?'

'I'll pay yuh to tell him you're backin' down. C'mon, how much d'ya want? Everyone's got a price.'

'Are you offering me a bribe?'

'Call it what the fuck you want to.'

'No, Hal, I ain't got no price.'

'But everyone has.'

'I ain't like everyone else.'

Conrad looked me in the eye saying, 'Ah've bin around a long time, an' you're the first son of a bitch ah've ever come across who couldn't be bought off.'

'So what you gonna do?'

'Ah'm just gonna have to find out what it's gonna cost me.'

As Hal left the room he said, 'Paddy, you're one very strange son of a bitch but at the same time ah can't help but admire your loyalty to Muhammad.'

The Irish Board's senior officials went backwards and forwards, all doing their best to talk Muhammad out of having me as his second. In desperation, the General Secretary himself came out to the hotel. They had a meeting in Muhammad's room and everybody who was connected with the promotion piled in. It dragged on until I got so pissed off with all the crap from the Board that I decided to chuck my penny's worth in.

Firstly, I told Muhammad that I appreciated him standing up for me and that his offer had been a privilege but to save any more aggravation it would be best to forget it – I'd watch the fight from the audience like everybody else.

Then I spoke directly to the General Secretary, 'Look, mate, I'm tired of listening to all this official shit, so you heard what I just said to Muhammad, let's forget about the whole thing.'

'Ah, well, now,' he said, 'I'm pleased you've seen reason and it's all been sorted out at last. You see, there was just no way it could have been allowed, because rules are rules.'

Muhammad was looking at me, then to everybody's surprise, he spoke up. 'Screw your rules. Ah want Paddy to be in mah corner.'

As the Secretary left the room, Hal Conrad signalled for Angelo to go and have a quiet word with the official. But the word wasn't all that quiet, as we all heard him shouting: 'Look, when Muhammad makes up his mind to do somethin' he's gonna do it and if he wants Paddy to enter the ring with him and just be there in his corner, then it's okay by me as the chief second.' Angelo walked away, shaking his head and muttering, 'I didn't come over here just to see the scenery and if you guys don't back off with this official crap you're gonna be in deep shit, for sure.'

The General Secretary left red-faced, along with a frustrated Conrad, and we heard no more about it until the evening before the big fight when Hal came rushing in with the news that the officials of the Board had backed down and given their consent, no doubt reluctantly, for me to be in the ring.

Next morning, Ali handed me what must be a unique licence, and I've still got it. It was made out in my name, though they called me an Englishman, but 'in care of' Muhammad Ali and was 'for one show only'.

'Hang on to that, Paddy,' Hal Conrad said, 'any memorabilia collector will let ya name your price for that.'

'So how did you get the Board to back down?'

'Well Paddy, ah gave 'em a load of bullshit last night. Ah went to 'em an' told 'em that Muhammad said that as you were prevented from entering the ring with him he'd called the fight off.'

'And did they believe that?'

'They believed it, how the fuck d'yuh think you got that crazy lookin' licence? They even sent it out by courier direct to Ali first thing this mornin'.'

This turned out to be the one and only time that the Irish Board of Control broke its own rules. But all the fuss they kicked up was totally unnecessary, 'cos if you ever get the chance to see a tape of the fight, you'll see that I had no real function in Muhammad's corner other than as a sort of mascot. Still, I'll always regard it as an honour and a privilege to have been in the ring alongside the man.

During that week in Ireland, a lot of people came to our hotel to pay their respects to the man and to wish him well. And no matter who they were, he treated them all the same. Former Member of Parliament, Bernadette Devlin, was the most impressive and respected of all of them. Other visitors included legendary film director John Huston, who asked me to take a couple of photographs of him with Ali. John had been a real fight fan and a fighter as well when he was a young guy. Another one was the actor Peter O'Toole. Muhammad greeted him with, 'Hey, Lawrence,' referring to the character he'd played in *Lawrence of Arabia*. I could go on and on; there were pop stars, groups, sporting celebs, politicians and at least one person who was on the dole.

Muhammad showed a real interest in Bernadette Devlin and invited her and her husband to join him for dinner at the hotel. He had a great admiration for her stand in Northern Ireland. It's no secret that the admiration was mutual. She was a big fan of Ali's and had screamed herself hoarse when she was at the ringside the time Muhammad first fought Joe Frazier. Her and her husband were seated next to Muhammad at dinner and I was directly opposite. After that dinner, he said to me, 'She is one of this world's great ladies.'

Muhammad and I arranged to meet one morning and have a ride into Dublin because he wanted to have a look at the city and visit Croke Park Stadium where the fight was going to take place. We'd said we'd have an early start, but to me that meant about nine o'clock, so I was still asleep when Muhammad banged on my door at 5am.

On our way into the city Muhammad asked the chauffeur to drive us to the Post Office in O'Connell Street that had figured in the 1916 Easter uprising. He hopped out of the car and rubbed his hand over the bullet holes and marks on the pillars. 'All that killin' that went on was bad,' he said. 'All wars are wrong, Paddy. An' all this time ... an' it's still goin' on. This beautiful little country has paid its price for freedom an' it shouldn't be a country divided. It's wrong, all the killin' it's wrong.'

We took a look at Croke Park Stadium and in a side street close to it we came across an old man limping and pushing a barrow that had a shovel and broom sticking out of it. Muhammad got out of the car and walked over to talk to the old man, who looked up open-mouthed at this young giant who towered over him. Muhammad put his hand on his shoulder and it was obvious he was talking to him, but I couldn't hear what was said. All I did catch was, 'Okay, sure – God bless ye.'

The chauffeur was sniffing like he a bad dose of the flu, but I think it was more in disgust at what he was seeing than anything wrong with his nose. He spoke to me over his shoulder, 'I've never seen the likes of this before.' Then he spouted out a list of superstars and celebrities that he'd driven about in the past.

'None of them would ever dream of asking me to stop in a little back street like this to talk to anyone, let alone a road sweeper. I should have thought that Mr Ali would have been the last person on earth to do such a thing.'

I think he thought that I was going to agree with him, but instead the snobby bastard gave me the hump, 'Oh yeah and just what makes you think that?'

'Well – he's so rich and surely he's the most famous person in the world. For him to stop and talk to such a low class nobody like that – well.'

'Listen here, mush,' I said to him. 'If that old fella was to die tomorrow, d'you think God would turn his back on him, just because he wasn't rich or famous?'

'No – but ...'

'Then shut your mouth you fuckin' twat.'

In his own way of trying to cut the meeting short, the chauffeur drove the car right up to the two of them just as Muhammad was saying goodbye. Ali got in while the old fella kept repeating, 'God bless ye, Muhammad, God bless ye.' As we drove off I looked back and the old road sweeper was waving his cap in the air. Ali leant out of the window and waved back. I slapped him on the knee and said, 'Nice one, pal, you've made his day.'

He said, 'Now, that was jest a li'l thing for me to do but it meant somethin' big to that old fella.'

On the way back he remarked on the beauty of the countryside. 'Ah never seen so many different shades of wrong ... Christians fightin' against Christians. Protestants against Catholics ... It's crazy. Ah sure am glad ah ain't no Christian.'

During his time in Ireland, Muhammad never visited a gym. He'd done most of his preparation beforehand and the training during that last week was just a couple of early morning roadwork sessions. But by fight time he'd picked up a very heavy head cold. I've read in the papers and heard on TV that his cold was 'a bit of a sniffle'. They didn't have a fucking clue, but I did, and I can swear now that it was one of those colds getting close to the flu. His camp put out the word that it was nothing to worry about, but being with him every minute I can say he was looking and feeling pretty rough as the fight approached.

Angelo had a full-time job on his hands just seeing to it that Muhammad got as much rest as possible. He was asked dozens of times if he could get Ali to make a personal appearance but he didn't have any choice but to keep repeating, 'he just wanted to rest him up.' Then he got a request from a children's home and with it a telegram that they'd got back in answer to a similar request to somebody else.

'Hey, Paddy,' said Angelo, 'look at this.' It was only a couple of lines from a celebrity's manager, but the fee that was being demanded was unbelievable, plus as much again in travelling expenses. It was almost a take it or leave it message. The home couldn't afford it, and they wondered if Mr Ali could make an appearance at a cheaper fee. Angelo was sympathetic, but apart from Muhammad's cold, the fete was too close to fight time.

Angelo was acting in Ali's best interests, but when I brought that piss-taking telegram up in conversation with Muhammad, mainly to show my disgust at certain celebrities, he called Angelo up to his suite and asked him to get in touch with the organisers right away saying, 'The day Muhammad Ali won't personally lift a finger to help li'l kids, then that'll be the day he'll hang his head in shame.' He turned up at the fete for absolutely nothing. We ended up on a stage in the grounds of the children's home. Ali spoke into a microphone to the crowd and they shouted back, 'We love you, Ali.'

'Thank y'all folks, ah love y'all, too.'

And then, as the people rushed forward, some of them

climbed onto the stage and it collapsed under their weight but nobody was hurt. Muhammad visited a ward of tiny handicapped children. He spent the next hour by picking up each child in turn and cuddling and kissing every one of them. Some of those children were so badly deformed that it would have hurt most people just to look at them. Every now and then, Muhammad would ask for a cloth so as he could wipe dribbles from their mouths and as he held each and every one in his arms he'd kiss their little faces. I'm telling you, it was pretty moving. But I couldn't see all that was going on because, just as when I flew back from America, I got some grit in my eyes.

Then there came another invitation, this time from Jack Lynch, the Prime Minister of Ireland. Muhammad was given a really over-the-top welcome and after we had all been introduced, I found a quiet corner and settled myself quietly out of the way. After a bit I heard him ask his brother Rahaman, 'Where's Paddy?'

'He's right over there behind you, Muhammad,' and with that he signalled for me to come over.

Muhammad introduced me to Jack Lynch, who said. 'Oh, yes, Paddy Monaghan.' He shook my hand again. 'I've heard people talk very highly of you. It's a great pleasure to meet you.' I thanked the Prime Minister and then stood back while him and the ministers carried on talking to Muhammad about boxing and chucking questions at him right and left. I knew from experience that this was a subject he didn't like talking about; boxing as a subject bored him rigid. He turned the conversation round to the troubles in Northern Ireland and Bloody Sunday:

'Ah can't understand why Christians kill anyone, let alone their fellow Christians. Why can't the good people of this beautiful li'l country be left to live in peace and harmony? Ah'll tell you somethin' now, if President Kennedy was alive today, there would not be one British soldier on Irish soil.'

When it was time to leave and Muhammad had finished his autograph session, the Prime Minister said to him, 'I've met some great men in my time, but you are the greatest.'

Muhammad lowered his head pretending to be embarrassed and then said, 'Oh, ah just knows it.'

That got a good laugh out of all of them. As we walked away Jack Lynch called after us, 'I'll be cheering for you at the fight, Muhammad.'

Quick as a flash, Ali came back with, 'What? Why, Al Lewis told me that you said that to him as well.' And, just as he left, Muhammad called, 'Hey, they jus' found out that Lewis is an Irishman.'

'I'll still be cheering for you,' Jack shouted back.

Fight time arrived. In the dressing room, Muhammad stretched out on the rubbing table while his masseur Luis Saria went to work toning up and easing out the tension from his muscles. He lay back, cracking jokes and every now and then sitting up so he could have a good cough or sneeze.

Suddenly a familiar figure appeared at the door. It was Eamonn Andrews, the TV chat show host, front man for *This is Your Life*. I'd never spoken to or been introduced to Eamonn, though he'd visited our hotel a couple of times. He nodded to Muhammad, then walked over to me saying, 'Paddy Monaghan, this is your life.'

I was paralysed for a bit. I couldn't speak, I just thought, for fuck's sake ... Me? What have I done to deserve getting on one the most popular shows on television?

Ali raised himself up on his elbows. 'What! Hey what you gonna do now, Paddy? You on *This is Your Life*. Hey Eamonn, if Paddy's gonna be on the show that mean ah'm gonna be on it, too. Right?'

'Of course you are Muhammad, if you remember we've got your pre-recorded interview.'

Then Eamonn turned to me. 'You'll have to come to the studio now, Paddy. A car's waiting outside.'

'Oh, no ... I don't mind doing the show but it'll have to be after the fight.'

'No. You must come now. You know how the show works.'

'Well, then, you're gonna have to forget it, 'cos I ain't going nowhere until after the fight. I'm working in my pal's corner.'

'C'mon Paddy, you'll be spoiling the enjoyment of millions of viewers if you don't turn up. No need to be nervous.'

'I'm not fucking nervous – sorry about the language, Eamonn.' Christ knows why I said that, but it didn't seem right cursing in front of the god of television. 'No way can I miss being in my mate's corner, especially as you've no idea what it took to get the chance.' I was getting all flustered and wound up and suddenly them two are pissing themselves. The penny dropped; I'd been done up like a kipper. I looked at Muhammad, then at Eamonn, and couldn't help bursting out laughing myself.

'You pair of bastards.' That was all I could think of to say.

This was all down to Muhammad, he'd arranged the whole thing with Eamonn beforehand. Before he was called away, Eamonn said, 'I'd appreciate it if you both keep this to yourselves. In my position, I'm not supposed to go round having a joke at the show's expense. If it gets out I'll be back on the radio as quick as you like.'

As he left the room, Luis Saria carried on warming up Muhammad's muscles, and at the same time giving Spanish speaking lessons to anybody who'd listen. The fight doctor, Ferdie Pacheco, injected cortisone into each web between Muhammad's fingers to give him some temporary relief from the pain that he suffered since his comeback. These injections had become routine before every fight.

The final routine was the most important one to him. His manager, Herbert Muhammad, and his brother Rahaman joined him in prayer to Allah. Then there was a knock on the door and a voice called, 'Whenever you're ready, Muhammad.'

As we made our way out to the ring, the noise from the crowd was like the rumble of thunder. That's a bit poetic, but there's no other way to describe it.

'Ah-lee! Ah-lee! Ah-lee!'

What an atmosphere. It was fantastic. And by the time he had climbed up and into the ring, with me proud as fuck beside him, the stadium became a storm of sound. As for me, well, no one, absolutely no one on earth, could've been more chuffed. And with that licence in my pocket I was an official corner man to the greatest of them all. It was something to tell the grandchildren about.

In the opposite corner stood the menacing figure of Al 'Blue' Lewis in his trademark blue robe. This contest was for the North American Federation championship and the referee was Lew Eskin. I shan't bother to give a description of the fight, because it's history now, but, in a nutshell, the ref stopped it in Ali's favour in the 11th round. But how that actually came about I'll explain for the very first time.

We all thought that the fight would be over in the fifth when Ali put Lewis flat onto his back for the longest count of nine I've ever known. Big 'Blue' keeled over. Then came the bell.

In the sixth, Ali dominated with beautifully timed right hand leads. Lewis's legs were buckling, but he was as game as they come. In the seventh it was all Ali – jabbing away at 'Blue's' middle. Those jabs carried a lot of power.

The eighth, Ali went back to concentrating on a right-hand lead. Now the ninth and, for the first time in the fight, Ali really opened up with fast and powerful combinations, punching to head and body. This brought a roar from the crowd that you could almost feel.

The tenth, and again it was all Muhammad's but the fight wasn't as one-sided as it sounds because Al Lewis always made a fight and he was, like every other opponent Ali ever fought, in the best condition of his life. But he couldn't match Ali, even slightly out of condition. Remember, my man had been taking a lot of liquids because of that head cold. At the end of the tenth, as I swung his corner stool under him, he slumped down and, right above my head, I could hear him moan. Angelo thought Muhammad had been caught with a low blow.

'Did he catch you in the balls champ?' Angelo asked him.

'Naw, mah nuts are okay, but gee, ah sure am bustin.'

Me and Angelo got a fit of girlish giggles. 'Ah can't believe this guy, he needs to go to the can,' said Angelo.

'What's the next round, Angie?' Muhammad asked.

'The eleventh.'

'Well ah'm gonna have to open up on him, oth'wise ah'm gonna piss all over that canvas.'

And sure enough, in the eleventh he opened up. And fuck me, did he open up. Then the referee jumped in to stop the fight. It was just as Ali had told us in the corner, this was the round he was going to have to stop or knock out big 'Blue' Lewis – just because he was desperate for a piss.

I don't think a boxer has ever pulled out all the stops so dramatically, all because of his bladder. And I don't think a winning fighter has ever left the ring so fast before. He ran to the dressing room, barged straight into the toilet and I heard him let out a roar, 'Ah!', and we could all hear his impression of Niagara Falls.

CHAPTER NINE
Firm Friends

So what was I up to when Muhammad wasn't on the scene? Well, I was still chasing my dream of being top of my own fighting profession. What else can I call it? A hobby? Getting my face rearranged one night a month? The truth is, I did a lot more rearranging to the opposition, and I'd had 78 consecutive wins. Yeah, I was a very popular fighter at the Barn, though, when it came to betting, I was fucking the system up because it was believed I could never lose. You can imagine the odds were shite.

In June 1972 I was matched against Welshman Phil Mahoney, and these fuckers from the valleys are tough old boys. Probably down to their ancestors knocking lumps out of coal faces since time began. Give him his due, he gave me a good bit of aggro until I knocked him spark out in the fifth.

I had a particular way of psyching up when I got in the ring. My mate Lenny McLean, a great fighter I first met in the Barn, told himself to *hate* his opponent – I'll nick a quote from his book, 'You interfered with my children. You hurt my wife.' Me? Nothing so drastic. What I did was mentally take the whole Monaghan clan into the ring with me. Crazy? No more crazy than wearing a lucky pair of shorts or a fucking rabbit's foot tucked inside your cod piece. I'd stand in my corner and imagine all my ancestors crowding round me, saying, 'Go on Paddy, do it for the family – get stuck in.' It might sound odd but it hadn't failed me once in those 78 fights.

If you're a fan of Billy Connolly you'll understand why I had a bit of a chuckle when I heard who I was fighting on 3 August that year. His name was Jobbie Wilson and he came from West Ham. His first name might have been Billy's funny term for a turd, but this guy wasn't to be laughed at. He hadn't built up an awesome record by being an easy target, so I reckoned I was going to have to pull everything out of the bag to wipe him out.

We were pretty evenly matched and neither of us got the better of the other for at least five rounds. This was a gloved last man standing contest and I knew inside me who that was gonna be. Again I took most of his punches on the top of my head and that was down to my fighting stance. I'd crouch low, tuck myself in keep my guard up like a shield and he just couldn't get through. It was a waiting game and I was prepared to chip away for as long as it took until he made a mistake. He made it in the seventh. A slight drop of his arms and I was in like lightning and dropped him to the canvas with one punch. The place went fucking mad. What I haven't mentioned – keeping the best until last – was that this was a championship fight and that one devastating punch had earned me the title of British Bare Knuckle Boxing Middleweight Champion. Result-and-a-half Paddy, my old son, but look out because that ain't enough for me.

Still, like legal boxing, once you've picked up a title you have to defend it if you get a challenge; so I had only three months to rest on my laurels before defending my new title against Holloway fighter Jack McCann. Another last man standing bout. Nobody was going to nick that championship off me, so me and the clan battered this guy around the ropes until in the fourth round when the ref had to step in before Jack got too badly hurt.

You might be wondering whether Muhammad ever watched me fighting. Well, one, his schedule would never have given him time for anything like that, and two, can you imagine the uproar if ever that straightforward and clean-living man was to show up at an illegal bare knuckle fight? Apart from anything else, those fights in the barn were a closely guarded secret for obvious reasons. The chaps knew what I was up to once a month, but the rest of Abingdon must've thought Paddy got a bit accident prone every few weeks. I'd go out about lunchtime and by the time I got back, around six, I'd usually managed to pick up a cut eye, a bruised face, or occasionally something worse.

Though we were both fighters, the gap between our worlds was as far apart as the North and South Pole. Like I said, his was way out in the open, mine was seedy by comparison. We still chatted about it though and he showed a lot of interest in this side of boxing that he'd heard of but never seen. It might have been criminal but at the end of the day, the skill, dedication and fitness level was no different to the legal art and I've got to say that, although I would've preferred to have to have taken up boxing proper, I've never been ashamed of what I did. In fact, looking back over my record, I've got every reason to be proud of what I achieved.

So, once a month I got off my arse to have a fight. The rest of the time I spent either in the gym or with my family, pottering about the house or keeping up with my reading. Tell you what, any poor sod who can't read is missing out on one of the most magical experiences because, as I found out, it opens up a world you can't even imagine. Yep, those horrible fucking teachers would be amazed that I spent so much of my time with my nose in books of every subject under the sun.

And I was still following my man's career as he fought off every contender who wanted to take his title away. A long way from being his corner man, I'd have to settle for going to the Hammersmith Odeon on a 183 bus to watch him live on close circuit TV. Sometimes, after those big fights, the commentator, Reg Gutteridge, would interview Muhammad and he'd lean towards the mike and say, 'Ah wanna say hello to mah best friend over there in England, Paddy Monaghan. He's mah main man. Hi, there, Paddy. Call me, an' ah look forward to seein' yuh again real soon.' He'd give me a wink as he looked into the camera and then turn to Reg saying, 'Now, what'ya wanna know about the fight?'

I'll admit that I often felt like saying to the bloke sitting next to me in the pictures, 'Hey, that's me he's talking about,' but experience had taught me to keep my mouth shut.

I'd sit there thinking that it was a great honour that I was in his thoughts minutes after a crucial fight. When recordings of those contests were shown on regular TV, for some reason my mention was edited out. This happened after both the Floyd Patterson and Bob Foster fights.

Another time, me and Sandra were watching the Sports Personality of the Year programme when Princess Anne was there to present the trophy. The BBC had a live link-up with Muhammad and I think it was Harry Carpenter who said, 'Hullo, there, Muhammad. We can see you on our TV screens here all over Britain. Can you hear me clearly at your end?'

'Yes, I can.'

'Good. Well, Muhammad, we are honoured by the presence here today of Her Royal Highness Princess Anne.'

'Oh, yeah, hi, Princess. First though, ah wanna say hello to mah friend over there in England, Paddy Monaghan.' Then, with his usual wink at the camera, he said, 'Hi, there, Paddy.'

That was a time when the editors couldn't cut me out.

Then the phone started ringing from friends of mine from all over the country.

'Paddy, were you watching TV?'

'Yep.'

'Muhammad's just been on.'

'Yep.'

'Wasn't it great?'

'Yep.'

'He mentioned your name.'

'Yep.'

'We're all chuffed.'

'Yep.'

'Ain't you?'

'Yep.'

I was too, and they'd never know how much. Hard to believe, but he'd more or less told one of the royal family to hang on while he said 'Hello' to me. No matter how I felt inside, I wasn't going to make a big thing of it.

Another Christmas was getting closer and, although I always tried to put a front on, I never failed to a get a hollow feeling in my stomach when I knew I was going to have to explain to my children, especially Clare, The Moo, that Father Christmas wouldn't be bringing them the things they wanted. The Moo would have a moan as usual, 'Why not? He's bringing all my friends what they want.'

'Because, Clare ... because ... ' I was stuck for words as she handed me her letter to Father Christmas.

''Ere, Dad, if that Santa don't get us what we want, then he can stay away, an' I ain't gonna leave any mince pies out for him. So there.'

Later, me and Sandra opened the letters they had scribbled out and all Clare wanted was a puzzle, a new drawing-book and some crayons and a bell 'that goes ding-dong'. She had added a sort of PS: 'and if you got anyfink else, leave it.' Tyrone just wanted a pair of boxing gloves and little Saydee was only two, so she didn't care what she got.

We laughed over their letters. They didn't ask for much, so we told them that Father Christmas would be coming. I wondered why The Moo wanted a bell that goes ding-dong; me and Sandra thought she was bloody odd. We had no idea where she got that from.

Christmas morning, we heard Clare hollering out: 'Now!' followed by ringing of her bell. Then 'Stop!' and more bell ringing. Then I saw what was going on. Tyrone was stood there with boxing gloves on and Clare was telling him when to start and when to stop his shadow-boxing. So I'd got the answer. Definitely gonna follow in Dad's footsteps.

There were more strange goings-on in the house in early 1973. This time we woke up to find that the same old thing had happened all over again, but with a couple of differences. Two dirty plates and two cups Sandra had left in the sink overnight had been washed up and were stacked on the draining board. This was the only automatic dishwasher we ever had. The other difference was that the hatch to the loft had been taken off.

The priest came out to the house for the second time and told me that the loft had been the only part of the house that he hadn't blessed on his first visit. I gave him a leg up into the loft and followed him with a torch, making sure the silly old twat didn't step between the joists. He sprinkled holy water all around the roof space, then did the same to the rest of the house again.

Not long after that, we had a visit from a man who lived on his own in a three-bed council house in Saxton Road. He lived opposite Sandra's parents and he'd heard about the poltergeist. He wanted a smaller house and was willing to swap tenancies.

We told him straight, then and there, that it was okay with us and said, 'Look, you've obviously heard about the strange goings-on in this house or you wouldn't be here. We've had the place blessed so the problem should be sorted, but if it ain't, don't come knocking on my door.'

'Don't worry Paddy, I'm quite happy whatever the outcome, that sort of thing doesn't bother me at all. Anyway, at my age, any company is better than none.'

So it was a done deal and we were well pleased to get out of Borough Walk and into the bigger house in Saxton Road. It was just one long street of terraced properties, but it was one of Abingdon's worst areas by reputation.

My Sandra and the kids were as polite and well brought-up as any you'd meet, but me, even though Ma and Da brought me up the right way, well, what can I say? I didn't have the nickname of Rough Diamond for nothing. So my friend was Muhammad Ali. I'd toured America with him and I'd recently become British champ in what I did. *So fucking what.* None of that made me any different from the sort of guy I'd always been. With me, and I'm not bullshitting, what you see is exactly what you get. Did I try to talk 'posh' in the States? Did I put on airs and graces because I was mixing with celebrities? Did I bollocks. I wouldn't know how to and I think that is why everybody in that street welcomed us. They all knew who I was, what I'd done over the last years and what I was capable of doing if ever me, my family or my friends were wronged or harmed. I've always had respect in the town generally, but once I moved into Saxton Road it became more than just respect.

I had people coming to me with their problems, as if I had some special qualification to deal with more than violence. I lived up to it though and dished out advice like a proper agony aunt. The simple answer is that often you can see a problem from a different angle if you look from outside – I didn't do anything special. Again, because I was known to step into the ring, though they didn't know about the Barn, that made me an expert in minor injuries. I'd have a steady stream of mothers bringing their kids to me if they'd been cut or grazed, particularly in the summer. Out would come my boxing bag and I'd do what was needed with my iodine, swab sticks and adrenaline.

If there was any trouble between rival gangs, I'd get a call to act as a go-between. If anything was wrong, it was always, 'Go and get Pads, he'll sort it.' That's the way it started when we moved there and that's the way it stayed until we moved away from the town many years later.

Good news for me was that Muhammad was going to tackle Ken Norton and it was going to be shown live on TV. On the night, my house was packed with family, friends and neighbours, all wanting to watch the fight with me giving a running commentary, I supposed. Towards the end of the second round, I was crunching on a boiled sweet and I broke a tooth. Shit me, it hurt like buggery, but nothing like what Muhammad suffered at exactly the same time when he had his jaw broken. It was just a coincidence I know, but a coincidence that was so weird and uncanny I've never even told Muhammad about it.

When Ali came out for the third round, only those in his corner knew what had happened to him. I could sense something was badly wrong. Time and again, as the fight went on, I'd say to everybody, 'Something's wrong with Ali. Don't know what but I can feel it. Something's definitely wrong.'

Muhammad's performance wasn't up to his usual standard, but when the bell rang at the end of the 12th round, everybody had the same opinion, 'Yeah, Ali's won but he wasn't at his best.' Being completely unbiased I thought that Ken Norton had done enough to get the decision and didn't expect Muhammad's arm to be raised, so I wasn't at all surprised when it was announced, 'The winner, Ken Norton.'

I wasn't being disloyal to my pal by predicting a Norton win before the announcement, because I've been around fights too long not to have picked up a judge's eye view of an outcome. No matter how much I wanted Muhammad to win, it wouldn't have made a shit's worth of difference to the result.

Straight away the papers were sticking the knife in and writing him off with headlines like, ALI IS FINISHED and THE LIP IS FINALLY BUTTONED. These same c**ts had been cheering for him the day before. Reporters never stopped ringing and there was constant knocking on the front door. I was asked by TV people to make an appearance on prime time, just after the six o'clock news, when the question was put to me, 'Do you think Ali will retire now?' I hadn't been in touch with Muhammad and there was no official statement, so I told it how I saw it.

'I can promise all you millions of people out there that Muhammad Ali will be back to beat Ken Norton and he'll go on to regain his title from George Foreman.'

I didn't really give a monkey's about the decision in favour of Norton. My main concern was for Ali the man and my friend and not for Ali the boxer.

Lots of fans wrote saying: 'Paddy, do something.' But what the hell could I do? Just who or what did they think I was? I got so much mail in the end that the only way to deal with it was to draft a standard letter explaining that there was nothing that I or anybody else could do. I told them to be patient, ignore all those reports in the papers about Ali being washed up and, though I didn't have anything to go on from Muhammad, told them that it was my firm belief that he'd be back to regain his title.

Around this time a lady turned up on my doorstep one afternoon and told me that she intended to write to all the fan club members because she felt that this was the time for all of us to show our loyalty. She said that as I had named Ali 'The People's Champ', there were a number who felt that a Muhammad Ali Fan Club trophy should be designed. If I was willing, I would present it to him.

While she was talking I was thinking, no way can I afford to buy a ticket to America. She either read my thoughts or I'd said what I was thinking out loud, because her next words were that she was organising a collection to pay for the trophy *and* my fare to the States. I knew that Ali had been presented with more trophies than anybody could imagine because he'd shown me a cellar full when I was over there. The fans had the best intentions in the world, but the truth was I'd be making the presentation more on their behalf than his.

I rang Muhammad to let him know I'd be coming over and his reaction was, whispered through his wired jaw, 'That's great news man, yeah, git your ass over here.'

As before, I took a big sack of mail, along with The People's Champ trophy. There was one letter in particular I'd separated from the rest and for safety I'd tucked it inside my passport wallet. It was from two Oxford dons, asking if he would accept the honorary title of Professor of Poetry at the University.

As usual I was picked up from the airport and driven to Muhammad's home in Cherry Hill and got a lovely greeting from his mother and his wife Belinda.

'Hi, Paddy it's real nice to see you agin. Mah boy has been expecting you and he's looking forward to seeing you again. Take a seat and make yourself at home.'

Belinda told me: 'He's in another room having a business meeting right now, but ah've to tell you he won't be long.'

I was jetlagged and could feel myself nodding off, in fact I think I did for a few minutes. Next thing I know I was gripped in a powerful hug that nearly choked me. He'd crept up on me from behind and was bellowing in my ear, 'Ha-ha. Paddeee Monaghannn. Gotcha.'

I struggled to breath and shouted back, 'Get off me you big lump or I'll ... Suddenly he let me go, stepped back into the centre of the room and shadow-boxed with those massive fists aimed at me. Growling through clenched teeth he said, 'Or else you'll do what? C'mon, Paddy, whatcha gonna do?'

'I dunno ... but I'll think of something.'

He started to laugh then groaned in pain instead. I said, 'Yeah, that's what I'll do. If you don't watch it, mate, I'll make you laugh.'

He welcomed me and we gave each other a friendly hug.

'Well, mate, how d'you feel?'

'Like someone with a broken jaw. Ah'm tellin' ya Paddy, the older ah git, the harder it is to pull mahself back into shape. But ah still got enough left in me to come back again an' whup Norton or Foreman or Frazier – or anyone else. An' ah'm gonna git mah title back.'

Then he gave me a wink, saying, 'Ah shall return. But hey, Paddy, you ain't seen mah son yet. He's eleven months old now. C'mon through an' take a peek.' We joined the family in another room, where he said to me, 'Here he is an' his name's Muhammad Ali Jnr.'

Ali's mamma was trying to support the baby on his feet and she said, 'Here he is at nearly a year old and he ain't even considerin' walkin' yet.'

I told them that my mamma told me I didn't walk until I was eleven months old either. Then as I sat down, Muhammad took over from his mother and tried to balance the boy upright. I clapped my hands together, held them out and he took a couple of stumbling steps towards me. Muhammad, to put it in my words, was well chuffed. 'Hey Paddy, he jes' bin waitin' for you to git here.'

Over lunch, I couldn't resist digging Muhammad out. As he sipped some sort of soup through a straw, I chewed and swallowed every mouthful of my food, going, 'Mm, this is fantastic ... Ah, tastes wonderful.' He looked at my empty plate and said, 'Man, why don't you just shuddup?'

Once we'd gone through into the lounge I thought that then was an ideal time to give him his People's Champ trophy, telling him that the fan members had set up a collection to have it made. 'You mean mah fans had a collection to have this made for me? Man, this is somethin' else.'

He held the shield for quite a few minutes without saying a word, then he shook his head and mumbled: 'This is gonna be in mah mind every time ah'm trainin' from now on, 'cos this is somethin' special to me.' He passed it to his mamma with, 'Hey, Bird,' his special name for her, 'take a look at this.'

'This is a beautiful thing, Paddy,' she said. Then to her son, sounding a lot like my own ma, 'An' you better take good care of this an' not go losing or misplacing it.'

He was well pleased when I passed over the letter from the two Oxford dons. They had made the gesture as a token of their admiration and there was no doubt Muhammad was touched by the thought.

'Whaddya think 'bout that? Me, being a professor.' He pointed to the letter. 'This is a great honour for me but ah can't accept it right now. It's more important that ah should come back and whup Norton for all mah fans.'

The next day, he wrote a polite and rhyming note to the two dons.

Pay heed, my children and you will see
While the time's not right for your University.
Not because of the pay, although it is small,
It's because I have to show the world I can still walk tall.

Muhammad Ali

After a couple of quiet days spent at his home, he asked me to go with him on a trip to Canada where he was going to make his first public appearance since the Norton fight at a press conference in Toronto. As we were having breakfast on the morning we were to leave, I noticed that he was unusually quiet. He was giving a lot of thought to a note that had come in the morning mail. After a while he passed the crumpled piece of brown paper across the table for me to read. It was typed and unsigned and in verse. It read:

The butterfly has lost his wing
The bee has lost his sting
You are finished, you loud-mouthed braggart and it's a great day
for America.

We just looked at each other, shrugged our shoulders and he chucked it in the bin. Shit like that didn't deserve any comment.

When the pair of us arrived in Toronto, the airport was just like all the others we'd been to. The place was rammed with an enormous crowd waiting to see him. Travellers, who'd been passing through and didn't expect him to be there, dropped their bags and ran towards him. Everybody sympathised with his broken jaw, but not many of them knew that his hands were still very painful and naturally wanted to shake them. Painful as it was, he never turned away from an outstretched hand. Some of the people told him that they thought he'd been 'robbed' by the decision being given to Ken Norton, while a lot of others said, 'It was close but you did enough to win.'

One man asked him, 'Muhammad, is there gonna be a rematch?'

He was only able to mumble but the message came across pretty clear, 'Yeah, sure is, man, an' ah'm gonna whup his ass good.'

We were staying at the Sonesta Towers Hotel and he asked me to sit in on a business meeting in the coffee lounge. Two men were waiting for him, puffing away on big cigars and giving out the impression that they weren't used to being kept waiting. To me, their attitude said they were arrogant bastards. They put the big smiles on for Muhammad, nodded towards me and asked, 'Who's he?'

They didn't know it, but their attitude ruined their chances of getting anything at all out of Muhammad. 'Aw he's just a Russian promoter who wants me to fight in Moscow. His name is Padowski Monaghov. He can't speak a word of English, he won't bother us ... His interpreter is around here somewhere.'

I thought to myself, Oh, what the fuck's he got me into now?

Then one them said suspiciously, 'If he can't speak the language shouldn't his interpreter be sitting in on this meeting?'

Muhammad's shot back with, 'Nah, no need, 'cos ah can talk Russian.'

At this, he turned to me and mumbled out some garbled crap that nobody else in this world could've understood, let alone me. But I had to play along with him now that he'd started and made out that I knew what he was saying, nodding my head and answering with, 'Ja, ja,' hoping that that meant 'Yes' in Russian.

Still rabbitting on, he signalled for me to take a seat. I clicked my heels and answered him back with a load of his own weird language. Thinking about it now, I was doing an impression more like a German than a Russian. He nodded his head and it was his turn to mutter, 'Ja, ja.'

They started to talk about some business deals they had in mind, along with some promotional offers they wanted Muhammad to consider. He cut them off, 'Well, mah friends, you'll jus' have to talk to mah manager, Herbert Muhammad.'

The two men tried again to get their offers accepted when a

young waiter came up to the table and asked, 'Would you like some more coffee, gentlemen?'

The guy couldn't have been more polite, but for some reason it seemed to piss off one of the Canadians who growled at the young fella, 'Can't you see we're talkin'? Why don't you just fuck off and leave us alone?'

The waiter went bright red in the face and stuttered an apology and no doubt was thinking that that was his job down the pan. The poor guy didn't know whether to have a shit, shave or a haircut and turned to walk away. Before he'd taken half a step, Muhammad said to him, 'That would be real nice, yeah, ah'll have a cup of coffee, an' ah want you to take a seat here right next to me an' pour one for yourself, 'cos you deserve a break.'

The waiter stuttered, 'That's very kind of you, Mr Ali, sir, but the management doesn't allow staff to sit at the table with the guests.'

'Is that so?' Muhammad said. 'Well, that's all changed now, 'cos you gonna sit down at this table an' drink a cuppa coffee jes' like anyone else. You go an' tell your boss man that Muhammad Ali says so.'

The waiter disappeared and there was a dead silence between Ali and the businessmen. I stayed quiet. Then they tried to break the silence, but Muhammad ignored them. The waiter came back and told Muhammad that the manager had said it was okay.

Ali said to him, 'Well, if he hadn't give it the okay, ah'd have bought this dam' place and he'd have bin lookin' for a job.'

Muhammad made a big show of making the waiter feel comfortable by asking him about his job, his family and anything else to stick two fingers up to the two ignorant twats. The two businessmen tried their hardest to back-peddle by trying to be friendly to the young fella. But it was just an act and Muhammad knew it. He got up, gave me a wink, asked the waiter to go with him and took off to sign autographs.

Completely ignoring me, the foreign dummy who couldn't speak their language, one of them nodded towards Muhammad, who by then was out of earshot. Remember, as far as they were concerned, I couldn't speak or understand one word of English. 'I'm glad that Norton broke his fucking jaw,' said one. 'Hey, I ain't gonna sit here and let him make us look like a couple of pricks.'

I leaned over the table and said, 'Too fucking late you pair of ignorant c**ts. What do you think he's been doing since you opened your big mouths?' They were completely speechless. In fact they looked like a couple of goldfish with their mouths opening and closing while they tried to think of some clever answer. If they thought of anything, I wasn't there to hear it because Muhammad signalled to me that it was time to leave.

In the car I told him what they'd said and what I said back to them and he slapped me on the back saying, 'Paddy mah man, you should've given 'em one o' yo' famous right-handers, then *they'd* know what it feels like to have their jaws wired up.'

When we got back to the house, there was a long list on his desk of all the people who'd tried to get in touch with him. He handed me the list to read – talk about a who's who of America's most famous. There was Marlon Brando, Charlton Heston, James Brown, Bill Cosby, Sammy Davis Jnr, Sidney Poitier, Clint Eastwood, Elvis Presley, Ella Fitzgerald, Ryan O'Neill and Barbra Streisand. If that wasn't enough, there was a separate sheet with the names of state governors, senators and foreign heads of state, plus a list of worldwide TV and radio stations and well-known reporters looking for interviews. I gave the list back to him and he casually threw it in a tray ready to be binned. Then having second thoughts, he picked it up again, scanned through it and called through to his wife,'Hey hon, can ya call Bingham an' tell him to give Elvis mah new phone number.'

That list definitely gave me something to think about. It really made me remember just who he was, apart from being my pal ... It didn't matter to me that he was famous, but here I was, living with him and travelling around with him, while all those celebrities and plenty of others like them all over the world were queuing up and busting a gut to get to speak to him. Here I was, a VUP (Very Unimportant Person), a bare knuckle fighter, privileged not only to meet the man but to gain real friendship.

After spending another couple of weeks with Muhammad, instead of the couple of days I'd originally planned for, I finally returned home to an enormous pile of mail from Ali fans, as usual. Not for the first time, I found that I couldn't answer the letters unless the senders had put in a stamped addressed envelope, which luckily most of them had; otherwise, I just didn't have the money for the postage. I answered mail all day long and well into the night. Often sitting up until four or five o'clock in the morning.

Though I've had thousands of letters from genuine Ali fans over the years, I've had my fair share of threatening letters and crank mail too. I've already mentioned the Ku Klux Klan, but there was the National Front as well and their letters were much the same. One example is: 'You lazy Irish bastard, on the dole and poncing off decent people. Get yourself a job and take your trash back to Ireland where you belong. God Save the Queen.' One Christmas I got a bomb-threat inside a Union Jack card. I treated this one like all the rest and after showing Sandra went to throw it into the bin.

I said to her, 'Sandra, these people are all cowards. If they meant what they said, they'd do it, not waste time sending cards and letters; don't worry.' But she did worry and was all for calling the police. I reminded her that we never went to them – I've got my own code. But it didn't make her feel any better. So in the end, and solely for her, I rang the law.

The next morning a sergeant turned up and Sandra showed him the Union Jack card and the threatening message. I heard him say to her: 'Oh, it's probably kids having a joke and if it's not, you leave it to us, Mrs Monaghan, you'd be amazed what evidence they can get from bomb fragments these days.'

That left Sandra feeling worse than she'd done before, so as he stepped out of the front door, with the card in his hand, I tapped him on the shoulder and said, 'You shouldn't be a copper. You should be on the stage, 'cos you're a fuckin' comedian.'

Then there were the crank letters. One man from Auckland claimed that he had discovered the secret of eternal youth and that he was willing to sell it to Muhammad for $50,000. Another guy, an Asian, claimed to be a good Muslim who prayed five times a day. So would Muhammad send him the money to buy a house? It goes without saying that no good Muslim would ever write anything like that. There were also begging letters which went on at great length about poverty and hardship and if only Muhammad could see his way to sending money it would solve all their problems. I could go on and on with examples, but luckily this sort of crap was about half a percent of the thousands I got from decent people showing respect and best wishes towards him.

I was also becoming a target for the national Sunday papers because of my friendship with Ali. They got in touch all the time with offers of big money. The *News of the World* and the *Mirror* dangled blank cheques for me to grab if only I'd dish the dirt on Muhammad's personal life in an exclusive interview. But I never have and never will accept any of these sorts of offers, no matter how skint I might be.

I'm reminded of a character who I introduced to Ali, thinking he was a genuine and very keen fan. His name was Tom Kappo and he asked if he could come and visit me in Abingdon. Nothing unusual in that and loads of fans had done it in the past. So I wrote back saying that I'm always ready to welcome fans into my home, after all, what better way to get to know people? Kappo turned up at my door and seemed a nice type of fella. We spent quite a few hours chatting away while Sandra kept the tea and biscuits coming. He asked me if it would be possible for me to introduce him to Ali next time he came to London. He seemed well surprised when I told him that he didn't need an introduction because anyone, no matter who they are, can walk straight up to Muhammad and he'd be pleased to say a few words. There weren't many celebrities you can say that about.

Then he started to quiz me on every detail he could get out of me. 'What's he like, is he easy to talk to? Oh it would be the greatest day of my life just to shake his hand.'

A good while after this I saw a copy of *Tit Bits* magazine on the shelves in our local paper shop and on the cover it said, 'Inside this week, Muhammad Ali's close friend and confidant makes the most intimate revelations only to Tom Kappo.' It takes a lot to wind me up but I can tell you, when I read all that fucking shite from Kappo about Ali, I wanted to tear his bastard head off. The article said that Kappo had gone over to visit his 'close friend' at his 'private training camp'. Muhammad had this camp especially built at Deer Lake, Pennsylvania and it was about as private as Woolworths. Anybody could walk in during sessions and have photos taken with Muhammad and that's obviously what he'd done, except that he went there with a plan to take advantage of Muhammad's generosity.

Kappo wasn't the only good for nothing I came across. There have been too many to count over the years. I've had the hangers-on, the businessmen, big and small, all trying to use me so they could make a few quid. But I never once co-operated with any of them, because it was too obvious what they were after. They didn't want me, they came to me thinking I could be bribed into getting a quick route to Muhammad through the back door. But I always gave them Ali's own get-out, that they'd have to contact his manager Herbert Muhammad.

The offers of payment came in regularly and they were usually for more money than I could dream of having, but even though I was always flat broke, my short and very direct answer was always 'fuck off'. People have told me that I'm crazy in having that attitude but it's very simple, at least to me. If I'd ever accepted just one offer, it would've meant that I was taking advantage of our friendship and that would make me as bad as, if not worse than, all those ponces looking for a quick earner.

One day I got a letter from the Home Office. It was from the chief liaison officer, a Mr Weston, asking if I would consider turning up at Wakefield Maximum Security Prison in Yorkshire to give a talk about my own life and my friendship with Muhammad Ali. I'd long got over any nerves about public speaking, having been thrown into the deepest end you can think of those times when Muhammad used to hand me the mike in front of celebrity audiences, so it was something I couldn't turn down. Wakefield was a fair old distance for me to travel to, but allowing that many of the fan letters I'd received over the years had come from prisoners in various jails all over England, I reckoned it would be worth the effort to meet and give a talk to these lads.

I borrowed an old banger from one of my pals and I set off. That old heap of a car immediately started rattling and spewing oil and water from everywhere and I begun to doubt that the dodgy piece of crap would get me there, let alone back. I was thinking how it would seem if Old Bill gave me a pull and found the guest speaker on his way to the nick was almost as bad as those he was visiting: no tax, no insurance and driving a motor that was barely street legal.

I arrived without anything like that happening; Mr Weston met me at the gate and led me into a packed reception hall. As he escorted me along, I asked him what had made him pick me to give a talk.

'Popular request of the prisoners,' he replied, to my surprise.

As we entered the hall, all the lads greeted me with clapping and cheering and as I was introduced from the stage I noticed that there were no empty seats.

After the hour was up, Mr Weston came back onto the stage and told the lads that he was so pleased with their response that he'd let me carry on talking if I'd no objections. Well, I was there, so why not? When I said I would there was a load of cheering and whistling.

I was surprised by the interest shown, though I guess what I'd accepted as a reasonably normal life did sound more interesting when I put it in words for the guys. I didn't overplay the violence that was part of my life, because I had to remember where I was and didn't want to give the impression that knocking the shite out of people was the best thing to do with your life, especially when half the chaps I was talking to were serving long sentences for doing the same thing. The Muhammad Ali part of my talk must've been fascinating for them and if I hadn't been in the position I was, but instead was sitting where they were, I would've been interested to meet somebody who was a mate of one of the most famous men on earth. In the end I spent three hours there altogether.

Okay, when you're banged up, a couple of flies screwing on the wall can hold your interest for as long as it takes and, having spent a lot of time down the block when I was 16, I can vouch for that. But even if they were listening to me because there was fuck all else to do, the applause those fellas gave me had to be witnessed to be believed. Some time after, I was telling a pal of mine the same story and he came out with, dry as you like, 'Paddy, my old mate, you just don't get it do you? The reason they was clapping and cheering was *because* you finished.'

Just as I was leaving the stage, Mr Weston told me that he'd had words from the lads that they wanted to shake my hand and get an autograph. So I was asked to stand by the door and the prisoners filed past one by one and I think every one of them wanted my signature. That took about an hour and opened my eyes as to what Muhammad had to do every day of his life.

Mr Weston was well pleased by the way it had all gone and commented that he'd never seen a response like the one I had. I can only imagine that the other speakers must've lectured on flower arranging, rambling or stamp collecting. But inside I was secretly chuffed to bollocks that this uneducated Irishman, who 'would never amount to anything', could keep an audience interested for three hours, virtually non-stop.

On 29 July, 1973, Sandra gave birth to our fourth child, another girl, who we named Belinda Jane. She was always a very loving and caring child and now she's grown up into a fine young lady, still full of thoughts of caring for other people. But if anyone crosses her, look out, because she's well into boxing. When her big brother Tyrone was in training out in the back garden, she used to cry until I started training her too.

Come 10 September Muhammad had his rematch with Kenny Norton in Los Angeles. Okay, it's all sporting history now, but Ali reversed the previous verdict and won the fight on a split decision. Again, it was close, but Muhammad won it all right, no question. He took the first five or six rounds and then Norton came back into it, winning a couple of the middle rounds and sharing one or two. Ali stormed ahead towards the end, carrying on from where he'd left off during the first half of the fight to win the later rounds.

Lose or not, Norton proved that he was a great fighter, because for the next six or seven years he became one of the most dominant figures in the heavyweight division. He was to meet Ali for a third time, in New York, on 28 September, 1976. Again he was beaten over what was then the championship distance of 15 rounds.

After Norton retired from boxing, he was seriously injured in a car accident. And who was the first person at his hospital bedside – Muhammad. And why not? Friendship has to be put to one side when two guys are matched up and they climb into the ring. Once they climb out, it's back on just like before, no matter who won or lost.

There's an old saying in boxing that you can't compare champions of the past with those from the present. But if you look at Muhammad Ali's record it says it all, because he stands head and shoulders above any of his 63 opponents and, putting aside my own friendship and bias, there never will be another Muhammad Ali.

After his victory over Norton, Muhammad wanted to wipe out the other blot on his record. He wanted Joe Frazier. But before that, the official World Heavyweight Champion, George Foreman, was set to make a visit to London. I didn't particularly look forward to that because I felt that I'd have no choice but to front him up to boost the People's Champ. No other fan of Ali's would be expected to go up against Foreman and let him know who we felt to be the real champion. They would have been thought of as either very brave or very stupid. I don't think I'm either of these things, but I'd got myself into a position where I would have to make a show, both for myself and for the thousands of Ali fans out there. I also hoped my confrontation would have some psychological influence on Foreman that might affect him when he eventually had a showdown with my friend.

I expected to have to put up with smart-arsed critics who would take the piss about me standing up to Foreman and treat it as some sort of joke. Particularly as they all said that the older

Ali didn't stand a chance against the young giant. Well, let me tell you that standing up to people like these men wasn't a bit funny, and I can tell you that Joe and George didn't think so either.

I dug out my double-handed 'ALI IS OUR CHAMP' banner, something I thought I'd never have to pick up again, and headed off to London.

I met Foreman face-to-face when he arrived outside the Connaught Rooms in central London, where he was scheduled to make the presentation of a jackpot cheque to a Pools winner. When he got there I unrolled the banner and raised it up with both hands. Foreman looked up to read the slogan, did a sort of double-take, then collected himself and carried on walking towards the entrance of the Connaught Rooms. I stepped out and blocked his path, standing right under his nose, just as I'd done with Joe Frazier two years earlier. He stared at me, and then raised his eyes to take in the message. He clenched his teeth and gave me a menacing look. I stared right back at him to let him know I wasn't frightened of him and was determined to out-stare him.

It was stalemate for about twenty seconds, then I said, 'Ali's our champ, George, and he's gonna fuck you right up.'

Fuck, he was a lot meaner and tougher-looking in the flesh than I'd ever thought he could be. Especially when his face twisted up and he snarled, 'You better git outa mah way ya li'l bastard, or you's gonna git hurt.'

'Yeah, I might do, but not as much as Ali's gonna hurt you when he fucks you up,'

He walked through me, knocking me backwards and to one side without answering me. I wasn't done with him yet, because I'd heard that he was to come out and pose for photographs with the lucky pools winner on a motorbike he'd bought before he even got his hands on the cheque. So I waited to heckle, picket and give him as much aggro as I could.

I didn't know it, but plain-clothes policemen had been called in. So when George came out with the smiling winner all ready to pose for the pictures, I ran over waving my banner. Then I was jumped on and dragged back by the coppers, who told me that if I didn't move on they'd arrest me.

'On what charge? If it's a crime to tell George Foreman that Muhammad Ali is our champion, then go ahead – arrest me. 'Cos I'm gonna carry on telling him the truth.'

When Dick Saddler, Foreman's manager, overheard the law threatening to pull me in, he very quickly and with a bit of sense said to a policeman, 'Oh no, man, don't you arrest him. It'll be bad publicity for George. Ah'll cut short this photo session, we leavin' here right now.'

That gave me an idea. If this is bad publicity for George, it can only be good publicity for Muhammad. So I said to the copper, 'Yeah, go on then, go ahead and arrest me.'

Saddler had waved the cameras away and bundled Foreman into a waiting car. As it pulled away I tapped on the rear window and I shouted, 'Remember, George, he's gonna fuck you up.'

Although Foreman took my confrontation in a more reasonable way than Joe Frazier, he was very annoyed. Luckily for me he controlled his anger. I don't know what affect our meeting had on him, but I believe that I gave my mate a psychological edge at the time. Well, I like to think so anyway.

I don't know what affect my similar campaign had on Joe Frazier, but it was soon time for his return fight with Muhammad. Both the time and place were set – it was the new Madison Square Garden in New York City on 20 January, 1974.

I was ready to settle for just watching it on TV in one of the London cinemas, but often I found things turned out better than I expected, and this was one of the occasions. I got a phone call from the manager of another charter flight company called Dolphin. He asked me for a list fan club members in Britain and

Ireland and in return offered me a return flight to New York with accommodation at the Royal Manhattan Hotel. He explained he couldn't get me a ticket for the fight.

No problem. I knew that once I met up with Muhammad it would be easy to see the fight. As soon as I put down the phone I started to make a list of some of the names and addresses. If I was more organised, sometime earlier I would've got my printer mate to run off copies of my address book, but instead I sat up into the early hours slowly copying them out by hand in an effort to get them posted off the next day. It looked like I was off across the pond again.

CHAPTER TEN
Ali vs. Frazier

I was going to go and see the return fight between Joe Frazier and Muhammad and I lost no time in getting my flight arranged. At least this time flying wasn't so new and daunting an experience, but I still had a few problems to overcome before I could think about getting ringside. I thought Muhammad would be staying at some hotel in New York, but didn't have a clue where. There was nothing I could do until I reached the States.

I phoned his training camp at Deer Lake and was told that Muhammad was at the Royal Essex Hotel. I found my way there and met up with Angelo Dundee, who gave me a friendly greeting. 'Paddy, glad you could make it. We never knew you were coming.' 'No,' I said, 'neither did I.' I told him about the charter flight company contacting me.

Angelo was called to the telephone and at the same time Muhammad's brother Rahaman came into the crowded room and came up to me saying, 'Great to see you again, Paddy. Mah brother is gonna be real pleased that you're here. He never told me you was comin'.'

'No, Rahaman, I didn't know myself, until ... ' and I went over the story. 'Where's Muhammad?'

'Oh, he's staying at a private apartment block nearby. C'mon, ah'll take you to see him. Ah know he'll be special glad to see yuh.' On the way, I asked him about the bit of rough housing that had gone on between Muhammad and Joe Frazier during a TV interview. It looked like things were getting really heated, but I figured it was a phoney set up to gee things up a bit.

'No, Paddy, believe me, that was for real. Frazier lost his cool. He just went crazy. Yeah, that sure was for real.'

When Rahaman and me walked into the apartment, Muhammad was genuinely surprised to see me. He jumped up from his chair and welcomed me with open arms and a back-breaking hug. There were several other people in the room. Some I'd met before, but a lot of fresh faces, and they all looked at me, raising their eyebrows, wondering why Muhammad was making such a lot of fuss over me. Fuck 'em. I've seen them all come and go over the years.

Ali asked: 'How'd'ya git here?'

'In a canoe, how d'you think?' I told him about the charter flight company, but pointed out that they couldn't give me a ticket to the fight.

'What? You should know bah now that you don't need to rely on any air charter company. Ah've told you before you kin come to any of mah fights anywhere, at any time, in any country in the world. Ah'll take you anywhere, you know that. All you have to do is pick up the phone but you never ask for nothin'.'

'Yeah and that's the way it'll always be.'

He put his fist on my chin, grabbed me in a headlock and put on an angry growl. 'Why you such a stubborn man Paddy? Anyways, what you tawkin' 'bout tickets for? You's with me, and now you are here, ah want you to be with me in mah corner when ah fight Joe Frazier.'

I thought, Fucking hell, me in his corner? I mean, what an honour, but all I said at the time was, 'Okay, pal.'

Muhammad turned to Rahaman and said: 'Have Paddy checked into the hotel,' meaning the Royal Essex, where he intended to move to. I told him that there was no need to bother as I'd already checked into the Royal Manhattan, along with the rest of the charter flight group. He told me what time to be at the apartment block, because he wanted me to ride with him in the limo to Madison Square Garden for the fight. Everything was fine.

As I was leaving, he followed me to the door, stepped out with me and very quietly asked me if I was okay for bread, meaning money.

I just said, 'I'm fine. No problem at all.'

He gave me that look, 'You such a proud man, ah don' know if ah kin believe you.'

'Believe me, pal. I ain't short of a shilling.'

I lied. I was in New York City and I didn't have a penny in my pocket. I walked back to the Royal Manhattan and was told that meals, apart from breakfast, had to be paid for. I should have checked into the Royal Essex as Muhammad had suggested. My guts were rumbling and now I had to try to work out just how the hell I was going to eat.

In the dining room the waitresses were setting out the tables. I watched as they put heaps of bread rolls in little wicker baskets on every table, then, as soon as they disappeared into the kitchen, I nipped in and stuffed my pockets with as many as could get in. After a quick look around, I walked across the lobby, hid myself in a sort of recess and got stuck into the rolls. Fuck me, was I hungry? I'd eaten about four rolls, stopped for a breather and, looking up for the first time, noticed I was being watched by an attractive, though very posh-looking woman who was behind the counter of a hotel jewellery counter. Now I'm bolloxed, two minutes and she'd be calling the manager to grass me up. Attack is the best form of defence, so I got up and wandered over to the counter and pretended I was interested in the very expensive display. It probably looked more like I was going to rob it.

She said, 'Can I help you, sir?' But it was so obvious that I didn't have a pot to piss in, she couldn't help herself giggling out loud.

'Okay', I said, 'you got me bang to rights as they say back home, are you going to report me?

'No, your secret's safe with me,' she said, then added, 'Do I take it from your accent you're from England? Are you over here for the big fight?'

'Well that's my plan, if I don't starve to death before the bell.' I could've kicked myself, because I sounded like a fucking beggar, so I said quickly, 'Only joking.'

She gave me a sort of thoughtful look, but didn't make any comment about that; she only said, 'You seem a keen fan, who are you rootin' for?'

'Who else but Muhammad Ali? The man is unbeatable, but I don't suppose a lady like you is very interested in what goes on in the boxing world.'

'You'd be surprised,' she said. 'You could say I have been involved in the fight business over the years. You say Ali is unbeatable – how do you think he would have fared against, say, someone like Jack Dempsey in his day?'

'Well, they say we shouldn't try and compare the boxers of today with them in the past, but as you've asked, absolutely no argument, Muhammad could've taken him with one hand tied behind his back.'

The lady put her hand over her mouth and giggled at that. A few customers were browsing around the counter, so I thought I'd disappear and finish off the rest of the rolls, so I excused myself and turned to walk away.

Just then she said, 'Oh, just a minute ... I think, after seeing you eat those rolls, that you would appreciate a good meal. Right?'

'Not 'alf,' I came out with, then groaned inside at my Dick Van Dyke accent and quickly said, 'Yes thank you, a proper meal would be great.'

'Well, I would like to invite you to join my husband, my daughter and myself for lunch.'

I was gobsmacked that this high-class woman would think of inviting a stranger to join her family. Pride almost made me refuse, then I thought of the food and reached across the counter, shook her hand, introduced myself and thanked her for the invitation.

'I'm very pleased to meet you, Paddy,' she said. 'My husband owns a restaurant on Broadway, just around the next block and it will be easy for you to find. And I'm Mrs Deanna Dempsey – Jack Dempsey's wife.' You could've knocked me down with a bag of chips, and the look on her face told me she'd enjoyed the joke.

A few hours after the invitation, I made my way to the restaurant, arriving bang on the time suggested by Mrs Dempsey. The place was packed. Eventually, through a small gap, I noticed Deanna Dempsey. Fortunately, she remembered me, as I'd worried in case she might not and I'd be stood in the restaurant like a prick without the price of even a cup of tea in my pocket.

'Paddy,' she said. 'Glad you came.'

I thought, Blimey, she's even remembered my name, this is one very classy lady.

She introduced me to her daughter, then handed me a menu. 'Here, order whatever you want.'

I felt a bit unsure about this and she must have gathered as much from my expression, because with a smile she whispered in my ear:

'Shh, don't worry. It's on the house.'

Inside I thought, Thank you, God, then to her, 'I'd like to have well done steak and chips if that's okay?'

'Chips? Oh, you mean fries.' She ordered for me. 'A large T-bone steak, well done, with fries, for our guest.'

I had difficulty in believing that all this was happening. Before long I caught my first glimpse of her husband: the legendary Heavyweight Champion of the 1920s. Leaning on a walking stick, he was a shadow of the man he used to be, but I hope I still look as good when I reach his age. He was standing by the counter, talking to a photographer. Then he joined his wife and step-daughter and Mrs Dempsey introduced me to the great old man. He shook my hand with a 'Pleased to meetcha' and peered at me through watery eyes. I said he had a nice place and was surprised when he said, 'After all these years I gotta close down.'

'Why's that, business not so good?'

'Business ain't bad, ain't bad at all, but I've only got this place on lease an' the damn landlady, well, she's just upped the price and I just can't afford the crazy price she's asking.'

'Well can't you have a word with her, she might cut the price for somebody like yourself.'

'Well mah friend, I somehow don't think the lady in question would wanna meet an ol' worn out boxer, an' ah think it maght be difficult to walk up her driveway.'

'Sounds a bit of a strange businesswoman to me.'

'Mah wife sez yer from England. Well, ah dunno if she's strange or not, but she's your Queen.'

'The Queen of England? You're joking with me.'

'Do you see me laughing?' He looked me in the eye again. 'I'm telling you, she's gonna put me outa business.'

'Bloody hell, I bet people back home don't know she owns your restaurant and that you're gonna have to close down.'

'Ain't jus' mine, she owns half of Broadway. And that half she don't own she very soon will. Right now she's got everything, from the most expensive theatres on the strip, right down to the cheapest clip joints.'

Well, now, I thought. That's a bit of info they've kept a bit secret. Not that I keep up with royal investments; perhaps ever other fucker in England has known about it for years and never bothered to tell me. Or maybe it's all bollocks. I don't know.

Our little chat was interrupted by a crowd of diners who had come up to shake Jack's hand. He was open, friendly and didn't seem to mind answering endless questions. Put me in mind of Muhammad, but with Jack there was a very good reason for him to make himself available and that's where the comparison with my mate ended. I'm not knocking the guy, after all he had a business to run and if his fame and glory brought the punters through the door, well, why not? I noticed Jack signing books and menus and posing with a big smile for anybody that approached him, but I also noticed money changing hands after every person walked up to him.

What prices they were charged I haven't the slightest. But I remember when Jake La Motta did a tour of Britain, it was his life that the film *Raging Bull* was based on. Anyway, he charged a tenner for a photograph and if you tried to take a sneaky one without paying, you soon found yourself confronted by a fucking great minder who would gently place his hand over the lens.

The waiter stuck in front of me the largest T-bone steak I've ever seen and even I had to laugh when Mrs Dempsey, quite loudly, said, 'Oh, Paddy, help yourself to the bread rolls.'

Jack was doing his bit of business close enough to my table so I could see and hear what was going and it passed the time between mouthfuls to listen to the questions put to Jack by whoever approached him.

The most often asked question seemed to be, 'Who'd ya figure's gonna win the fight, Jack?' and his answer was always the same: 'Frazier will win by a knockout.'

But that didn't surprise me because boxing books had taught me that Jack had the same sort of style as Joe.

Another pretty obvious question was always going to be, 'Yuh figure you coulda beaten Muhammad Ali?'

He'd answer in that lazy drawl, 'Well in ma'h prime, I think I could've taken real good care of him.' But once he got that out of the way he'd go on to praise Ali. 'Before that lay off, there ain't no-one who could have licked him, but all those years without a real fight has messed him up. I know, I was three years out of the ring mahself without a serious battle and I know it's true what they say, "They never come back." Ali always talks about what he's gonna do an' most times he does jus' what he promises, no mistake about that. But now he's talkin' too much. No matter how great he was, he can't ever come back ... an' I know, 'cos I've tried it.' I've often thought about Jack Dempsey's words and they show what separates an all-time great boxer from the greatest of all time.

It was time for me to make a move, but before I slipped my coat on I did something right out of character for me. I dropped a gentle hint to Mrs Dempsey that I would've liked to have a photo, but ... I didn't even have to finish what I was going to say because she'd known I was skint ever since she saw me nicking those rolls. She put her finger to her lips. 'You just leave it to me.' She asked the photographer to take some pictures, with me as the guest at the table, then picked up some empty photo folders and got Jack to sign a couple, 'To my pal Paddy'. As she handed them to me she promised, 'I'll bring the pictures to my shop in the hotel tomorrow' and she did.

Although I had the privilege of meeting this great legend, we never knew each other apart from that brief meeting. I found out a long time afterwards that he wrote the word 'pal' or 'friend' with most of the thousands of signatures he dished out on photos to all the strangers who paid to pose with him. Because of that there are quite a few chancers out there who say: 'Oh yeah, Jack Dempsey was my pal. See, I've got the photos.'

When the night of the fight arrived, I was sitting beside Muhammad as we headed up to the stadium through a massive crowd. Just outside the place, dozens of fans mobbed the car in their excitement. They jumped onto the bonnet, and then the roof, whistling, screaming and cheering. I thought, Fuck this, we're either gonna be flattened or torn to bits, but Muhammad sat there as though it was just another quiet drive. Angelo Dundee must've thought the same as I did because he yelled at the driver: 'Move, you asshole! Move, move!'

'How can I? I can't see a thing.'

'Nah, an' you never will see a fuckin' thing again, if you don't move this heap. Now – c'mon – move!' Eventually the limo eased its way through and parked inside the building.

It was a relief for all of us once we got inside the dressing room, well, all except Muhammad, who seemed to get a kick out of any sort of excitement. Those allowed into the dressing room after the clearance call were Ali's brother Rahaman, Angelo, Bundini Brown – the 'court jester' – Walter Youngblood – 'Blood' for short – Luis Saria, Gene Kilroy, the fight doctor Ferdie Pacheco and last and very least … Yer man, Paddy.

The clearance call was very strictly monitored, but in the case of a couple of special young fellas, the rules were relaxed, at least for a short while. They were John F. Kennedy Jnr, the son of the late President of the United States, and his cousin Edward Kennedy, who was on crutches because recently he'd had part of his leg amputated through cancer. Muhammad was their hero and they'd asked if they could have some photographs taken with him. Muhammad did the photos separately and told the boys to make out like they were having a fight with him. The faces he pulled because these young kids seemed to be knocking seven bells out of him were the funniest things I'd seen for a while. No doubt those pictures would be hung on their bedroom wall forever. Sadly, John and his wife died in a plane crash in 1999.

People were continually fussing around him in a right flap, but Muhammad ignored all that and sat jawing away with the two young guys. Then he excused himself while he went through his bag, sorting out all his gear ready for the off. I was standing beside Edward and, because he'd noticed Muhammad and I were very close, he must've thought I was the best bet to ask a favour. He whispered to me, 'Do you think you could ask Mr Ali if he would let me have his trunks after the fight as a souvenir?'

'Don't worry,' I said, 'I'll ask him for you right now.'

I had a word in Muhammad's ear and he didn't hesitate. Turning to Gene Kilroy, his Mr Fix It, he said, 'Kilroy, ah want you to see to it that young Ed here gits mah trunks after the fight.'

'Okay, champ, will do,'

'But before you hand 'em over, ah wanna write a personal message on them, so make sure you find me one o' them special pens.'

It was getting close to the call and the room had to be cleared except for his official corner men, his masseur and me. Muhammad was the calmest person in the place. He stripped down and stretched out on the rubbing-table for the pre-fight ritual of a massage-cum-Spanish lesson from Luis Saria.

There had been rumours that Ali had sprained or damaged his right hand during training. There were no breaks, sprains, or bumps, but I could see he was concerned with his hands, particularly the left one. I'd often seen him rubbing or sucking his knuckles. He was forever prodding at the middle knuckle of his left hand. It was obviously troubling him, though he never complained.

Ferdie Pacheco noticed him picking at it and said to him, 'Will ya leave them damn hands alone? Here, let me take a look at 'em before they gits taped up.' Ali sat up on the table and held out his *left* hand – so much for the rumours. The doc sprayed the backs of Muhammad's hands, then injected cortisone between the webs of his fingers to take the edge off the arthritic pain.

While this was going on, Bundini Brown, a very funny fucker, strutted around the dressing room, going on and on about what he was going to do to Joe Frazier. Anybody who didn't know better would've thought that he was going into the ring instead of Ali.

'Ah'm gonna dance – ah'm gonna sting. Ah'm gonna ...'

Ali egged him on. 'Whatcha gonna do, eh?'

Bundini strode backwards and forwards like a man possessed and Muhammad just watched and laughed at him. I take people as I find them and I liked Bundini. He was a proper character, a crazy eccentric, but great company for all of us, particularly when everybody, except Muhammad, was suffering pre-fight tension.

Herbert Muhammad entered the dressing room and he, Rahaman and Ali went into the shower-room for prayers to their Allah. Muhammad warmed up with some shadow-boxing and dancing. Then as ever, he rested for a bit and repeated the same process.

Giving me a wink, he said, 'This one's for you, Paddy. Ah'm gonna whup his ass for when he got heavy with you in London.' I was surprised he even gave it a thought, but that's Muhammad Ali.

Angelo reminded him to watch out for Frazier's head: 'You know he uses it as a weapon and gets away with it.'

With minutes to go before the knock on the door, Muhammad sat quietly on a chair he'd swung round so as he could lay his head on his crossed arms, draped over the top of the chair back. After a few minutes, he raised his head, took a deep breath and rolled his head one way and the other. Then came the knock we were all waiting for.

Angelo said, 'Time, Muhammad. You ready?'

'Yeh, man, ah'm ready.'

Muhammad turned to me and said: 'Stand close to me, Paddy, when we get out there. Ah don't want you gittin' lost. Jes' stay with Angelo an' the others in mah corner.'

We left the dressing room and made our way down a long corridor lined with policemen. Suddenly I was jumped on from behind and found myself tied up in an arm- and headlock by a cop who demanded to see my pass. The copper was good at his job, because I couldn't move. Just as well, I might've lamped him in the heat of the moment and ... Well it doesn't bear thinking about. So I shouted out, 'Oi, Muhammad.' He came stomping back quickly to rescue me. I'd never seen him flare up so quick.

He yelled at the cop, 'Take yo' damned hands off him. He's mah friend and he's in mah corner, so let him go now.'

His face was so full of anger; he frightened me, let alone the copper. As I straightened myself up and we carried on, I could hear Bundini shouting, 'Yeah, he mah friend, too, yuh big motherfucker.'

With every step we took, the noise of the 21,000 crowd got louder and louder. I'd never experienced anything like it at any of the places we'd been to before. The cheers, screams, whistles and roars were deafening. I'm not exaggerating when I say it was like an express train screaming through a station at 120 miles an hour. When the spotlight flashed onto Muhammad, the chants of 'Ah-lee! Ah-lee! Ah-lee!' hit us like a wave.

Frazier was already in the ring, bouncing and hopping around, looking as menacing as ever. He was the meanest-looking fucker I'd ever seen in my life. Muhammad looked across and poked his tongue out at him.

Soon enough the fight started. Muhammad came out dancing with jabs and combinations. Frazier advanced, bobbing and weaving. There was no clowning around from Ali. This time it was down to business. Ali dominated the opening round on all the score cards. When the round finished, the lights went on in the auditorium and on top of all four ring posts, in case either the fighter or the referee couldn't hear the bell.

In the second round, Frazier was saved by the bell that never rung. Ali forced Joe into a neutral corner and threw a powerful, chopping right-hand punch to the jaw. Joe definitely felt it and it looked like his legs turned to jelly. With only thirty seconds of the round to go, Ali moved in to finish his man off. The only way I could've been closer to the action would've been if I was in the ring beside the ref, so I saw exactly what was happening.

Not only were Joe's legs gone, but also his eyes had rolled up in their sockets as he rocked backwards and staggered. Ali was just about to put the finisher on him when the ref jumped in between them, waving his hands with a criss-cross signal, like they do when they move in to stop a fight and save a boxer from further punishment. It's the same signal refs use when fighters are throwing punches after the bell has rung. Yet the bell hadn't rung, and the lights never lit up on the tops of the posts or in the arena to show the end of the round.

You can imagine, us guys in his corner were over the moon. Angelo yelled, 'Beautiful. He's gone, Muhammad. You've stopped him.'

Bundini was jumping around with excitement and giving me a great big bear hug. 'Yuh see that Paddy? Yuh see that?'

But after a dozen seconds passed, Perez, the referee, brought both men to the centre of the ring to carry on boxing. It was only then that the corner posts lit up and the bell rang to signal the end of the round.

Perez was quoted in the papers the next day as saying, 'I thought I heard the bell.'

In my mind, right or wrong, by jumping in I think he might've prevented Muhammad from scoring a two round knockout. And after the fight, Ali understandably made some comments of his own in the papers.

Anyway, it didn't matter what we thought. The ref's decision, right or wrong, is always final and the fight carried on.

It was only through being right up there with the action that I got a proper idea of the violence and raw power of two awesome heavyweights. I could hear Ali talking to Frazier during a clinch in the fourth round, saying, 'You ain't nothin' but shit.' Frazier barged Ali with his right shoulder, then threw a left hook that was way off target. 'You sucker!' laughed Ali. Then he danced in to throw a combination to Joe's head.

Frazier's corner men were soon at work with the ice bag, applying it to the swellings that were a result of Ali's jabs. Joe was never hard to hit, though it seemed he was hard to hurt. In the seventh, round, during another clinch, Frazier growled, 'Ah'm gonna kill ya.' Then – bang. Ali caught him with a beautiful inside uppercut and I heard him say to Joe, 'You crazy, man, you crazy.'

Ali often came down off his toes and onto the soles of his feet, planting them firmly on the canvas to out-slug Frazier, beating him at his own game. He was landing four, five and sometimes six punches to Joe's one. Between rounds, Angelo kept reminding him, 'Watch out for his head. We've only got a coupla rounds to go and he's getting the worst of it. But you've got it all to do.' He was bang-on, because not once did the referee warn Frazier for using his head. I thought Muhammad out-boxed and out-fought Joe. Ultimately Muhammad was a clear cut winner by 10-2. Or, in Paddy-speak, he knocked the holy shite out of Frazier.

After the fight we were led to a room under the terraces of the Garden, where Ali sat sucking on a chocolate lolly. 'Now who said ah was all washed up an' too old?' he asked the reporters. 'Eat your words, you suckers.' Back in the dressing room, the very first thing he did was to pray and give thanks to Allah.

The next morning I had breakfast with Muhammad and Rahaman. Ali was in great shape, but his hands were very painful. You'd never have dreamed he'd gone 12 rounds with the mighty Joe only a few hours before. That morning we drove to a press conference at the Felt Forum. Joe Frazier had arrived 45 minutes late for his session and he was still there, sitting up on the stage with his trainer, Eddie Futch. Muhammad arrived bang on his scheduled time.

I walked in with Muhammad, right up to the stage, hoping that Joe wouldn't recognise me. I didn't get on the stage with Ali, just stood at the front while he climbed up to a round of applause from the world's press, celebrities and VIPs.

Muhammad looked the bollocks, all suited and booted, without a mark on his face. In contrast, Frazier looked as if his face had been through a meat-grinder. He wore a large hat and tinted glasses to hide his closed right eye. Swellings covered his forehead and lips – he was a mess. If he'd gone to the zoo, he'd have had to buy two tickets: one to get in and one to get out.

Frazier told a reporter that he thought he'd won the fight. Then Ali was asked, 'What's your response to that claim?'

'Were you at the fight?' asked Ali 'Did you see it?'

'Yes, I was there,' said the reporter.

'Then ah don't need to tell you what you already know.' Frazier looked dead uncomfortable and mumbled, 'Ah thought ah won, man.' Muhammad looked at the audience with a look on his face that said it all.

I was leaning on the platform just below them, when Frazier

suddenly caught sight of me as he was answering a question. He cut off in mid-sentence and for the rest of the conference he kept glaring at me. I knew he'd recognised me, but I was hoping he didn't remember it was me that had dug him out at the airport. My foot was resting on a big lump of wood left over from building the stage and I thought, If that big bastard starts anything he'll get it across the head before he kills me. As he left the stage, he walked down the steps towards me and I made sure the piece of wood was ready to pick up. Frazier stopped in front of me and studied my face, 'Where have ah seen you before?'

'Ah ... never, mate,' I said.

'You ever bin ta England?'

'No, too cold.'

'That's strange, 'cos you kinda remin' me of some li'l pissant ah had dealings with. So where you from?'

'Australia.'

'What's yo' name?'

'Er ... Bruce Smith.'

'Yuh sure we ain't ever met before?'

'No, never, but I hope to see you in Australia sometime.'

He gave me another frightening glare, grunted and walked away. I wiped the sweat off my face and thought, 'Fuck's sake, Paddy, you don't 'alf look for trouble.'

Ali missed all that because he was still on the stage surrounded by the press. They asked him about his future plans, and one of them brought up George Foreman and the touchy subject of the official World Champion.

Muhammad said, 'Oh, yeah, ah'd be glad to give Foreman a shot at me.' Then he said something that was very special to me alone. 'Ah'll put mah rankin' on the line against Foreman. George is only the World Champion of the boxing commissions. So what? Ah'm the People's Champ.'

One of the biggest names in British sport, football manager

Brian Clough, was sitting in the audience, or so the commentator Reg Gutteridge told me. God knows why Reg wanted to plug Brian Clough, but I noticed him trying to get Muhammad's attention and heard him say, 'Please, Muhammad, will you mention the name of Brian Clough?'

That was ignored and another reporter asked Ali to name the best fighters in the world today. He said, 'You got one of them right among you tonight. His name's Edward Kennedy Jnr. Stand up Ed an' take a bow.'

While the applause for the young fella was going on, Gutteridge again plugged Cloughie: 'Please mention Brian Clough's name.'

Muhammad put his hand over the mike. 'Brian who? Who the hell he?' When the applause for Kennedy had died down, Muhammad announced: 'We have a Brian Cloof in the audience.' Brian Clough stood up to the most indifferent, lukewarm applause I've ever heard. Soccer, as they call it, means hardly anything in the United States. To be fair, if some famous baseball player was mentioned in a similar situation back home, the result would've been much the same. Well, not quite, because the British are so polite they'd have made an effort even if they didn't know why.

Then Muhammad surprised the shit out of me when I heard him saying, 'Ah've got someone here who's a bit special. Ah would like you all to meet him an' to tell the world about him. He's a man who has proved over an' over, many times to me, that he is a true friend. In this life we kin count on the fingers of one hand our really true friends. Now ah want you all to meet and greet him as ah introduce him to you. He's mah friend an' mah brother Paddy Monaghan, an Irishman livin' in England since he was a kid, but he always calls himself Irish ... Come up here, Paddy, an' stand by mah side like you always done. Let 'em see who ah'm talking about.'

I climbed up onto the platform to an applause that must've had Brian 'Cloof' hiding under his seat. Afterwards John Kennedy Jnr gave me a recording of the event as a way of thanking me for getting those fight trunks for him.

Back home, Sandra had kept all the press reports of the fight. But none of them covered the press conference. Instead, we got a picture of Ali with Brian Clough that gave the impression that they were the best of friends. Not a word was printed about the long speech that Muhammad had made about me, but so fucking what? I was used to that sort of thing by then.

If you'd asked the average man to name the Heavyweight Champion of the World, nine out of ten of them would have said Muhammad Ali. George Foreman wasn't stupid. He knew what everybody thought and going into his title defence against Ken Norton, I think he made his mind up to let all those people know that he was a force to be reckoned with and a better man than Ali.

I don't think there was any doubt that Foreman was going to claim a victory over Norton and it was proved when he knocked Norton spark out in a couple of rounds. He really did hand out some punishment and that's when the warnings started about what was going to happen if Ali ever got in the ring against Foreman. Newspapers were pushing fears for Muhammad's safety. A bit odd, because I didn't remember they were ever concerned for his safety in the past. What they were predicting, and probably hoped for, was complete disaster for Ali.

Fans assumed that, if it was in print, it must be true and letters poured through my letterbox, all worried about Muhammad's safety. I sent out a newsletter to the fan club members throughout the world, telling them to ignore all that crap in the papers and as a footnote added that I was confident that Muhammad Ali would defeat George Foreman inside the distance and that he'd regain his title. It wasn't wishful thinking – I honestly believed what I wrote to the fans. I'd seen close up what Ali was capable of doing when he fought Joe Frazier.

When he phoned me from his training camp, he couldn't have seemed more confident. He said, 'Paddy, after ah've put Foreman on his back, so thet he'll never git up agin, ah'm gonna drop by your house an' take a visit.' I appreciated the thought but honestly didn't give it a lot of thought. The man would've had one of the most important fights of his career and, though the intention might be there, I reckoned he'd have a lot of other things to do before showing his face in the downmarket place I lived on the ragged side of town.

The fight was being promoted by businessman Don King. Muhammad called it 'The Rumble in the Jungle' and it was to take place in Kinshasa, Zaire. It eventually kicked off on 30 October, 1974. It was supposed to have taken place earlier, but Foreman cut his eye in a training session, so the fight was put off for eight weeks. I heard George wanted to go home, but they wouldn't let him. I would've loved to have been there supporting my mate, but with no change in my life and none in my pocket, there was no chance of that. Well, not strictly true, because one phone call to Muhammad and I could've been there at ringside all expenses paid but, as I keep saying, that's not my style.

Thanks to Ma and Da digging into their pockets for me, plus a few shillings of my own, I got enough cash to buy a ticket at the Odeon, Hammersmith and see the fight. It was a blinding contest and the highlight for me and every fan in the world was watching Muhammad come off the ropes and place a beautiful short right to Foreman's jaw. It sent him straight to the canvas – face down. Foreman did his best to get up but didn't make it before he was counted out. Muhammad Ali had knocked out George Foreman in the eighth round.

In the cinema I looked round and watched the people

go crazy. They stood up and cheered and chanted, but I just sat there, closed my eyes and said a mental prayer of thanks to God.

Outside the Odeon it was like a carnival, as people formed circles and chanted, 'Ali's the greatest – Ali's our champ.' But there was nobody on this earth happier than Paddy Monaghan. I left the celebrating crowds and set off on my 50-mile trek home. I was lucky and a lorry picked me up after about ten minutes and dropped me off just outside Abingdon. That left me a couple of miles of walking, but I got indoors by seven o'clock.

I got bags of telegrams and letters from all over the world. One telegram simply read 'To Muhammad Ali – Hip, hip, hooray.' As soon as I knew Muhammad would be back in the States, I phoned him at his home.

'Hello champ.'

'Paddeee. Mah number one, mah main man. Didja watch the fight on TV yet?'

'Of course I did. Well done mate.'

'Hey, can you remember the fun we had when we used to go out for a drive, an' ah put on that accent to the people in the streets?'

'Yes, mate. We used to have some great laughs.'

As I've said before, me and Muhammad hardly ever spoke much about boxing, but I had to bring up a few things about the fight and tell him about the reaction from his fans in London – all dancing and singing in the streets outside the cinema. I asked him how his hands were.

'Oh, they a bit sore but ah'm used to the pain by now. Ah never had trouble with mah hands until after the long lay-off – that's what caused 'em to soften up. It's only since mah comeback they started to trouble me – but ah can still whup ass when ah hev to.'

'So what are your plans now?'

'Gee, Paddy, they want me to be here, there an' everywhere.

Ah've jes' accepted an invitation from President Mobutu, back in Zaire, to be the guest of honour for the country's 14 years of independence celebrations.'

'When are you going back there?'

'Coupla weeks from now, ah reckon,' he told me.

As we finished our conversation, he said the same words he'd said to me before the Foreman fight, 'Ah'll be comin' ta visit you real soon.' I thought it was his way of saying, 'See you later' or 'See you around'. We all use those phrases, but usually just as a way of signing off, not seriously.

CHAPTER ELEVEN
Welcome to my Gaff

While Ali had enhanced his reputation still further with the Foreman result, my own career, such as it was, was doing really well too. Having clinched the British Bare Knuckle Boxing Championship title, I was determined to aim as high as I could. It's always difficult to predict where you want to be in my version of the fight game, because it's much more dangerous than legal boxing. Give or take rare accidents, you don't expect too many severe injuries in regular boxing. I mean, how many straight boxers get their nose almost bitten off? Still, putting aside the chances of not being able to pursue my career through injury, I set my sights on becoming European champ and I didn't have long to wait.

After defending my title against Jack McCann, I took on a guy from Hungary and he had to throw the towel in after six rounds because I tore into him so bad he couldn't take anymore. The next was an Italian who I knocked out in the eighth. That fucker was hard work and I came out with a few lumps and bumps of my own. I did Earl Stewart from Sheffield in the third. He was

213

another one without enough experience to give me any problems and, to be honest, I could've put him away a lot quicker than I did, but sometimes you have to give the punters their money's worth. Quite honestly, I fucked around with him. He dropped his guard more times than a whore's knickers, but I didn't take him up on it until the third round when I got bored, opened up with three or four lefts and rights and stretched him out.

That was in April and a month later I got the chance I was waiting for when Tommy told me he'd arranged for Peter Benichi to fly over from Italy to fight me in a gloved defence (last man standing) of his European BKB Middleweight title. I was over the moon. I remember telling my pal Lenny McLean that this was a big one for me. His advice based on his own training schedule was simple, 'Pads, my son, train hard for this an' you'll knock the bollocks outa 'im.'

I thought I'd better stick to my usual training, so I headed off to Croydon to stay with Tommy and his wife Renatta. I was up at five every morning running round the town and I worked out solid the rest of the day at Charlie Shorey's gym at 'The Cottage'. At the end of the day, it's all about stamina. There's no good having a wicked punch if you can't breathe after a couple of rounds.

Give Benichi his due, he definitely looked the part. Wouldn't have been out of place in a film on the mob, hard-faced and tough looking. As I found out in the ring, he didn't just look tough, he was as hard as fucking nails. Well, as reigning European Champion, he was hardly gonna be a pussy. To be honest, by the seventh, I was beginning to think that no matter what I threw at him, he wasn't going to go down. I was hurting him, no doubt about it, but he was fucking well hurting me as well. My head felt twice the size, my ribs were on fire, and my hands were starting to swell up. I've got the Monaghan clan in the ring with me and they're all saying, 'Fer feck's sake Paddy, will ye git yer finger outa yer arse. Yer feckin' granny could have finished 'im by now!' Yeah, like bollocks she could. The eighth was pretty equal, then half-a-minute into the ninth I thought, 'That's enough,' and knocked him spark out.

Fuck, that hadn't been easy, but no pain no gain, and with that I'd gained the BKB European Middleweight Championship.

I had six months to get over that before I had to defend my title against Bermondsey boy Chris Johnston, but he was out of his league and retired in the seventh. Oh yeah, two months before that I had a go with another Frenchman, but with the ref stopping the fight in the fourth, it was hardly worth talking about.

In February and March, 1974, I put away a couple of fighters in a KO and a points win. They were just a warm-up for something I'd been aiming at for a number of years. I'd long progressed beyond taking on the Sunday afternoon bouts solely for picking up a few quid. As I put win after win behind me, it was my manager, Tommy Heard, who put the idea in my head of aiming to be the best. Once that seed was planted it was all about more than the money and, as I've already said, I aggressively protected my successes. Now I was aiming at Jean Paul Durrell, a name I won't forget. A Canadian from Quebec, he was top of the tree and a lot of people said I'd got no chance of beating him. Fuck 'em, I'd been in situations before when I was told that I was committing suicide, but I showed them all different then. I'd had 86 fights and 29 of them had ended in knockouts, but every one of them was a win for me – not a bad record if I was to retire then and there. That wasn't going to happen though because I still had a long way to go.

What can I say about that fight in May 1974? I could give you a blow-by-blow account, but one punch is pretty much like another unless you were there in the stink of sweat and tobacco smoke. One punch is like another unless you're on the receiving end of it under the hot lights with the crowd screaming, catcalling, swearing and shouting advice. One punch is like another until you throw the one that puts your opponent on the canvas. That one special punch came for me in the eighth round, straight to the point of the chin. It jarred my arm from knuckle to shoulder and sent Durrell's brain crashing to the back of his skull. His eyes rolled up while he was still standing, then he fell backwards, lay down at my feet and never heard the count that meant Paddy Monaghan had had taken his title away. Yes, I was now BKB Middleweight Champion of the World and nobody would ever take that away from me. But how many knew it? In the closed world of my kind of fighting I was the dog's knackers, outside of it I was just another face. No headlines, no hysteria, no screaming crowds of fans. Absolutely fuck all, but that's life – or my life anyway.

I'm saying I got fuck all out of becoming World Champion, but, on second thought, that's not strictly true. Inside I had a terrific buzz that is indescribable, and just in case I forgot the peak I'd reached – not much chance of that – I had the very tangible reminder in the Champion's belt I'd been presented with. Was I proud of that or what? I wanted to wear it around town so that it screamed 'look at what this know-nothing, illiterate labourer has achieved.' I wanted to track down that teacher who knocked the spirit out of me daily and spank him around the head with it while shouting, 'You said I'd amount to nothing you bastard.' I didn't do none of these things, but, in short, I can honestly say it was my most prized possession.

About a year after taking the title I was invited to New York for a press conference in the Royal Essex Hotel – what a gaff! Expensive, luxurious and in a prime position overlooking Central Park. What was the first thing that went in my suitcase? Yep, my belt, wrapped up like a mummy in case it got scratched.

Anyway, I've done the business as far as the American press were concerned. Gave a bit of a speech; answered questions that were being fired at me like machine gun bullets; and posed this way and that for the photographers, making sure my belt was in every shot. I'm talking a very heavy belt here, so having held it above my head for what felt like a hundred pictures, I laid it on the sofa behind me while I had a breather. Some breather, those journalists never stopped shouting questions.

What a contrast between home and the States. Yeah I'd been in the local paper more than once, but that was over being nicked for the Denton business and various motoring offences. Yet here in the Royal Essex, where what I was and what I had achieved was no secret, they couldn't get enough of me. Eventually I held my arms up to let them know that I'd had enough and it all quietened down apart from a couple of latecomer photographers shouting, give us some shots with the belt Paddy. I've said, 'go on then,' turned to pick up the belt and it's gone. Disappeared from two feet behind my back.

I didn't panic straight away because it was feasible that one of the guys was having a closer look or that it had been passed round the group. Within a minute I'd established that wasn't the case and my insides turned to water. Distraught ain't a big enough word to describe how I felt. Honestly, I felt like crying, but this particular venue was hardly the place for that. Very quickly my despair at losing that symbol of my success turned to anger and I wanted to rip somebody's head off. But whose?

Cut a long story short, I steamed down to the manager's office and threatened, one, to throw him off the roof, and two, to burn his poxy shithole of a fuckin' doss house to the ground. This guy was bricking it 'cos he knew who I was but all he could stammer out was, 'sorry champ ... sorry champ.' I told him to pack up calling me fuckin' champ or I'd brain 'im. It was my anger and hurt talking 'cos I'm never normally that aggressive and lairy out of the ring. Still, didn't matter how much I raved and swore, the belt never showed up that day or any other day in the future.

Soon after Muhammad's win, a lot of the mail I got was concerned with new Ali fan clubs. This seemed to bother the members of our club more than it did me. I let everybody know that these other clubs had nothing to do with me and at the same time pointed out it was a free country and that my friendship with Muhammad didn't give me any monopoly. I added that I wouldn't be offended if any Ali fans bought stuff I couldn't supply, such as photos, posters, badges and t-shirts, from these new clubs. Give them their due, those fans were as loyal as you could find anywhere and I've still got most of their letters. One from Newcastle said:

> Where were these other fan clubs when Ali needed support? Where were they when you fought for Ali for years with your ALI IS OUR CHAMP campaign? Where was the organiser when you practically put your life on the line with those two head-on confrontations with Joe Frazier and George Foreman? I'll tell you where. They were following Frazier and Foreman all round London, trying to creep their way in to be part of their entourage. We shall never forget that you, Paddy, were the only one who kept faith with Ali. Your loyalty is unprecedented and it is an insult to you that anyone else should appoint himself as the President of a Muhammad Ali Fan Club.

There was another one from France:

> We want only one champion and we want only one fan club and we thank you, Paddy.

From Finland:

> I now hear about an Ali fan club in my country, but if it's not your project, then I don't want to know about it.

From Japan:

> If this club in my country is not yours I shall not write to them.
> They use only Muhammad's great and honourable name, but they
> bring dishonour upon themselves. You did not use his name for
> your glorification. You fought for his name and you fought for the
> man. My countrymen and I will always respect you. You are a man
> of honour.

Campbell Town:

> Fuck 'em, Paddy. They are boycotted. You're a hard act to follow.

I think it must have been round about at that point, with his
picture on most magazine covers, that he really did become the
most famous living person on this planet.

Perhaps the Pope or the President of the United States were
more famous, but how many ordinary people would actually
know both their names? Yet take a canoe up the Amazon with a
photo of Ali and I'll bet most of the native people would know
who they were looking at.

Christmas was coming up fast and it always depressed the shit
out of me. In a way, it's one of the best times of the year if you've
got a young family, but then again it was the young family that
gave me heartache because I couldn't afford to get them what
they wanted and what I wanted to give. One job after another
had folded. Regular employment was never regular for longer
than a couple of months. And Tommy had no title defences for
me lined up at this time of year. Then, out of the blue, I got the
chance that would solve my worries about Christmas.

A neighbour of mine called in to say goodbye before moving to
another part of the country. He'd been working on a building site

in Oxford and, knowing I was looking for any kind of work, suggested that it would be a good idea if I got myself down to the site and put my name up for the job before it got advertised.

I told him I'd set off walking there first thing in the morning, but he said, 'I'm leaving at 5am, so if you want a lift I'll drop you at the site. But, as it'll only take 20 minutes in the motor, you'll have a fair old wait because nobody turns up until at least eight o'clock.'

'Don't worry mate, I'd appreciate the lift and the wait won't bother me. I can't afford for anybody to beat me to that job.'

And that's how I came to be waiting, in the dark, at the building site, freezing my nuts off well before dawn on one of the coldest October mornings on record. When the site foreman eventually turned up, I was too cold to speak even though I was used to outside work. My usual uniform of jeans and a light denim jacket didn't do me no favours as far as keeping warm. The foreman lit a stove in the site hut and put a kettle on. Thank Christ for that because I'd emptied my flask about two hours before. It was a while before I could stop my teeth chattering long enough to explain why I was there.

'Fucking hell, son, you must be dead keen on getting a job if you've hung around here for nearly two hours in this weather ... I'll get the ganger over to see if the job's still going.' He came back to the shed in a couple of minutes with the ganger following him. Before this ganger even opened his mouth I was already thinking what a miserable-looking bastard he was. I wasn't wrong. Without a 'Hello, how are you?' or a 'Kiss my arse,' he snapped out, 'Job's taken.'

'How can it be taken? It's just become vacant.'

'You have to give notice when you leave here. We got two weeks from the other labourer and the job was filled next day.'

I'm a guy who gives respect but I like to get a bit of respect in return and the way this prick was talking to me made me want to put him on his back ... But ... He was the man who could make or break Christmas for my kids so I stayed calm.

'Look,' I said, 'I've worked on building sites before and I can turn my hand to most things. Surely there's ...'

'You're not fucking listening are you? There ain't no work available.' With that he stormed out, slamming the door, leaving me alone with the site-foreman, who was sympathetic. He offered me a couple of quid to tidy up and sweep out his office and that small gesture went a long way to restoring my faith in my fellow man – they ain't all c**ts. Still, I couldn't take money from his pocket. He probably had a family as well, so I thanked him and set off on my seven-mile journey back to Abingdon.

I felt sick at the thought of breaking the news to Sandra. I hadn't felt hungry since leaving home at five that morning but after three miles on the way back, my stomach started rumbling. Then I remembered the wrapped-up bag of sandwiches Sandra made up for me the night before. At that point we had been in good spirits and both felt we'd turned a corner as far as work was concerned. Opening the bag, I pulled out a sandwich, and at the same time found a note. It was from Sandra and the message choked me up: 'We don't need Father Christmas. All we need is you.'

By the time I got home I was knackered and feeling even more pissed off than I'd been before that job had been mentioned. Bills were mounting up and mixed up among the letters from Muhammad's fans were more final demands than we'd ever had before. Only the week before bailiffs had again tried to get a foot in the door and I'd had to kick them out. We were pretty used to having it rough but this was a real low spot. I sat with my head in my hands for ages trying to come up with an answer to our financial difficulties, then Sandra came in and said quietly, 'Don't worry, Paddy. Something will turn up.'

Something will turn up. Fucking hell, if I had a pound for every time I told myself that same thing, I wouldn't be so deep in the shit. I'd tried my hardest to get any sort of work at all. Seems laughable now, but I even tried to get a job delivering papers. Whichever way I turned I got a smack in the teeth. Christ. I'd wished so often that something would turn up, but it was no bloody use.

I heard a knock on the door and looked out of the window. Oh, fuck. A big, flash car was parked right outside and the only people in Abingdon who drove motors like that were officials on business – that could only mean trouble for us. My heart sank at the thought of getting an eviction notice just before Christmas. Then I thought, Okay, we haven't paid the rent for a bit but that didn't mean I had to roll over and take a load of shit from some stuck-up twat coming to my home and giving it the big 'un. When the knocker rattled I jumped up, almost ran to the door, ripped it open and found myself face to face with my friend Muhammad Ali.

For once in my life I was completely lost for words. It was unbelievable. There he was, as large as life, standing on the step of my run-down little council house. I was so shocked that one of the stupidest things I've ever said came falling out of my mouth.

'Muhammad – Muhammad, me ol' mate – is that you?'

'Hi, Paddy, ma'h friend.' He took off his tinted glasses and we had a proper cuddle.

There's no point in trying to describe how I felt. All I can say is that it was and always will be one of the highlights of my life. I'd started the day deep in desperation and depression. Now I felt absolutely on top of the world.

Muhammad Ali walked across my doorstep for the very first time, and with him was Howard Bingham, along with Pat Patterson and another fella I'd never met before. By now,

Sandra and the kids were back downstairs and I introduced my family to Muhammad. First, I started with Sandra, but when she moved her lips, nothing came out. She looked to me. 'Paddy, I can't speak.'

'Well, you jes' have,' Muhammad joked.

'I can't believe this is happening, but it ... it is ... Oh, thank you for coming to visit us, Muhammad.' Then she flew off into the kitchen to knock up some tea, coffee and sandwiches.

Now the kids were all over him. I mean all my kids knew him as well as they might know a favourite uncle because he'd not only been part of my life so long but theirs as well. Only difference was they'd never actually met him in the flesh. Muhammad loves children, and the little ones took it in turn to sit on his knee. While he was making a fuss of the kids, I was talking to Howard in the kitchen and he told me they'd just arrived from Zaire for a five-day visit to England. I told Howard that when I'd spoken to Ali on the phone he'd told me that he was going to call by and see me soon but that I'd never taken what he said too seriously.

'Paddy,' said Howard, 'you oughta know by now, with Muhammad, anything kin happen.'

After he'd finished fussing over the kids, Muhammad pulled out a crumpled piece of paper from his shirt-pocket. 'Hey – Paddy ... Ah wrote this out on the plane. It's a li'l ol' poem just for you. It's called "Paddy told 'em an' Ali showed 'em".'

Then he started to recite,

When Frazier and Foreman came to London Town
They couldn't make Paddy put his banner down.
It spelled out to them ALI IS OUR CHAMP
And he told Joe Frazier he was just a tramp.
He told George Foreman he was just the same
When the title changed hands he was just another name.

The true – and the People's Champ – had far too much class:
I went to Africa and I whupped George's ass.

'"Paddy told 'em and Ali showed 'em", by Muhammad for Paddy.' He laughed as he handed me the poem, saying, 'Yeh – we done it, brother, we done it. You told 'em, ah whupped him. Here, you like it?'

'Mate, I'm chuffed,' I said.

'Whazzat mean?' he asked.

'Chuffed? It means I'm well pleased with it.'

He repeated the word to himself like he was making sure he remembered it.

Sandra asked if he'd like another cup of tea and he gave me a crafty wink. After saying, 'No, thank you,' he turned to Howard and in a terrible imitation of a cockney accent said, 'Hey Bingham, d'you wan' anuvver cuppa char?'

Howard looked up, thinking his ears had deceived him, 'What did you say?'

'Cor, strewth. Oi sez ya wan' anuvver cuppa char?'

Howard, who talks with a slight stutter anyway, appeared to be quite puzzled by Ali's cockney questions. 'Ah do-don't know w-w-what you talkin' 'bout.'

'Oi sez a cuppa char – cuppa char.'

'What's a cuppa cha?'

'Man – you ignorant. Well, if you don't know, ah ain't gonna tell ya.'

While Howard was downing another cup of tea, Muhammad surprised me with: 'Paddy, you got anything planned for the next five days?'

'Well mate, I'll have to look in my engagement diary.'

'You kiddin' me man, right?'

'Yeah, I am, 'cos nothings changed over here, I ain't doing nothing.'

'Well,' he said, 'Ah'd like you to come with me while ah'm on the road here in England.'

'Right, mate, I'd be well chuffed.'

'Well chuffed, well chuffed? There ya go again. That's well pleased. Right?'

'Right,' I told him. 'Spot on.'

Sandra butted in with, 'Paddy, you can't go with Muhammad looking like that.'

'What you on about? Looking like what?'

'Just take a look at yourself.'

I stood up, spread my arms and looked down at my working gear. Bit of a joke, really, as work was the last thing I was going to do, though when I'd got dressed that morning I'd had high hopes that things were going to change on that score. I shot off upstairs to change into some decent clothes.

As I got dressed, I couldn't help thinking back to the day when Muhammad and me first met. His first words to me had been, 'Hi, man, how you doin'? What's your name?' He thought he'd met me before and I felt I'd met him somewhere before but knew I hadn't and now here he was drinking tea in my home.

The suit I put on was one of those that Muhammad had bought for me when we were in Oklahoma City and, as I stepped into the room, I could see he was surprised to see that I still had it. I don't particularly like wearing suits, so Sandra packed me a clean pair of jeans and a denim jacket. I put them into a carrier bag to take with me. Then Howard reminded him that he had a business appointment with a couple of businessmen who had made themselves a few million out of working in the world of British boxing.

Waving his hand, Ali said: 'Oh, shh. You call 'em Bingham an' tell 'em ah'm held up right now with some very important business. Tell 'em they can drop by an' see me later.' He sat back in the armchair with a smile that said it all. 'Ah like it here, anyways.' Howard got onto the phone to put off the meeting and told whoever it was that that he'd call back when Muhammad checked in at the Hilton.

I leant over and whispered into Ali's ear, 'You ain't nothing but a bullshitter.' He tried to get me into a headlock, but I backed out of reach. He seemed relaxed and happy in a home that was a million miles away from the lifestyle he was used to. And yet I never once felt that he looked down on our very basic living conditions or gave the impression that he felt it was any different from the New York Hilton or his own luxury home.

Before we left, he said to me, 'Paddy, ah wanna have a private word with you an' your wife.' The three of us went into the kitchen. He put his hand on my shoulder and looked at Sandra. 'Sandra, ah know Paddy here would never accept money from me. But it'll soon be Christmas. Now, we don't celebrate that festival, but ah know you do. Ah want you to take this an' buy your children some presents.' He handed her $600. Then he called out for Howard to come through. When his friend came into the kitchen, Muhammad said: 'Hey, Bingham, gimme a coupla hundred.' Howard passed him two hundred dollar bills and then went back into the front room.

'Now, here's eight hun'red for the little kids' presents. Ah'm givin' it to you, Sandra, 'cos ah know he'd never take it.' Sandra thanked him with tears in her eyes and gave him a big hug. I didn't need to say a word – he knew me well enough by now to know that sometimes words aren't necessary.

We looked each other in the eye, then tapping me on the shoulder, he said: 'C'mon, Paddy, we gotta go soon.'

I thought, Bloody hell, eight hundred dollars. And Ali was right, I'd never accept money from him personally, but this was an exception. It was for the kids and it came from his heart. I tell you it was a great feeling being able to tell the kids that Father

andra, Mamma, me, Tyrone and Clare 'The Moo' enjoying a night out
t Abingdon Fair.

Above: With Ali in my backyard.

Below: Ali and my son Tyrone squaring up under the clothesline to entertain the crowds that had gathered in my back garden. The cute little girl in between them is my youngest daughter Sarah.

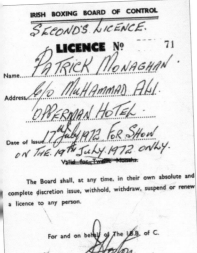

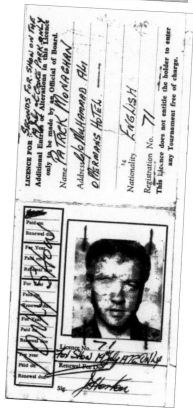

Some memorabilia.

Above left: Muhammad Ali's roadwork training boots.

Above right: My painting of Ali vs. Frazier: 'The Thrilla in Manila', signed by Muhammad.

Below left and right: The second's licence the Irish Boxing Board of Control reluctantly issued to me in July 1972. This unique licence entitled me to sit in Ali's corner during his bout with Al 'Blue' Lewis – I've been offered a lot of money for it over the years!

Above left: Presenting the People's Champ Trophy to Muhammad, New Jersey, 1972.

Above right: Catching up with some old pals. *From left to right*: John H. Stracey, a former World Welterweight Champion, Les Stevens and Ricky Porter, a former Southern Area Welterweight Champion.

Below: Sandra, Muhammad and me dressed up to the nines for a testimonial gala at the Grosvenor House Hotel in Park Lane, August 1977

Above left: Muhammad and my daughter Clare.

Above right: My old mate holding my beautiful granddaughter Nirvana.

© T. Bailey

Below: Outside my gaff with Tommy Heard, my former manager and best friend.

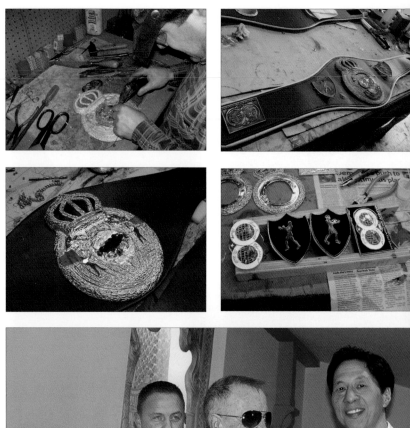

Above: The making of my replica World Championship Belt. Johnny Najjar, of Masis Boxing Belts, spent over 160 hours working on it.

Below: Sifu Samuel Kwok presenting my belt to me. Behind are my frien Naim Munshi and my son Tyrone.

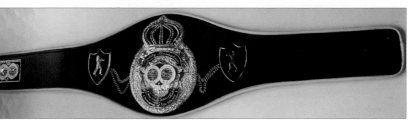

My replica World Championship Belt in its full fantastic glory.

Above: My good friend Thomas Mollan, me, my granddaughter Ella and my son Tyrone.

© Tony Frempong – Enniskillen

My dear friend posing for a snap with my wonderful family.

Christmas would be coming that year. Only Sandra knew how much that meant to me. As I kissed her on the cheek and told her that I'd see her in five days time, she looked at me and said quietly, 'Paddy, I still can't believe all this is happening.'

'Well, love, you'd better believe it.'

We eventually got away and I took the sack of mail and the telegrams with me. A chauffeur-driven Rolls Royce was parked outside the house and my neighbours were gawking at it. Saxton Road was the last place that anyone would expect to see a Roller. If a car like that was parked in any other street in the area the owner could expect to come back and find it balanced on a pile of bricks without its wheels. Outside Paddy Monaghan's house it was as safe as if it were parked in the Bank of England.

The neighbours were stunned when they saw who was coming out of my house. Who could blame them? If I didn't know the man and he turned up in a local street I'd have been first in the queue to have a gawp at him. There was no cheering or clapping, just an overawed silence as he climbed into the Rolls, raised his hand and waved at everybody, 'Hi, y'awl.'

I leaned back on the soft leather seats, a mind-boggling contrast to that seven-mile hike in the freezing cold. But there I was, sitting beside Ali as his Rolls Royce drove towards the Hilton Hotel in Park Lane. I was given my own room right next to Muhammad's VIP suite on the tenth floor, the last place where anyone would expect to find an unemployed labourer getting his head down.

Ali's first engagement was his first-ever talk show in Europe, at the Victoria Theatre. I didn't know he'd been due in England, because I hadn't read a newspaper for a couple of weeks – to tell the truth I had better things to spend my money on than newspapers. Every single seat in the theatre was sold out.

First, there was a film of his fight with George Foreman. He hadn't seen it, so the organisers reserved half-a-dozen seats at the back of the theatre with security guards in front and at the sides. When the lights went down, we slipped in without being noticed by the audience. Gasps and cheers went up as everyone watched him sucker Foreman time after time, drawing George into throwing wallops that missed.

I heard some bird sitting not far from us say, 'Isn't he gorgeous?' And different males voices whispered, 'He's the greatest ever.'

Muhammad tapped my arm and crouched lower in his seat, with his knees on the back of the seat in front. He had something up his sleeve and it wasn't long before I found out what it was. He disguised his voice and began to join in with remarks of his own. 'Oh, he's just got to be the greatest ... Oh, look at this, look at him now ... Ooh, what skill.'

I remember hearing a gravelly voice coming from just a few rows in front: 'Oi, mush. You at the back. Knock it on the 'ead, will ya?'

Muhammad's diary was packed solid with functions and all kinds of appearances. Everywhere we went he always made it clear to the organisers that I would be beside him, so there was little chance of slip-ups, though I never knew where we were going from one day to the next, or on what day to wear my suit or my denims.

One time I went with him to a London sports club where he was guest of honour at a dinner organised by Mickey Duff. The place wasn't really a club for sportsmen in the true sense of the word. It was more of a businessman's meeting place for those who had the right credentials and dough. It was that type of gaff that had thick carpets and crystal chandeliers and smelt of brandy and fine cigars. I couldn't have got in on my own in a thousand years. I remember the looks I got from the members. I was a stranger to everybody, but that didn't explain the shocked expressions and the stares that were directed at me. I found out the reason for this later. I had broken the club rules by not wearing a dinner suit and a tie. I was in my denim jacket and a pair of jeans and I must've stuck out like a sore dick.

Mickey Duff explained the club's rules about dress and asked if I would mind taking a seat towards the back of the room. It was a table right to the rear and my seat was against the wall. Muhammad was at the top table. By his side were people like Sean Connery, David Frost, Henry Cooper, racing driver Graham Hill and loads of other celebrities.

Muhammad took his seat, then looked around the place. He waved Mickey Duff over to him with a signal that meant he'd like a word. After a few words, Duff nodded his head and pointed his finger towards me. I gave Muhammad a wave and he waved back.

I gave a nod and a polite, 'Good evening' to the members sitting at my table. Not one of them stuck up c***ts acknowledged me. They looked up, gave me a blank stare and then more or less turned their backs on me. I knew that if I tried to kick off any sort of conversation I'd be ignored, so I only opened my mouth to make the most of the food on the table.

Now, I might not have had much education, but I didn't have any problem behaving in company. All the credit for that goes to my Ma. No messing when it came to her when we were kids. No elbows on the table, no talking with our mouths full, knife and fork at right angles to the plate when you're finished and so on. So with that drummed into me I could be taken anywhere ... and be invited back.

So by the time this lot, who still hadn't said a word to me, were delicately dabbing their lips with napkins, I'd had enough of their stuck-up ways, so I deliberately wiped my mouth with my sleeve and gave a noisy belch. If I'd slapped my old chap on the table I couldn't have got a better reaction.

It all went quiet and they all looked at each other. Then one of them took it on himself to be spokesman for all of them and said, 'I say, tell me this, just how on earth were you allowed in here tonight?'

With a serious look on my face I said, 'Probably because them on the door thought I was with Muhammad Ali.' They fell about laughing, thinking it was the most unlikely and funniest thing they'd ever heard. I didn't give a shit. I had my own silent chuckle and left it at that.

Then it was time for the after-dinner speeches and it was soon Muhammad's turn. I couldn't even look at those wankers on my table or I would have burst out laughing as he gave me a sign to come and stand beside him. He put his arm round my shoulder and introduced me to all the toffs.

'Paddy's friendship,' he said, 'means more to me than that of any other person here tonight. Ah've got business associates among you, but a relationship based on business must not be confused with the relationship of a true friend. True friendship is all about givin' without expectin' nothin' in return. "Friendship" is a word that is used far too lightly. True friendship has a very special meaning, and if it's not understood then we will never know the meaning of it. Ah'm happy to be here, to talk to y'awl and see y'awl here tonight on such a grand occasion and ah say that with all sincerity. But the most sincere part of my stay here in England will be when ah visit Paddy an' his family again at his home in Abingdon ... Why? 'Cos Paddy Monaghan is my true friend.'

Muhammad's speech received a great reception from all the toffs. I shook his hand and whispered into his ear: 'Thanks, mate, appreciate it.' But then, as I went to leave the platform, he gripped my shoulder as tight as he could. Still smiling, he whispered, 'Shit you ain't goin' nowhere my man.' Then he spoke into the microphone. 'C'mon, Paddy, and say a few words.'

Caught on the hop, I didn't have too much to say. 'Well, first I'd like to add my congratulations to Muhammad for regaining his title a few weeks ago. A title that he won but never lost in the ring; a title that certain people robbed him of back in 1967. Since then he has won another title, one that is even more important than the Heavyweight Championship of the World. What's more, it's a title that is his and his alone and one nobody can ever take away from him – Muhammad Ali, the People's Champion. I can think of no greater honour than to share with him a true and lasting friendship. Thank you, Muhammad.' The members of that club gave me another nice reception and I slipped away quick as I could.

The following day we went to the Mayfair Theatre where Muhammad appeared on a TV programme presented by Michael Parkinson. We were just making our way back to the car when I heard puffing and panting from behind us and a voice calling out, 'Muhammad, Muhammad.' Looking over my shoulder, I saw Brian Clough pushing his way through a load of other celebrities who were trying to get to catch up with us.

'Muhammad, please, just one minute ...'

Ali stopped and turned to Cloughie, who had two children with him. He wanted Muhammad's autograph for them. Ali scribbled his signature, tapped the two youngsters on their heads and got into the car. He was hurrying to get back to the hotel, as he was expecting an important phone call from the States.

Obviously, Muhammad hadn't recognised Clough from their meeting at the press conference in Madison Square Garden's. I said to him: 'You see that geezer there?'

'Which one?'

'Him, the one with his face right up to the window waving at you.'

'What about him?'

'He's one of the biggest names in British sport.'

'What sport is he into?'

'He's a football manager.'

'You mean soccer? What's his name?'

'Brian Clough.'

'Never heard of him.'

Telegrams poured in for Muhammad over those few days. So many came that it would've taken long enough to count them, let alone read them. Within a couple of days there were quite a lot addressed to me. Some were from Ali fans, but others were from national newspaper editors, all much the same: 'Dear Mr Monaghan. Am interested in your story, exclusively. Please telephone to negotiate terms.' I wasn't interested and I didn't follow them up.

But, despite how busy he was, Muhammad still found time to come to my house again before he went back to the States. He told me that he'd visit my family on the day before he left. That day he was due to appear at the Royal Albert Hall and Howard later told me that the big noises in London didn't like the idea of his visiting Abingdon at all because of potential delays. In fact, they couldn't understand why he wanted to travel to my home on any day. He'd never visited any of their posh homes, so why should he visit mine? My attitude was, 'Fuck 'em all.'

Before the Abingdon trip, Ali said to me: 'Paddy, phone your home. Ah wanna say hello to your children.' I spoke to them all and then passed the phone to Muhammad and he chatted to them one by one, then said that he'd see them the following day.

When my youngest, at the time, Belinda was on the phone, I could hear her cooing, so Ali said into the receiver, 'Coochi coochi coo.' He laughed and sat back, then handed me the phone and I had a chat with Sandra. But before I signed off, Muhammad called over, 'Paddy, tell Sandra, Bingham says to have anuvver cuppa tea ready for him.'

Around three o'clock the following afternoon, we left Park Lane and headed for Abingdon. After just over an hour's drive the limo turned into Saxton Road and, as we drove towards my house, I could see a large crowd of people outside it. Muhammad stepped out of the motor and was met by a deafening cheer. We almost had to fight our way through the people to get to my door. Sandra, Mamma and the children stood in the hallway. Men and women, young and old, were reaching out to touch him.

My wife, kids and Mamma welcomed Muhammad into our home. Ma had always been a great fan of his, not a boxing fan but a mother who could appreciate what a fine, clean-cut man he was. When she was introduced to him, she broke into tears, overjoyed that he was really there. She held his hand and said with her broad Irish accent: 'Look, will yer look. It's yerself. Aah – God bless ye.'

I noticed a large, life-sized poster of Muhammad on the wall that wasn't normally there. Sandra said the children had kept at her to put it up to make him feel welcome. She looked at Howard. 'Right, Howard. I'm going to make "anuvver cuppa tea" for you and Muhammad.'

Muhammad sat in the armchair, surrounded by the children, and they all took it in turns to sit on his knee. When Sandra came out of the kitchen with the tea and sandwiches, I asked her, 'How come there's a crowd of people outside? 'Cos no one knew he was coming.'

She said, 'You might ask. They've been there since Muhammad flew in because they'd heard rumours he'd be coming back here but they didn't know when. They've been out there waiting every day since.'

'No kiddin'?' said Muhammad, 'You sayin' they have been waitin' outside your home, for me, every day since ah arrived in the country?'

'That's right, Muhammad, every single day.'

The chanting outside the house became louder and louder. Then Muhammad stood up and said that he'd talk to the people from the doorstep. I opened the front door and couldn't believe that what had been a large crowd half-an-hour before now filled the street from side to side as far as the eye could see.

The local group of Morris dancers had turned out in their traditional gear and he was blown away when they broke into a routine for him. Somebody in the crowd started singing that song that used to be about the Beatles, but they changed the name just for Muhammad, 'We love you, Ali, we love you too, Ali we love you ... ' In no time the whole street was joining in. But when he raised his hand, you could have heard a pin drop.

'Why, thank you ... an' ah love y'awl, too.'

This brought shouts of, 'Speech. Speech.'

He gave a few words to the people of Abingdon thanking them for such a warm and friendly reception and then told them, 'Mah visit here to Paddy an' his family at his home here is the most important item on this trip to England. Ah've taken time out to come to your li'l town to honour my main man Paddy. Until ah met him, ah'd never even heard of Abingdon. And from Paddy, here in this country, from this town, from this place, came mah title: the People's Champion. It's a title never heard before, but now it's known all over the world. An' as befittin' mah title, ah represent the workin' class people of the world, regardless of colour, or creed or nationality. Ah'm with you.'

This brought another loud cheer. Ali reminded the crowd of his tight arrangements and that he had to keep an important engagement in London that night.

'But before ah go ah jes' wanna spend more time with Paddy

an' his family inside.' About to close the door, he called to the crowd: 'D'ya want Paddy to invite me back here again?'

'Yes!' they screamed.

He put one hand to his ear. 'Whatta ya say? Lemme hear it again.'

'Yes!'

Before he closed the door, he called out, 'Ah shall return.'

And he has returned – on almost every trip he's made to England since.

Back inside he carried on chatting with me and my family in the sitting room against a background of chanting from outside. I was well chuffed with the welcome the people in my street had given him. As far as the family were concerned, they all had a very special place for him in their hearts and they loved him dearly. As for me, well, what can I say except that he was family?

I went back to London with him for our last night together and we spent it at the Royal Albert Hall, which, like every other occasion, was a sell-out.

The next day we said goodbyes at the airport as he set off for his trip back to America.

CHAPTER TWELVE

Good Times, Bad Times

I t's a strange life … when Muhammad Ali comes over to your house for tea. After the whirlwind of his visit to the UK, things settled back to normal quickly and soon it was as if he had never been there. Then, exactly one week later, I picked up a newspaper and on the front page was a photo of Muhammad and Gerald Ford, President of the United States, shaking hands in the Oval Room of the White House. What can I possibly add to that?

The people of Abingdon, my friends and all our neighbours were delighted, bless 'em. It was a different story for the councillors and other officials in the town. They were criticising me in the local paper and on local radio for not introducing them to Muhammad, yet these were the very same people who'd said in 1967, 'Why is Paddy Monaghan creating such a fuss for someone he's never met and is never likely to meet?' They knocked me and no doubt, behind my back, thought I was due for a straitjacket.

It reminded me a bit of *Little Red Hen*, one of the kids stories I learned to read with – you probably read it when you were five, rather than 17. This hen asked all kinds of animals to help her plant the corn, clear the weeds, then help to harvest the crop. They all said, 'No', but when the bread was made from the corn they all wanted to eat it. Little Red Hen told them to fuck off. Okay, those last words are mine, but I knew how she felt and that's exactly how I felt about those stuck-up officials. They had to eat their words and I hoped it choked them.

Their criticism was a bit out of place anyway. Muhammad's visit to me was private and personal. He didn't turn up to make a public appearance, though he was good enough to speak to the people that mattered outside my house. Something else. Saxton Road was a notorious no-go area. You could've stood at my front door for 12 months and you'd never see the mayor or any of the local big shots walk past – apart from election times, and even then they were few and far between. So, there you have it. Apart from the odd few, the whole town was delighted. As for my family, they were overjoyed.

Muhammad Ali has visited my home on eight different occasions since. His visits have become a normal part of every trip he makes to this country. When I was with him in the States during 1991 he promised that when he pays another unofficial visit to England he'll stay at my house for a week.

In 1975, the People's Champ went on to make four successful defences of his title. The first was against Chuck Wepner and he stopped him in the very last round. Then he beat Ron Lyle in the eleventh round. And next he out-pointed Joe Bugner in Kuala Lumpur.

Ali always liked Joe and I did as well. He was a decent sort of guy and I don't think he got the credit he deserved from the British press and public. In the same way that Gene Tunney was never forgiven for licking a living legend, Jack Dempsey, back in the 1920s, the media and the fans never forgave Joe Bugner for beating Henry Cooper.

The final defence was to be made against my almost-sparring partner, Joe Frazier. This was the third clash between the pair. Never before, and never since, has there ever been a World Championship fight to compare with it. Perhaps there never will be a fight to match it. Muhammad won when Joe Frazier's trainer took the gloves from his man's hands at the end of the 14th. Frazier had taken so much punishment that Futch wouldn't allow him to answer the bell for the 15th round. But don't imagine that the fight had been one-sided. Right to the end, the outcome was in doubt, with Joe battling back. Ali was the master, but when Frazier was forced to retire, Muhammad almost collapsed with exhaustion.

I always thought that these two rivals brought out the best in each other. But boxing is a young man's sport and Ali was 35 years old. I often think about what Ali might have done to Frazier in his prime, and I come to same conclusion every time: he would've beaten him long before the 14th round.

About a week after their fight, I telephoned Muhammad.

'Hello, me old friend,' I said.

'Paddeee. How you doin', man? Glad you called.'

'How you feeling mate?'

'Still achin', man, still achin'. Ah never had to fight like that before in mah life.'

'How did you feel afterwards?'

'With the heat of those TV lights, an' in that kinda climate with no air-conditionin' and then havin' Frazier in the ring makin' me fight like that to whup him – well, afterwards I jes' felt exhausted. But ah guess it was even worse for Joe.'

'But you're okay now – yeah?'

'Sure, I'm okay. Still a few aches an' bruises around the ribs and hip sockets where he hit me low – arms, legs, back, front, head, hands, feet … a broken ear drum.' He laughed, 'Want me to carry on? Nah, don't worry, Paddy, ah'm okay. Jus' wanna rest up a little, an' ah'll be fine. Hey, didja like the fight?'

'It was the greatest heavyweight fight I've ever seen, but, no – I didn't like watching it.'

'What's that supposed to mean?'

'Well, you're my friend, right?'

'Right.'

'Well, nobody would want to see his friend in the ring with Joe Frazier.'

There was a silence. Then he said, 'Yeah, ah git your meanin'. But it musta bin harder for a friend of Joe's to watch than it was for any friend of mine. Right?' Then he changed the subject. 'Hey, Paddy, give mah love to all your family.'

'They all send their love, too,' I told him. 'Well, what you doing now?'

'Ah'm talkin' to you on the phone. Why you talk so dumb?'

'You know what I mean. What are you gonna do after you've had a rest?'

'Next week, they want me to attend a United Nations reception in New York. After that, I'm gonna sit down an' sort out what's happenin' next. Ah've got so much goin' on around me, but ah'm used to it by now. Ah kin handle it okay.'

He finished with, 'Take care, Paddy. And ah'll call you an' let you know whenever ah'll be comin' to England again.'

'Okay. God bless you and I'll see ya when I sees ya.'

I felt a lot better knowing that he was all right, in spite of his aches and pains. It was the greatest, but the most brutal, heavyweight title fight in history. In all the many years I'd spent watching Ali in the ring, I'd never felt such concern for his wellbeing as at that time. If Frazier had managed to last the full 15 rounds, I've no doubt in my mind that Muhammad would've won on points. Even so, he took a proper battering from one of the toughest hookers who ever threw a punch.

It was early in the new year that Muhammad rang me one

morning – at about 4am, he must have forgotten the time difference – to let me know that he'd just bought a farm near Berrien Springs, a small town in Michigan. He invited me over, paid for my trip and showed me all round the 88 acres of beautiful scenery. The whole place was so quiet and peaceful and a long, long way from the bright lights and roaring crowds.

The place had been built by none other than Al Capone, the Chicago gangster. I suppose films like *Scarface* and others and his catchy name made him stick in the public's mind. It seemed strange that I was sitting in the old house of a world-famous guy, having it described to me by another world-famous guy. Straight as he was in a business dominated by 'families', I think Muhammad got a kick out of who'd owned his house 50 years before.

I remember sitting in his lounge and him saying, 'An' the guy who ah bought this house from told me that the place once had tunnels leading up to it from the river, so that Capone could have his bootlegging deliveries an' p'raps a squealer or two brought straight up to the house outa sight o' the cops and Feds.'

At first, I thought Ali was winding me up, like people do when they say there's a ghost in your bedroom. On a later trip to the farm, I found out he'd been telling the truth. Floyd Bass, a local guy, who for some reason was also known as Hodge, used to be caretaker there and he put me straight on the tunnels and other bits and pieces. But, I've got to say, as hard as he tried, he never managed to convince me that Capone wasn't all bad.

'Ah s'pose you heard an' read a lot of bad things about Capone?' he asked me one day.

'Well, I hear he was a pretty nasty bastard.'

'Sure, he done a lot of bad things, but he done some good ones, too. Believe it or not, he helped a lot of people who needed it. He was one of them guys who set up free soup kitchens for all them poor and destitute people in Chicago an' other places durin' the Depression.'

'Well from what I've seen in films he was a murderer and about as bad as he could get.'

'Can't argue with that Paddy. He killed other gangsters, but all in the way of business and most of 'em deserved to be bumped off. He also saved a lot of innocent people from dyin' of hunger. An' it may surprise you to know that around these parts there are folks whose grandparents knew him. They all have their stories about Al and they got plenty of good stuff to say about him. Does that surprise you?'

I enjoyed meeting Hodge. He was a friendly and cheerful character and I looked forward to seeing him again. But it's hard to think of Al Capone as a Robin Hood type, or maybe I was just a bit too cynical to be won over completely. As far as the farm goes, I've heard it said many times that Muhammad bought it in 1980. But the truth is he actually bought it in 1976 before he moved to Los Angeles. He moved back to settle on the farm whenever he could. A great deal of his time was spent in travelling, due to the demand for his personal appearances throughout America and the world.

The reason I know for sure that he owned the place in 1976 was that me and him watched the 1976 Montreal Olympics on the giant TV screen he had put in the farmhouse. We saw a young Leon Spinks win the Olympic heavyweight gold medal, and I can remember Muhammad's actual words during the finals: 'If that kid gets the right trainer an' the right manager, he'll make it big some day after ah retire. His main fault right now is that he fights with his mouth open. He gotta get outa that habit, 'cos he could get his jaw broke like that.'

Ali was always a guy who seemed to be able to look ahead – at least a little, but surely he couldn't see what was going to happen two years in the future when he came up against Spinks himself.

One of the things I enjoyed at Muhammad's home were the meal times. I've never eaten such beautiful dinners in my life as those cooked by his Muslim cook, the late Lana Shabazz. She was the greatest cook in the world and I even include my mamma in that. Whenever I'd turn up at Muhammad's home, Lana would always welcome me with a big smile and the words: 'It's soul time for Paddy Monaghan.' As well as being a great cook, Lana was also a great lady. A wonderful person and I was very sad to hear of her death in 1990.

One afternoon during my first visit to the farm in 1976, Muhammad and me were sitting outside on a little curved stone wall. We were in the shade, chatting and joking, when he heard the phone ringing. Ali answered it in the kitchen. I heard him say, 'Okay, drive on in.' Then he pressed the gadget that opened the gates away in the distance at the front of the farm. He came outside saying, 'Shit, it's Don King. Ah done him a favour once, when he came outa prison. Ah helped him get on his feet when ah boxed an exhibition for him in Cleveland an' he's bin on my back ever since. An' look where he is today. Ah made those guys – him an' others, includin' Bob Arum. Instead of working with each other they fight with each other. Ah'm getting fed up with all these dudes.'

A few seconds later, a fancy car pulled right up where we were sitting. Don King got out with a fixed smile on his face and that comical, 'I've just had an electric shock' hairstyle of his.

'Muhammad Al-lee – mah main man – mah brother – mah best friend in the whoooole wide world.'

Muhammad whispered in my ear, 'Listen to this cat, he's full o' shit.'

King jabbered on, but Muhammad cut him off.

'Okay, cut the shit. What you doin' here uninvited? For all you knew ah might not been at home.'

That knocked the smile off his face for a bit, but he soon stuck it back on. 'Heh – heh – heh. Ah knew you was here, champ, ah knew.'

'Well, jes' how did ya know?'

243

'Oh, ah got friends, champ, ah got friends.

'Yeah, ah knows that. Jes' how much d'you pay 'em to be your friends?'

'What, champ? Everyone who knows you cares for you, man, an' they all know that no one cares for you more than ah do. Ah had some business to deal with down in Indiana, an' ah was just drivin' by, so ah jes' had to drop in an' see you, mah brother, mah champ, 'cos you mah main man.'

'You jes' happened to be drivin' by – yeah, yeah.' As they walked towards the house, Muhammad signalled for me to follow them, and inside I'm laughing my bollocks off because it was so obvious King didn't want me around. I mean that smile of his turned on and off like a light as he looked me up and down, thinking: What the fuck is he doin' here?

He gave me the cold shoulder and when he said that he wanted to talk in private, Muhammad told him: 'Anythin' you have to say, go ahead. 'Cos he's mah friend.' So I stayed put. Don didn't like it but he did go ahead. It was there and then that I first heard the news about the possibility of a forthcoming Ali-Norton fight. King wanted to promote the fight, but more than that, I think, he didn't want Bob Arum to promote it. Tough shit for Don King because Arum eventually did.

Seemed that Don King didn't like the idea of Muhammad's manager, Herbert Muhammad, doing business with Arum, a white promoter. Not surprising when the other guy was coining a few million that Don thought should go into his own pocket. King did his best to wipe Arum out with the old black and white shit and made it clear that he didn't like Herbert.

'Us brothers gotta stick together, champ,' King said, 'Ah can't understand why Herbert tries to separate us by dealin' with white trash like Arum. Ah care for you, champ. Like ah say, you mah main man, mah brother. Ah care for you more than anyone else. You knows that.'

I thought he was talking such a load of old crap that I felt like getting up and having a walk, but at the same time I have to admit I was enjoying how uncomfortable Muhammad was making him, so I sat tight. Muhammad was putting him right in his place. 'Look, ah've tol' you before: if you got any business you wanna talk about, then do it with Herbert. You gettin' greedy, man. Ah remember you when you had nothin' but holes in your pockets. If it wasn't for Herbert an' me you wouldn't be here today. You were a better man when you had them holes in your pockets. Now you walk about in thousand-dollar suits, drive fancy cars, buyin' up fancy property and there ain't nothin' wrong with that, but your success has turned to greed for power an' control. Herbert an' me were glad to see you make it, that's why we helped you, but now you disappointed us with your greed.'

'No champ, no ... There's a conspiracy against me. Some people have been tellin' you bad things about me. They're lies, all lies. Why, ah got nothing but care in mah heart. There ain't no greed. They been tellin' you lies, mah brother. They jealous 'cos ah'm the biggest, the best, the blackest an' most beautiful promoter in the world an' the white man, he don't like that. Right on, brother.'

'Ah don't care if they black or white,' Ali told him, 'or pink or yeller or even if they li'l ol' green men from Mars. Anyone who wanna do business with me will have to go an' talk with Herbert first – an' that includes you.'

'Hey, champ, this is jes' a social visit, brother. Ah jes' dropped by 'cos ah wanted to see you. You're mah main man.'

I don't think King had the slightest idea that he was making a prick of himself or how false everything he said sounded.

I could see my mate was getting the right arsehole but good manners were such a part of life to him I doubt it even crossed his mind to tell Mr Haircut to fuck off. Taking the piss though was something else. Ali looked over at me and winked, always a signal that he was up to no good. I knew something was ticking over in his head, but I didn't know what.

'Have you met mah ol' friend Ringo before?' he said to King, who had a puzzled look on his face when he glanced at me. Keep it in mind that he'd cold-shouldered me all the time he'd been in the room.

'No, ah don' think ah have, champ.'

'Whassa matter with you? You bin livin' in a cave all your life? Can't you see who he is?'

'Ringo? Ringo? Now ... the face looks familiar, very familiar.'

I sat there, playing along thinking, What? My face familiar? What a load of bollocks.

'That's Ringo Starr, of course,' said Ali 'He's one o'the Beatles. Now don't tell me you ain't ever heard of the Beatles.'

King let out a roar. 'Aah. Of course. Ringo Starr. John, Paul, George an' Ringo.'

Now I was in a fucking bear hug and I looked over King's shoulder to see Ali laughing. He coughed and put on a straight face. I look nothing at all like Ringo Starr, but King believed him.

'Sure, I knew it was you, Ringo. I was jes' waitin' for the champ to introduce us.' What a twat.

King handed me, his business card and said, 'If there's anythin' ah can do for you, Ringo, jes' call me any time. Jes' what are you an' the rest o' the Beatles doin' with yourselves these days?'

That threw me, but Muhammad jumped in with, 'Ringo's over her to see me 'cos he wants me to talk to John, Paul, an' George and get the Beatles back together again.'

Don practically fell off his seat, 'Wow, ah can jes' picture it champ. Imagine it. You introducin' "The Return of the Beatles" at the Hollywood Bowl. It'd be the biggest attraction in history an' ah could put it together in a package like no-one else. You know that, champ ... When you an' Ringo have sorted things out call me. It's gotta be done right an' ah'm the man to do it – right, champ?'

The way Muhammad came out with, 'Well, ah dunno. What do ya think, Ringo mah friend?' Almost had me thinking me and the boys were gonna get back into business. Trouble was, Muhammad's play-acting didn't come as easily to me as it did to him, so I kept getting stuck for words.

'I ... er ... ah... What do I think? Er... I'll just leave everything to you, Muhammad.'

'See, champ?' King burst in again. 'Ringo knows ah is the man for the job ... Why, this is gonna be the biggest show on earth. C'mon, champ, Ringo says it's up to you, an' you know there ain't no-one who kin put it on like ah can, my brother.'

'You still gonna have to talk to Herbert,' insisted Ali.

'Why do ah have to talk to Herbert about the Beatles? He ain't got nothin' to do with Ringo or the other Beatles, so why would I have to talk to him?'

''Cos he's mah manager, that's why.'

'Yeah – but he don't manage the Beatles.'

'If ah get the Beatles to make a comeback, then he's got everythin' to do with it. Right, Ringo?' said Ali

'That's right, Muhammad,' I told him.

'Okay – Okay.' King agreed. 'We can still all work something out, champ. Whaddaya think, Ringo?'

'Well, like I said – it's all up to Muhammad.'

'Yeah, Don,' Ali told him. 'Don't be too hasty, 'cos ah got to talk to the other Beatles yet, an' see if they ready to make a comeback.'

'If anyone kin bring 'em together again, it's you, champ. Ah've read that the Beatles are among your greatest fans. Right, Ringo?'

'Yeah. That's true.'

'Right. Now, you're willin' to make a comeback, even if it's jes' for only one show, if the other three agree. Is that right Ringo?'

'Yep. It's just all up to Muhammad to talk John, Paul an' George into it.'

'He'll do it, Ringo. He'll do it, They'll do it for you, champ. They love you. The world loves you. An' ah love you, mah brother, 'cos you're the greatest.'

Ali was twisting him round his finger. 'You still gotta talk to Herbert, Don.'

'Of course ... Why, you didn't' think ah'd try to get to you around by the back door, did you, Muhammad?'

'You ain't as dumb as you look,' Ali told him.

'Say, what a night it'd be if ah promoted your match with Norton in a package with the return of the Beatles on the same show. You think about it an' talk to Ringo. It would be the greatest event of all time.'

'Don't get carried away, now,' said Ali. 'Take it easy. An when the time comes you can talk to Herbert ... '

'Herbert? Yeah sure, Herbert. Say, does anyone else know you're here tawkin' to Ali 'bout getting your group back together again, Ringo?'

'No. No one.'

'No, man,' said Ali. 'Ain't no one knows about the Beatles getting back together again 'til ah talk to 'em all. So keep quiet, you the only one who knows.'

'Okay, okay, Ringo. That's good. Let's keep it that way. Later on, ah'm gonna do the biggest PR job in history. After ah talk to Herbert, that is.'

King went rabbitting on for another couple of hours, kissing our arses the whole time and telling Ali what a great fighter he was and then telling me that I was the greatest drummer since Buddy Rich, whoever he was. It was lucky Muhammad didn't have a drum kit or he'd have had me banging the bollocks out of them for hours. And guess what? He even asked me to sign my autograph on a photo of Ali. He asked me to write: 'To my good and close friend Don, from your pal always, Ringo Starr'.

I signed it along with Muhammad, who just wrote his name and dated the photo.

Muhammad had only recently returned from a tour of the Far East – Japan and Korea. In Tokyo he'd been disappointed in the fight with the World Heavyweight martial art Champion, Antonio Inoki. The guy had crawled around on his arse doing nothing the whole time except kick at Muhammad's legs. I asked him why Inoki hadn't stood up and fought and he said that the man was scared stiff.

When they had originally arranged for him to meet the wrestler, the Japanese promoters had wanted them to go along with a script. 'But ah said: "No fix. It gotta be for real." But ah never figured this would frighten the dude so much that he'd slide around on his ass, kickin' mah legs all night. Ah never wanted to hit an opponent like ah did that Inoki. Ah wouldn't have hurt him, ah'd have jes' played with him for a couple rounds and put in two or three good clean shots an' taken him out. But when he jes' crawled around on that canvas ah couldn't git a chance to pop at him.'

Muhammad showed me his legs and they were bruised from knee to ankle. If that had been me, I would've given him a kick in the nuts if that's the game he wanted to play, Japanese hero or not.

Ali was resting his legs up as much as possible, before starting preparations for a forthcoming defence of his heavyweight title, his third match with Ken Norton. Although there was a bit of a dispute over the scoring, he came out the winner after 15 rounds. Earlier in his career I reckon he could've finished Norton off in five rounds, and it was then I started to think it was about time my friend should consider retiring. Trouble was, I couldn't bring myself to tell him outright, so I'd drop hints every now and then, like, 'Well my old mate, you've done it all now. There's nothing left for you to do.'

Did he pick up on my hints? Did he fuck. He carried on boxing for another five years. And during that time he lost and then won back his title, and both times it was against Leon Spinks – the 'Kid' who he'd been so impressed with that day on the farm.

Muhammad Ali announced his retirement in 1979, undefeated champion, and I wish he'd stayed retired. But he just couldn't keep himself out of the ring. He came back in 1980 and challenged the reigning champion, Larry Holmes, who'd been his sparring partner years before. It was a very bad move and everybody, including me, who'd always had the greatest faith in him, realised he didn't have a chance against Holmes, who was younger and superbly fit. It broke my heart to see him humiliated when the fight that should never had started was stopped in the tenth. I'll tell you what, I've watched that fight on video many times since and I'm not ashamed to admit that watching my defeated friend, head bowed and slumped on his stool at the end, never fails to bring a lump to my throat.

Incredibly, he made another comeback, just over a year later, but after taking a beating from Trevor Berbick at last he decided to call it a day. He never mentioned it at the time, but a long time after he told me that before these two final fights he'd been diagnosed as being in the early stages of Parkinson's.

On the home front, me and Sandra were blessed by the birth of another beautiful daughter. We called her Sarah.

I retired myself at the end of 1980, as the undefeated BKB Middleweight Champion of the World. For something to do with the skills I'd picked up over the years, I took up being a licensed professional boxing trainer. One of the fighters I trained was David Pearce, who, I like to think, with my help went on to became a British Heavyweight Champion. Another Welshman I trained was George Sutton, 'the bad boy of British boxing'.

In 1981, during his training for a match against top featherweight contender Vernon Penpras, we'd moved to Cardiff and stayed with his parents. We'd been there a couple of weeks when I was woken up by a weird nightmare where I'd been dreaming I was dead. I seemed to be floating in the air and looking down on myself lying in a bed with my wife and family round it crying. I called down to Sandra and the kids, 'Stop crying. I'm not dead, I'm here. Just look up, look up and you'll see I'm okay.' But it didn't matter how loud I shouted, they still couldn't hear me. In the end I woke up, sweat pouring off me and frightened shitless because it had seemed so real. It haunted me all that day and only slipped into the back of my mind after about a week, but it was still there and it still is, even today.

About a week later me and Georgie came back from an early morning training run. At the same time as he said, 'Bung the kettle on,' right out of the blue I was doubled up with a crushing pain in my chest. Georgie thought I was larking about and through the pain I heard him say, 'Oh yeah, very funny. You making out that three miles running has fucked you up so bad you can't make a cuppa?' I raised my head and he saw the expression on my face. The sweat came pouring off me and I thought, Oh no, not that fucking blood pressure thing I'd had years ago.

Georgie wanted to get an ambulance and doctor right there and then, but I told him, 'No'. The pain was worse than it was the previous time in my front room and I guessed something a bit serious was going on, but stupidly thought I'd be better off back in Abingdon if I needed hospital treatment. I was thinking as well that I wanted Sandra and my kids around me.

Still doubled over, I told Georgie to get my gear into a suitcase because we were going to head back to Abingdon. Georgie and his dear old mum and dad were trying to make me see sense and agree to at least see a doctor, but stubborn bastard that I was I insisted that I was going to drive back home.

Georgie had the bags packed by now and said: 'But Paddy you can't drive in that state.'

'Don't worry, I'll do it, Georgie, I'll do it even it kills me.' When I said it, I didn't mean it literally, but I found out a lot later that's exactly what I came close to doing.

It was a two-and-a-half hour drive and the pain never stopped for a minute. What made it worse was being blinded by the sweat running into my eyes and the effort of changing gear with pain shooting down my left arm. There were times when I felt like pulling over and giving into whatever was wrong with me, but then I thought of my family, gritted my teeth and just focused on the road ahead.

In hindsight I should've driven myself straight to the hospital instead of practically driving past the place to get home, but my head was completely empty of any rational thought. All I could think was once I got home and saw Sandra everything would be all right. I made it to our front door and laid my head on the steering wheel and stayed like that until Sandra came flying out in a panic wondering why I was sitting there.

The next thing I remember was opening my eyes, seeing Sandra crying, like she'd done in that nightmare, and telling her she'd better ring the doctor because I had chest pains. She smiled and cried at the same time, 'Oh Paddy, I rang them three days ago. You're in the Radcliffe hospital.' I'd been unconscious for days and Sandra had stayed by my bed for the whole time. I was wired up like a Christmas tree with drips in my nose and arm.

When a doctor turned up he told me that I'd had a massive heart attack and by the time I was wheeled into the hospital I was minutes away from dying. When I told him that I'd had the attack in Cardiff he couldn't believe it.

'It's a mystery to me, Mr Monaghan, how you could possibly have driven back from Cardiff while suffering a massive heart attack. You're a very abnormal person.'

'Yeah,' I said, 'Me Ma always said I was an odd bugger.'

He said that he'd explain the difference between a heart attack and a massive heart attack, but I told him not to bother. I think the word massive said it all. The tests revealed that the attack was so serious that part of my heart was dead and that the old pump would never fully function again.

Ever since, I've had to rely on medication to keep me going. And do you know what I have to take daily, in order to keep me alive? Fucking rat poison. It's called warfarin but it's still rat poison, no matter what fancy name they give it.

The first of the two saddest days in my life was 26 July 1982. That was the day that my father died. The other was when my Ma passed away. I laid beside Da's cold body all night and told him so many things that I should've told him in life, but we always think there's endless time to do these things and sometimes we leave it too late.

What he knew, and never said a word to any of us about, was that he'd been diagnosed with cancer. While we lived in hope that whatever was wrong with him would soon be put right, he knew different and was trying to save us all pain while he kept that terminal secret to himself. What a man. May he rest in peace with God.

The happiest day in my life, of course, had been when I married Sandra. And other days that were highlights in my life were those of the births of my children and now my grandchildren. Nothing and nobody could mean more to me than my family. I've written a lot about my friendship with Muhammad because I know that people are interested in him and are curious as to how some insignificant guy from the sticks could strike up a genuine friendship with one of the most famous men in the world. There was always some sort of moral running through those kiddies' books I used to read, so I'll throw one in here of my own. What goes around comes around. If you do something without any thought of recognition or reward, don't matter how big or small, it'll come back to you in time, just like it did for me.

There isn't enough space here to mention my many 'ordinary' friends but they were and are equally as important as my friendship with Muhammad Ali. I only use the word ordinary in comparison to Muhammad but don't think I lessen these people because they're all extraordinary in their own way. One guy in particular comes straight to the front of my mind and that's big Lenny McLean, one of the most awesome fighters I ever came across.

Famous in his own right after the runaway success of his book *The Guv'nor*, when I first met him he was a young fighter like myself. He did the rounds of gypsy camps, horse fairs and the Barn. In his own words, he wanted 'to put steam on the table', exactly like all the rest of us.

The first time I met Lenny was at the Barn and even then he was either respected or feared, however you looked at it. I can remember thinking, Fuck me, he looks a bit tasty, and the guy he was supposed to fight that evening thought the same, because he bottled it and refused to get in the ring. Lenny stayed on and watched me demolish my opponent, and from that day on we were friends up until his final days.

He gave me a call one day to tell me he'd put my name down to fight the Irish Middleweight Champion, Benny Lafferty, and that on the same day he was taking on Irish heavyweight champ Sean McCaffery. Both of these bare knuckle fighters had unbeaten records, but then so did the two of us.

Before I put the phone down, Lenny told me to make sure I trained hard and got myself fit, not that I needed telling. After that I got a load of calls from him and they all ended with him reminding me to train hard. He was so keen that I should reach a peak of fitness, he wanted me to go up to London to the gym he used so that he could keep an eye on me. I assured him I was out running every day and in the gym sparring every evening. I felt ready for anything. I mean, the man obviously had my best interests at heart, but I often wondered why all of a sudden he was so insistent on me shaping up?

I got myself up to the Stowe-on-the-Wold horse fair and was met by Lenny, already kitted out in his usual fighting gear of tracksuit bottoms and t-shirt and, fuck me, the first thing he said was, 'You sure you're fit for doing this Lafferty?' I was either cocky or bloody confident, but I told him I reckoned I'd do him in a couple of rounds and he said, 'Well, make sure you do, son.'

I had to say, 'Lenny, I know you want me to win same as I want you to come out on top but why are you so concerned? You've been onto me for weeks to get fit an' really this is just one fight among many, so what's the deal?'

He gave that big belly laugh that was so much part of his personality, tapped the side of his nose and said, 'You do what you have to and I'll tell you later.'

Lafferty was one very hard man, but after I'd put two deep cuts over each eye and a rip in his forehead, the poor bastard was too blinded by blood to carry on and the fight was stopped a few seconds into the third round. I reckon that stop came a little late. I did what I had to do without mercy, same as he would have done to me, but I honestly think the fight should've been ended earlier.

But don't think I walked away without a scratch. Lafferty had a fearsome punch and I reckon I must've been black and blue from my neck down to my waist. Still, it was a worthwhile fight because I picked up a handy little purse: 150 notes. Not much by today's standards, but a nice little earner back then. I'll throw in here as a matter of interest, this fight never ended up on my record because as far as Tommy Heard was concerned it didn't comply with BKB rules. He was a stickler for the rules was old Tommy, bless him, but honest as they come and I can't knock that.

Lenny was the first to congratulate me, with one of his rib-crushing hugs, just what I needed when I was bruised to fuck. 'Nice one my son, you've just earned me a monkey,' he boomed. 'What a lovely way to pick up a bit of scratch.'

Yeah, no wonder he chased me to win – he had a side bet on me with some horse traders and picked up £500. After he'd knocked Sean McCaffery spark out in the first few minutes of round one, I found out that not only was his winner's purse a lot bigger than mine, he'd had somebody put side bets on himself. With very little effort Lenny had picked up something like three long ones.

'You're one cheeky bastard, Lenny,' I told him. 'You put my name down against Lafferty, I have to work fucking hard for my bit of dough and you make a fortune betting on me.'

'Name of the game, son, name of the game.'

Later, when I caught up with him before setting off home, he put his arm around my shoulder and said, 'Paddy my son, I've been thinking about what you said earlier.' Then pulling out a bundle of cash he peeled off 250 notes and put them in my hand saying, 'Go on, my son, buy your kids a bag of sweets, but I hope you've learned a lesson like I did years ago. The money's all in the side bets, the purse money is just enough for exes.'

That was Lenny all over; he never took the piss out of his friends and would help anybody without ever expecting anything in return. He was not only a giant physically but mentally too. I was devastated when he died back in 1998.

The last time I saw him was at Ronnie Kray's funeral in March 1995 and when we were catching up back at a pub he owned at the time, I mentioned I was writing my autobiography and that it was bloody hard work. Typical Lenny, he said, 'Well I ain't fucking surprised, you told me you couldn't read or write.'

I told him that we'd had that conversation about 20 years previously and since then I'd managed to learn at least the basics of the two RRs, though I never mastered the third.

He said, 'Nah! You're living on a top of a fucking mountain out in the wilds and I'll tell ya, by the time you get that book finished, you'll have a white beard down to yer knees and be dribbling in yer cornflakes.' By that time I had returned to Ederney in Northern Ireland, but even when I lived in Abingdon he classed that as being in the sticks, despite it not being much of a drive from London. He was always telling me to move nearer the city where the action was. 'Now listen, Pads, listen,' he continued. 'What you gotta do is have a word with my book man, Peter. He'll sort you out and make a blinding job for yer.'

Well, it's been many years, but if you're up there looking down Lenny, I took your advice eventually: nuff said.

I had a lot to thank the big fella for. Back in the early days he introduced me to lots of the main people on the London scene. I'm talking faces here and I became great friends with many of them. I had offers to work the doors in major clubs, but I always resisted the temptation of getting into the big money because I knew there was a downside to mixing in circles like that.

That said, I've been many things in my life and I would be the first to say I'm not whiter than white and I've got involved in minor bits and pieces that I wouldn't have wanted my Mamma to know about. But I've never been a criminal like a lot of the guys I rubbed shoulders with. Nevertheless, I regard a lot of the lads on the London scene as great friends. Diamonds, every one of them, but I was kept on the straight and narrow by the possibility of doing time and the fear of being parted from my family for years. I've always been skint, but being with Sandra, my lovely kids and now grandchildren has been worth millions to me.

CHAPTER THIRTEEN

How Time Flies

Muhammad was so strong and so full of life that I guess most people thought that he was indestructible and would go on forever. That's what it always seemed like. But he was only human and the constant activity – out of the ring as much as in it – had to take its toll. I'd been friends with him long enough to notice the change in his health when it happened.

It was towards the end of 1978, about the time he regained his world title against Leon Spinks that it became perceptible. At first I thought the slight slur he had when he spoke was down to exhaustion, because the man never stopped. I couldn't keep up with him. But in 1980 he was diagnosed with Parkinson's syndrome, the most obvious symptoms of which were his increasingly severe problems with movement and speech. The world got the news in 1984.

Not long after that, I made a trip to America, where I was to spend nearly two weeks at his farm in Michigan. I landed at Chicago and took a shuttle flight to a small airport called South Bend. Muhammad and his fourth wife Lonnie had been down in

Louisville to finalise the adoption of a two-and-a-half-month-old boy they'd already named Assad, meaning 'the lion' and he drove to the airport to meet me. He greeted me with that big smile that nothing seemed to wipe off.

'Paddeee, my friend. Hey, you're lookin' good.'

'You're looking great as well. I see you're still dying your hair.'

'Yeah, Paddy, ah gotta keep mah good looks, but hey, man, ah'm gittin' old, same as you.'

'Yeah, mate. I'm a granddad now.'

'No kiddin'? How many grandchildren yuh got now?'

'Three an' a fourth on the way.'

'No! Mah, how time does fly. Say, we wuz jes' a couple o' kids when we first met up. Remember?'

'Yes, mate, and now we're growing old together.'

'You are only as old as yuh feel,'

'I only feel old when I look in the mirror,'

'Hey – why ain't you got no wrinkles?'

He lifted his shirt up and grabbed a roll of flab around his belly. 'An' why ain't you got fat? Look at me!'

We were having a good laugh at one another's expense, but physically my friend was a long way from the man he used to be, even allowing for the years. His voice was a husky whisper and slurred, his balance wasn't good and it was sad to see that famous Ali Shuffle of the ring had turned into a foot-dragging reality. But as a friend he hadn't changed one bit. His piss-taking and sharp wit were the same as ever.

I often hear people saying how sorry they are to see him as he is today. All I can say to those people is: don't feel sorry for him. Parkinson's seems to bother them more than it does him. I can remember him joking about his illness by saying, 'It wasn't the boxing that did this to me, it was all those autographs.'

Still, it was obvious his illness hadn't affected his driving because that morning he'd driven all the way from Louisville,

Kentucky to pick me up and once we got in the motor he took off like a racing driver, heading for the farm in Michigan.

We hadn't caught up with each other for a while and what struck me most was how much deeper he'd got into his religion. I mean, he was always very sincere about his religion the whole time I knew him and, in fact, I used to feel guilty that I was a disappointment to Mamma in terms of my own. I don't know whether it was getting out of the rat race of the boxing scene, his poor health or just getting old that had led to him turning more to Allah, but there was no getting away from how he felt about his beliefs.

He prayed five times every day. Every morning when I eventually dragged myself out of my pit, I'd find that he'd been up for hours signing pamphlets or reading the Koran. I once asked him how many times he'd read it.

He told me, 'Many, many times. It's bee-utiful. Even if a person was to read it a thousan' times they'd always learn somethin' new from the Koran. There's a hun'red an' fourteen chapters containin' the words of God, as given to the prophet Muhammad. Ah'll tell ya Paddy, me bein' a true Muslim is the most important thing in the world to me. Ah'm workin' harder now than at any other time in mah life, 'cos now at last ah've found mah true vocation an' that's to try to help people live better lives in preparation for the beginnin' of eternal life.'

It's all pretty heavy talk to me, I'm just an ordinary geezer, but it was clearly very important to Muhammad.

We were looking after ourselves while Ali's wife was in Louisville. One morning I made breakfast. Now I'm as good at cooking as I am at dress making, so I filled a couple of plates with some American cereal, I think they were blueberry pop tarts. Then I shouted out, 'Breakfast's ready.'

'That was quick. What are we havin'?'

'Well, it ain't a fry-up but it looks good.'

Muhammad came through to the kitchen diner and we got stuck in. After we emptied the plates I said, 'Not a bad cook, am I?'

He looked at me, then without saying anything reached over, picked up the cereal box and filled them up again, saying, 'Here, now you try mah cookin'.'

After we'd taken a slow wander around his garden every morning, we'd go back into the house and Muhammad would spend time autographing the 814 limited edition prints of the painting I had made of him – believe me, it took him two and half days. For a break he'd drop onto autographing pamphlets or pictures fans had sent him, or answering his fan mail for an hour or so.

When I was with him I'd give him a hand, sorting out things on the desk. I noticed that after he'd quickly scanned through his letters he'd separate from the main pile any that used words like 'idolise' or 'worship' or were over the top in making him some sort of God. He'd reply politely enough to these, but would point out that people should never idolise or worship anyone but God.

'Ah can't understand why people say or write such words. There are no idols in Islam. These letters about idolisin' an' such is against all ah believe in. Ah conquered the world in the ring three times, an' it never brought me no real happiness. The only true satisfaction came to me through Islam by doin' all I can to please Allah.'

Around lunchtime, Muhammad would take his prayer-mat and walk across to one of the rooms above the garage, to say the second prayer of the day. After that we might take a drive together. The transport ranged from his big container lorry to his Roll Royce and that always depended on which set of keys he could lay his hands on. Have you ever heard of a man losing the keys to a Rolls? He did it all the time.

We'd head back to the farm for his afternoon prayers and take a stroll or watch TV before it was time for his next session of prayer. That's what we did the whole time and if that makes us sound like a couple of boring old farts, remember, Muhammad wasn't a well man and, come to that, I wasn't exactly bursting with good health myself. Over the years I had spent time with him we'd be tearing around all over America so in a way it was great just to chill out.

Having agreed that neither of us had a clue about cooking more than cereal, we'd eat every evening in the restaurant of the local Holiday Inn. It was a very large place and without fail he'd be mobbed by a crowd of people who would all line up to shake his hand. The man had been retired from boxing for years and still the public wanted a piece of him. It was obvious to me that the magic of Muhammad Ali would never be forgotten.

Towards the end of my brief visit, he took me into a big barn and showed me hundreds of trophies, plaques and paintings. Shelf after shelf of them. Taking pride of place was a heavy pair of working boots. I commented on how strange they looked among all the fancy glitter.

He said, 'They were mah boots for mah roadwork trainin', ah mus' be getting' sentimental in mah old age.' He picked them off the shelf and said, 'An' now they are yours, brutha.' Before I could say thanks, he handed me some other treasured memorabilia, including a pair of his bag mitts, used for working out with a punch bag, 'There you go Paddy, now you got some souvenirs to take back home.'

When we said goodbye he gave me a hug then, with his hands on my shoulders, held me at arm's length for about 30 seconds, just looking at me. I expected some sort of speech but, shaking his head, all his said was, 'Paddy mah friend, time is jus' like an airplane.' I asked what he meant and in whisper he said, 'Mah how it flies. How it flies.'

I thought about those last words when I was sitting on the plane back to Heathrow and can only think that, like me, he was thinking back over the years; thinking how long we'd been friends and, yes, how it only seemed like yesterday when we first shook hands.

He told me that he was supposed to be coming over to England sometime that September. But he added, 'I'm not too sure if ah'm gonna make it, though if I do ya'll gonna be the first to know. An' bet your life ah'll be dropping by your house to catch up with mah friend an' his lovely family.'

Time went by and I didn't hear anything from him. I accepted that for his own reasons he wouldn't be making that visit. I was puzzled that there had been a lot of publicity about an expensive dinner organised by the boss of Lonsdale Sporting Equipment and Henry Cooper. I understood it was to commemorate the anniversary of Henry and Muhammad's fight back in 1966.

I got a lot of mail from fans asking if I was going to be there and I pointed out they should save their money because Muhammad wasn't going to be there. Right up to the last minute that publicity pumped out and, sure enough, come the night it was a sell-out and packed with fans and celebrities – except the main man, who was in Abu Dhabi. It was a big disappointment to everybody, but not Muhammad's fault or anything to do with him. Lonsdale Sporting Equipment are good people. I know the head of the company, Bernard Hart, personally, and I have no doubt that they believed in good faith that Ali was coming – if only they'd checked with me!

Finally, eight months later, he did manage to get to England. He had told me he'd be bringing his wife Lonnie and daughters Jamillah and Rasheda with him. We arranged that we'd meet up at the Cumberland Hotel in Marble Arch and, as you can imagine, I was looking forward to it.

For once in his life his timing couldn't have been worse, his visit coincided with the death of Mamma. It was painful enough when

HOW TIME FLIES

I lost my Dadda because I loved and respected him, but even Dadda himself would have understood that my Mamma is somehow different. There's a special bond between you and the woman who brings you into the world that I haven't got the words to explain. Everything revolved around my Mamma. She was there for all of us no matter what. I thought back to the sacrifices she'd made, like going without a dinner when we were kids just so we'd have enough or going without nice clothes and things because she wanted us to have everything we needed first. The death of my Mamma was the worst day of my life. The strange thing is, I never shed a tear. I felt like my insides had been torn out and went through pain like nothing I'd ever suffered during over 40 years of fighting. I cried inside and lost almost four stone in weight, but stayed dry-eyed, even alone and in the darkness of my room.

As soon as Muhammad heard of Mamma's passing he was on the phone straight away offering me his sympathy and promising that he'd be by my side as soon as he could. Remember, this was a man who had commitments 24 hours a day and people depending on him to show up at pre-arranged functions. The fact that he made the effort to come and see me at that time of so much grief meant more to me than he ever knew.

Even among all that sadness, with my mate around there was still time for some lighter moments – in fact it helped to take my mind off things. The big motor outside my house was like a magnet to the neighbours. They knew who was there and in no time my back garden was filled with kids being entertained with magic tricks by Muhammad. Then he and my son Tyrone got the gloves on and had a bit of a spar to the cheers of all the kids. He's the only heavyweight champ ever to have fought in Madison Square Garden and my back garden.

That was 1992 and the last time I was to catch up with my friend in person. We spoke on the phone regularly until it reached a point where his voice had deteriorated so much it made conversation almost impossible. Now all we do is swap the odd scrawled note, though he knows that he's often in my thoughts and I'm in his.

Three years after Mamma passed away, we decided to move back to Ederney and live, as Lenny said, 'on top of a mountain'. Sounds like I've turned myself into a bit of a hermit, but it's not like that at all. Our house sits above the village and at weekends there's a steady stream of visitors turning up at my door to talk about Muhammad and about my life as a fighter. I'm not in the tourist book, but seems like I should be.

I retired from the fight game in 1980 and ever since I've been reliving my 40-year career for the benefit of my fans. Yeah, Paddy's got his fans all over the world and I'm catching up with Muhammad when it comes to signing autographs.

I left the story of my career earlier having just become world champ but that wasn't the end of it by any means. I carried on for the next seven years and in that time made fourteen defences of my title and saw off every challenger. At the same time I had 18 regular fights over the years. In total I had fought and won 114 consecutive fights.

I'm told that my long and unbroken fighting record is a record in itself and recently heard that Jimmy Vallient from Florida is going to put my name forward for inclusion in the Californian Ultimate Fighters Hall of Fame. Not bad for a guy who it was said would never amount to anything.

Thirty years on there's a fantastic footnote to that story about my World Championship Belt that was stolen from the Royal Essex. No it didn't turn up in some reporter's deathbed confession; and no it wasn't anonymously posted to Abingdon from somebody with a conscience. What it is, is that Sifu

HOW TIME FLIES

Samuel Kwok, a man who has trained with Bruce Lee and is considered the Martial Arts Grand Master of the world, has had a replica of the World Championship Belt produced and presented to me. The belt was made in America by a company called Masis Boxing Belts – apparently they're top of their game, and they don't bash a belt out for any old fighter. Second best? No way. In fact it's a double honour because I've got the greatest respect for Samuel Kwok and by his act of generosity he's showed equal respect for me and that's what it's all about in the fight game – legal or illegal.

Would I change anything about my life if I were given the chance to live it all over again? The short answer, as you might expect, is a definite 'No'. I say that because this guy sitting on a mountain today is who I am. If I'd got a decent education and never got up to the things I did, who knows? I could have been anything I chose to be. Something in the City, IT specialist, doctor even ... but – and it is a very big but – I wouldn't be myself. Paddy Monaghan the Rough Diamond.

My early life would've been taken up with carving out some career and I wouldn't have had the time on my hands to have even considered the ALI IS OUR CHAMP campaign. I'd never have had the fantastic pleasure of knowing and being a close friend of Muhammad Ali. I've never had a pot to piss in and have never missed it, but what I did have were the best parents anybody could wish for and a family that have never brought me a day's grief, only happiness.

I've lived a tough life but, looking back, enjoyed every single minute of it ... Well almost!

APPENDIX

Paddy Monaghan's BKB Fight Record (1962–1980)

Undefeated

114 wins

DATE	OPPONENT	FROM	RESULT	METHOD	ROUND
21.06.1962	Bobby Daniels	Cardiff	Win	Points	4
29.06.1962	Joe Crimmins	Basildon	Win	Points	4
06.07.1962	Doug Prince	Shepherds Bush	Win	Points	4
14.07.1962	Packie McCey	Govan, Scotland	Win	Knockout	2
25.07.1962	Mick Williams	Manchester	Win	Ref stopped contest	3
07.08.1962	Billy Drew	Hammersmith	Win	Knockout	1
14.08.1962	Alan Wheeler	Liverpool	Win	Points	4
23.08.1962	Jimmy Fuller	Walworth	Win	Knockout	3
31.08.1962	Dave Phillips	Brighton	Win	Points	4
09.09.1962	Ivan MuCulloch	Newcastle	Win	Points	4
18.09.1962	Sammy O'Connor	Manchester	Win	Ref stopped contest	2
03.10.1962	Brian Edwards	Shoreditch	Win	Knockout	4
18.10.1962	Johnny Gale	Hackney	Win	Points	6
30.10.1962	Harry Daniels	Putney	Win	Ref stopped contest	5

STREET FIGHTING MAN

11.11.1962	Ronnie James	Wembley	Win	Points	6
29.11.1962	John Hughes	Manchester	Win	Knockout	3
30.11.1962	Brian Tate	Harrow	Win	Knockout	5
08.12.1962	Ray Cullen	Shotton	Win	Knockout	2
15.12.1962	Terry Dobson	Bellingham	Win	Ref stopped contest	4
06.01.1963	Danny Pickard	Battersea	Win	Knockout	6
21.01.1963	Keith Richards	Dartford	Win	Ref stopped contest	8
02.02.1963	Bernie Taylor	Richmond	Win	Points	10
23.02.1963	Bernie Taylor	Richmond	Win	Knockout	3
04.03.1963	Sean O'Shea	Dublin	Win	Ref stopped contest	7
15.03.1963	Harry Powney	Doncaster	Win	Opponent retired	5
20.03.1963	Bobby Reid	Chelsea	Win	Knockout	3
04.04.1963	Alf Packer	Dartford	Win	Knockout	7
22.04.1963	Rene Duquesne	Lyon, France	Win	Ref stopped contest	5
17.05.1963	Pierre Schiller	Paris, France	Win	Knockout	2
01.07.1963	Jupp Stockmann	Kiel, Germany	Win	Opponent disqualified	6
25.07.1963	Jupp Stockmann	Kiel, Germany	Win	Knockout	2
20.08.1963	Gigu Stanav	Romania	Win	Ref stopped contest	4
30.08.1963	Ivan Otvos	Romania	Win	Ref stopped contest	7
06.09.1963	Olav Pitu	Romania	Win	Knockout	3
17.09.1963	Hans Wilheim	Germany	Win	Knockout	5
29.09.1963	Helmut Dieter	Hamburg, Germany	Win	Knockout	7
20.10.1963	Carl Kottych	Frankfurt, Germany	Win	Opponent retired	6
12.11.1963	Sav Grzensiak	Poland	Win	Ref stopped contest	7
25.11.1963	Des Limpart	Ontario, Canada	Win	Knockout	4
12.12.1963	Charlie Spangler	Chicago, USA	Win	Knockout	8
20.12.1963	Heini Ven	Berlare, Belgium	Win	Points	10
03.02.1964	Heini Ven	Berlare, Belgium	Win	Knockout	4
28.02.1964	Johnny Worthington	Walworth	Win	Ref stopped contest	5
03.03.1964	Bobby Newman	Hammersmith	Win	Opponent retired	3
15.05.1964	Mauri Bergloef	Helsinki, Finland	Win	Knockout	1
12.06.1964	Pete Coventry	Liverpool	Win	Knockout	6
22.07.1964	Dave 'Mad Dog' Davis	Swansea	Win	Knockout	9

11.01.1965	Alan Brown	Govan, Scotland	Win	Ref stopped contest	5
28.02.1965	Sammy Lendrum	Brighton	Win	Opponent retired	7
06.03.1965	Vic Barlow	Manchester	Win	Knockout	4
14.04.1965	Andy Hardacre	Manchester	Win	Knockout	3
27.05.1965	Bobby Tate	Newcastle	Win	Ref stopped contest	2
17.07.1965	Gary Reid	Hammersmith	Win	Points	10
17.07.1966	Bernie Woods	Walworth	Win	Points	10
10.09.1966	Al Drew	Shoreditch	Win	Ref stopped contest	3
21.11.1966	Bernie Woods	Walworth	Win	Knockout	4
20.01.1967	Tommy Edward	Bermondsey	Win	Knockout	2
22.02.1967	Gary Reid	Hammersmith	Win	Knockout	5
09.04.1967	Olav Ajoma	Helsinki, Finland	Win	Opponent retired	3
18.09.1967	Ivan Dinu	Romania	Win	Ref stopped contest	4
03.12.1967	Hans Zech	Hanover, Germany	Win	Knockout	6
07.05.1968	Kevin Wheeler	Shoreditch	Win	Ref stopped contest	5
23.06.1968	Jobbie Wilson	West Ham	Win	Ref stopped contest	8
20.07.1969	Bobby Baldwin	Bristol	Win	Points	10
17.09.1969	Bobby Baldwin	Bristol	Win	Knockout	5
04.11.1969	Eddie Fowler	Blackpool	Win	Knockout	1
03.03.1970	Don McMillan	Glasgow	Win	Opponent retired	4
21.04.1970	Harry Redfern	Liverpool	Win	Knockout	2
12.06.1970	Freddie Pearson	Pontefract	Win	Ref stopped contest	6
20.09.1970	Mickey Newman	Leicester	Win	Knockout	5
14.11.1970	Willie Quinn	Belfast	Win	Knockout	2
14.02.1971	Les Parris	Tottenham	Win	Knockout	4
02.07.1971	Joe Pain	Barking	Win	Ref stopped contest	6
15.11.1971	Johnny Murphy	Wigan	Win	Opponent retired	3
08.02.1972	Gordon Moore	Grimsby	Win	Knockout	1
10.06.1972	Phil Mahoney	Cardiff	Win	Knockout	5
13.08.1972	Jobbie Wilson	West Ham	Win	Knockout	7

British BKB Middleweight Champion

08.11.1972	Jack McCann	Holloway	Win	Ref stopped contest	4
13.01.1973	Luka Gedo	Hungary	Win	Opponent retired	6
08.03.1973	Guido Cattaneo	Milan, Italy	Win	Knockout	8
03.04.1973	Earl Stewart	Sheffield	Win	Knockout	3
10.05.1973	Peter Benichi	Italy	Win	Knockout	9

European BKB Middleweight Champion

12.08.1973	Emile Criqui	Paris, France	Win	Ref stopped contest	4
09.10.1973	Chris Johnson	Bermondsey	Win	Opponent retired	7
10.02.1974	Charlie Lawson	Bingham	Win	Knockout	1
18.03.1974	Davey McLaren	Glasgow	Win	Points	10
09.05.1974	Jean Paul Durrell	Quebec, Canada	Win	Knockout	8

BKB Middleweight Champion of the World

04.08.1974	Mickey Lowery	Boston, USA	Win	Ref stopped contest	9
20.11.1974	Maurice Raphael	Paris, France	Win	Opponent retired	5
14.02.1975	Ian Widley	Maldon	Win	Ref stopped contest	8
27.04.1975	Tony Gallana	Chicago, USA	Win	Knockout	6
15.08.1975	Joe Corsine	Chicago, USA	Win	Knockout	10
04.11.1975	Ferdi Chiocca	Chicago, USA	Win	Knockout	7
14.04.1976	Jose Ruiz	Madrid, Spain	Win	Opponent retired	5
03.08.1976	Aldo Sybille	Rotterdam	Win	Knockout	3
17.10.1976	Peter Benichi	Grosseto, Italy	Win	Knockout	10
22.01.1977	Packie Henderson	Glasgow	Win	Ref stopped contest	6
18.01.1978	Stevie Weller	Battersea	Win	Points	10
15.03.1978	Stevie Weller	Battersea	Win	Knockout	4
09.06.1978	Chip Robinson	Manchester	Win	Ref stopped contest	9
17.11.1978	Salvatore Gianelli	Milan, Italy	Win	Opponent retired	3
22.03.1979	Slav Gruescu	Romania	Win	Knockout	7

APPENDIX

14.05.1979	Duke Russell	Birmingham	Win	Knockout	5
03.08.1979	Curtis Quinn	Virginia, USA	Win	Points	10
07.10.1979	Curtis Quinn	Virginia, USA	Win	Knockout	6
03.01.1980	Giuseppe Sassarini	Berundi, Italy	Win	Knockout	8
28.03.1980	Manuelle Hernandez	Barcelona, Spain	Win	Ref stopped contest	4
15.05.1980	Tommy Boyle	Walworth	Win	Opponent retired	7
20.06.1980	Earnie Rasconne	Philadelphia, USA	Win	Knockout	2
27.07.1980	Rene Martinez	Madrid, Spain	Win	Points	10
30.08.1980	Rene Martinez	Madrid, Spain	Win	Knockout	6
29.09.1980	Herbie McMillan	Glasgow	Win	Ref stopped contest	5
30.10.1980	Bobby White	Manchester	Win	Points	10
24.11.1980	Maxie Deloy	Pittsburg, USA	Win	Points	10